Learning from the West?

Learning from the West? gives a fascinating insight into political life after the collapse of communism and the fall of the Iron Curtain in the late 1980s.

For Communist parties and their successors (CSPs), the challenge was perhaps the greatest – to redefine themselves within new, 'westernised' political systems. As these parties sought to adapt their programmatic appeals to their new environments, they searched for policies from abroad that could fit these new political structures.

The political parties of Western Europe provided a rich range of programmes from which policies could be drawn. This book analyses how, to what extent and under what conditions external influences came to bear on the programmatic development of CSPs. It argues that while some parties remain neo-communist in orientation, growling about the evils of capitalism on the far-left of their respective political systems, others have developed into social democratic actors, embracing programmatic ideals that often bear a strong resemblance to those of centre-left actors in Western Europe.

This book was previously published as a special issue of *The Journal of Communist Studies and Transition Politics*.

Dan Hough is a Lecturer in Politics in the International Relations and Politics Department at the University of Sussex.

William E. Paterson is Professor and Director of the Institute for German Studies at the University of Birmingham.

James Sloam is a Lecturer in International Relations at Royal Holloway, University of London.

Learning from the West?

Policy Transfer and Programmatic Change in the Communist Successor Parties of Eastern and Central Europe

Edited by
Dan Hough, William E. Paterson and James Sloam

LONDON AND NEW YORK

First published 2006 by Routledge
2 Park Square, Milton Park, Abingdon, Oxfordshire OX14 4RN

Simultaneously published in the USA and Canada
by Routledge
711 Third Avenue, New York, NY 10017

First issued in paperback 2016

Routledge is an imprint of the Taylor and Francis Group, an informa business

© 2006 Taylor & Francis Ltd

Typeset in Times by Techset Composition Limited

All rights reserved. No part of this book may be reprinted or reproduced or utilised in any form or by any electronic, mechanical, or other means, now known or hereafter invented, including photocopying and recording, or in any information storage or retrieval system, without permission in writing from the publishers.

British Library Cataloguing in Publication Data
A catalogue record for this book is available from the British Library

Library of Congress Cataloging in Publication Data
A catalog record for this book has been requested

ISBN 13: 978-1-138-97962-8 (pbk)
ISBN 13: 978-0-415-37316-6 (hbk)

Contents

1. Learning from the West: Policy Transfer and Programmatic Change in the Communist Successor Parties of Eastern and Central Europe   **Dan Hough**   1

2. Westernizing the East: External Influences in the Post-Communist Transformation of Eastern and Central Europe   **Marcin Zaborowski**   16

3. Learning from the West: Policy Transfer and Political Parties   **William E. Paterson and James Sloam**   33

4. The Communist Successor Parties of Eastern and Central Europe and European Integration   **Michael Dauderstädt**   48

5. West European Social Democracy as a Model for Transfer   **James Sloam**   67

6. Polish Social Democracy, Policy Transfer and Programmatic Change   **Piotr Buras**   84

7. Between Emulation and Adjustment: External Influences on Programmatic Change in the Slovak SDL   **Vladimír Handl and Vladimír Leška**   105

8. Choosing Between China and Europe? Virtual Inspiration and Policy Transfer in the Programmatic Development of the Czech Communist Party   **Vladimír Handl**   123

9. The Programmatic Development of the Eastern German PDS: Learning What from Whom and Under What Conditions?   **Dan Hough**   142

10. Conclusion   **William E. Paterson and James Sloam**   161

Index   169

Learning from the West: Policy Transfer and Programmatic Change in the Communist Successor Parties of Eastern and Central Europe

DAN HOUGH

Background

Communist successor parties (CSPs) have never been a homogeneous group of political actors.[1] Like their predecessors, the communist parties that ruled in each of the countries of the state-socialist world, initial perceptions of ideological coherence, programmatic similarity and organizational consistency apply in only the most superficial of ways. Some have 'reformed' much more extensively than others, but – as a group – CSPs remain significant as a politically influential family of parties, even if the ideological orientations and programmatic strategies of individual actors can vary quite considerably. In trying to pin down what these parties believe in, how they behave in the political arena and what differentiates them from other parties of the left and centre-left, the contributors to this collection define CSPs as those parties 'that were formerly the governing party in the pre-1989 communist regime and which inherited the preponderance of the former ruling parties' resources and personnel'. While it is clear that other definitions exist, this none the less succinctly sums up the parties with which we seek to deal.[2]

Until 1989, communist parties (CPs) in Eastern and Central Europe (ECE) espoused similar rhetoric and signed up to the same ideological doctrine, yet in practice the programmes that they sought to implement and the strategies that they adopted frequently produced very different political and economic outcomes. Some CPs remained loyal and unambiguous supporters of the Communist Party of the Soviet Union (CPSU), championing both its means and its methods in leading the countries of the Soviet bloc towards a communist

---

Dan Hough is a Lecturer in Politics at the University of Sussex.

utopia. The leaders of the loyalist Socialist Unity Party (SED) in East Germany argued, for example, that 'to learn from the Soviet Union' meant 'to learn to win', illustrating that the guidance of the great socialist brother in the east was vital in defeating capitalist (as well as any other) evils.[3] Other CPs espoused the same ideology and the same rhetoric in public, but, as and when opportunities presented themselves, they sought to broaden their practical aims and make use of small spheres of independence that materialized. At its most extreme this 'deviant behaviour' involved introducing elements of democratic multi-party competition (as in Czechoslovakia in 1968) and even backtracking from international security and defence commitments (as in Hungary in 1956), prompting various forms of Soviet intervention, the most extreme of which was to send tanks into the streets of East Berlin, Warsaw, Budapest and Prague. Some CPs none the less crafted a degree of ideological and rhetorical space for themselves, reacting to specific national constraints and considerations, from finding an accommodation with significant social institutions such as the Catholic Church (Poland) to exerting relative independence from the USSR (Romania).[4]

If before 1989 communist parties were a more heterogeneous group of actors than is widely perceived, then this is even truer of the parties that succeeded them in the post-communist era. In the years after 1989 some CSPs reformed at a pedestrian pace, reacting only slowly to the imperatives of democratic multi-party competition. Others actively chose to distance themselves from their predecessors more or less immediately. Some CSPs (most notably in the Czech Republic) stubbornly refused to be overtly critical of the failed state-socialist experiment and continued to espouse more or less unreconstructed Marxist-Leninist positions. Others (most notably in Poland, Slovakia and Hungary) either dissolved themselves (only to re-form soon afterwards under another name) or radically reformed, embracing democratic organizational structures and social-democratic programmes and policies. The new leaderships of reform-orientated CSPs therefore undertook wholesale ideological, programmatic and organizational reform. Young and intelligent former middle-ranking officials rose rapidly through the ranks to lead – in their own ways – CSPs away from their pasts, with the aim of turning them into organizations that could react to competitive party politics. The more conservative and reactionary CSP memberships were forced to accept that their once dogmatically anti-reform CPs were now embracing a form of market socialism, and at times preaching the gospel of their former sworn ideological enemies.

Yet, regardless of the initial type of self-preservation strategy, all the CSPs in Central Europe were forced out of government and into opposition in the immediate wake of 1989–90. Several observers intimated that if they were to stabilize themselves and halt electoral freefall – not to mention harbour dreams of returning to government – then they would do so as a reactionary force on the far left of the political spectrum. This was likely to entail giving political voice to those who were bitter towards the transition process (and had a strong sense of nostalgia for the social comforts of the state-socialist welfare system) more than any articulation of a revitalized political agenda. Add to this other groups that had suffered losses of personal status, or felt that their pre-1989 efforts to build a just socialist state (no matter how flawed) had been in vain (or indeed encountered both experiences), and – so it was hypothesized – the communist successor parties would be able to play a role in the new party systems. This role would principally be a reactive one, as they growled about the inadequacies of capitalism from the party system's far-left reaches.[5] Another indirectly linked strategic option would be for the CSPs to re-emerge as brazen populists, advocating the need for strong leaders to 'save' their countries from the capitalist charlatans who now ruled in their own interests.[6] Come what may, initial predictions for the CSPs were bleak and they were not expected to be significant political forces in their respective countries.

The second round of democratic elections that took place from 1992 onwards contradicted this gloomy scenario. There was evidence of both political and electoral rejuvenation as their popularity grew and they began to return to national governments. Observers have conventionally advanced one of two reasons to explain the successful metamorphosis of CSPs into efficient and effective political actors.[7] The first approach stresses the internal organizational reforms that CSPs initiated and the balance of power that resulted.[8] Those leaderships that centralized power in their own hands and remained firmly in control of party affairs were able to make their parties electorally attractive by adopting more overtly social-democratic programmatic positions. Leftist-retreat parties, on the other hand, underwent more radical processes of internal democratization, empowering frequently reactionary memberships before becoming bogged down in debates about the party's relationship with the past and what this should mean for its contemporary political activity.[9] Linked to this were theories arguing that the nature of the previous regime had a considerable effect on the ability of CSPs to adapt their structures to the democratic competition for votes.[10] The more liberal and pluralist the regime, the more likely the party would be to reform itself effectively in order to compete with newly formed democratic actors.[11] Post-communist leaders who received their political education in what Herbert Kitschelt termed 'national-consensus communist' states (principally Poland and Hungary) possessed more experience of guiding and dealing with independent forces of interest articulation, however limited, and were likely to be more adept at steering their parties in the post-1989 era. These leaders, and the CSPs that they represented, were more aware of the need to adapt to democratic norms and conditions, and subsequently found it easier to build legitimate and popular political platforms.[12]

The second approach to explaining the success of communist successor parties emphasizes factors external to the CSPs. It holds that they took advantage of an external political environment where weak competitors systematically made strategic mistakes, offering reformed CSPs a second chance. The success of these parties has had, so it was argued, more to do with external political conditions than internal reforms and adaptations to democracy. CSPs were seen as mobilizing feelings of discontentment and disenchantment and using their considerable organizational apparatus to lever themselves towards societal respectability.[13] In truth, both of these perspectives tell us something useful about the rebirth of the post-communist left – the CSPs have tended to be surprisingly flexible and versatile in the face of challenges from other parties, just as they have made use of societal conditions that were clearly in their favour. They have reinvigorated themselves internally while the problematic process of economic reform has offered them ample opportunity to portray themselves as defenders of a more just social and economic order.

While CSPs are clearly heterogeneous in terms of their aims, ideals and organization, they do none the less remain different from their political competitors in a number of significant ways. CSPs are not merely clubs of notables, with few members and limited organizational resources, as most of their early competitors were. CSPs were faced with a rather different set of challenges. They did not need to build up organizational networks; on the contrary, they needed to streamline bloated organizational structures that were both expensive and hopelessly inefficient in shaping and guiding programmatic and ideological change in a democratic polity. They also attempted to stop the haemorrhaging of party members – something other parties did not have to worry about as they were essentially building up party structures from scratch. While CSPs across the region lost millions of members between them, they frequently remained the most membership-heavy actors in their respective national party systems. Members did, in this sense, very much matter to the communist successor parties. The CSPs – whatever their stances on individual questions of policy and ideology – subsequently found an electoral lifeline, and began embedding themselves into the still nascent party systems of which they were becoming an ever more important part.

CSPs and Paths of Programmatic Reform

Analysis of CSPs through the early and mid-1990s, while fruitful and enlightening, clearly concentrated on understanding why and how CSPs had survived rather than what they now intended to achieve when they returned to power. This emphasis shifted towards the end of the 1990s, as observers began to analyse how they had relabelled and redefined themselves programmatically.[14] CSPs such as the Hungarian MSzP, the Slovenian ZSLD and the Polish SdRP were all, after spending a remarkably short period in opposition, re-elected to power on the basis of their conversion to democracy and their attempt to embrace market reforms.[15] CSP leaders also began to stress their ability to manage transitions that the reforming parties then in government were, in their view, badly mishandling. CSP leaders sold themselves as competent arbiters of change: a steady hand at the wheel rather than inexperienced learner-drivers. These parties sought to increase their external legitimacy by joining the international family of socialists and social democrats, expressed institutionally through membership of the Socialist International. This, they thought, would help them emulate the political and electoral successes of West European centre-left parties through the 1990s. These reform-orientated CSPs stressed the recklessness of the initial reformers in bludgeoning through wholesale economic reform, stressing that they had squandered at least some of the resources at their disposal when they took over in 1990. For these CSPs, the communist past was to be left behind and, where possible, rejected outright. They undertook radical internal reform, generally centralizing power in a small elite, ensuring that the reformers maintained a firm grip on the direction of the party. Party members were likely to be much more reticent in embracing reforms, while party leaders were aware that radical processes of democratization could hamper their own attempts to take the party away from its dogmatic past.

Yet not all CSPs have – as was indicated above and as is highlighted in some of the contributions to this collection – chosen to go down the reformist route towards social democratization. Some, most notably the Czech Communist Party of Bohemia and Moravia (KSČM) but also the Romanian PDSR, the Albanian PSSH and, to a certain extent, the Bulgarian BSP, have chosen to embrace their ideological heritage in a defiant and defensive gesture of self-confidence.[16] Their electoral performances in recent years illustrate that, even in genuinely free and fair elections (such as in the Czech Republic), there is still clearly a constituency for far-left parties, embracing genuinely communist aims. These parties have rejected the reformist agenda that other CSPs have embraced, and they stress the need to remain true to their Marxist-Leninist roots and to fight the capitalist enemy whenever and wherever possible. As a rule, the memberships have been empowered and processes of internal democratization have been wide-ranging. The leaders of leftist-retreat parties have to interact and negotiate with a variety of significant internal bodies when creating policy, and party leaders do not enjoy the same levels of autonomy that the leaders of the reformist parties do. The Slovak

SDL (Party of the Democratic Left), on the other hand, is an example of a CSP that, after initially moving down the path to social democracy, later retreated to a hard left position.

The further east and south one goes in the region, the more likely one is to see further manifestations over and above broad divisions between reformist social democrats and leftist-retreatists. Some CSPs have successfully reshaped the parameters of party politics and now compete primarily on a nationalist-liberal and cosmopolitan dimension of political competition. While the combining of socialism and nationalism may seem paradoxical, there are clear reasons why some parties have successfully synthesized these two apparently contradictory approaches. Both socialists and nationalists stress the importance of the state in solving political, economic and social problems. While the nature and extent of state intervention will vary, many socialists and nationalists agreed that the state was (and is) obliged to 'do something'.[17] CSPs in southeast Europe were not slow to recognize these commonalities and many were not averse to wrapping themselves in a nationalist cloak, portraying their competitors not just as ideological adversaries, but also as enemies of the nation-state. A vote for the CSP, it was argued, was a vote for national confidence and aimed to ensure the dignity of the nation.

Research on CSPs has not shied away from analysing this diversity.[18] In more recent times the emphasis has shifted to analysing how organizational change has affected programmatic development[19] and how the reinvigoration of some CSPs has affected broader party system dynamics.[20] Yet very little research has been conducted on where CSPs actually acquired their inspiration for programmatic renewal. Even where parties possess little room for ideological manoeuvre, they still have the option of looking across national borders for successful policies and ideas that appear to be bearing fruit elsewhere. They can also take heed of mistakes and errors that parties may have made in trying to achieve similar goals. It is therefore not too controversial to hypothesize that external forces are likely to be of some importance in explaining the specific programmatic developments of CSPs. This is plausible in tranquil times of peaceful normality, but is even more likely in times of political transition and upheaval. Actors in turbulent times instinctively look for road maps and policy pointers from elsewhere as they attempt to stabilize their own political identities and electoral fortunes. Put another way, there seems little point in expending time and energy on creating nationally specific policies when there may be other actors from whom one can learn. External factors and processes have provided important sources of compulsion, constraint and inspiration for CSPs. Of particular consequence have been the challenges posed by EU and NATO enlargement and the ways in which CSPs have actively sought to adapt their policies and rhetoric to forge links with West European social-democratic parties.

The political context of individual CSPs is still critical in determining both their openness to external ideas and the type of programmatic learning that takes place.[21] Party identity and national political systems have presented very different 'opportunity structures' for these parties in the construction of their programmes. This mixture of national opportunity structures (party system dynamics, historical constraints and so forth) and exposure to external influences led to an initial diversification of these parties before external forces again prompted a form of limited convergence. Hence, even though CSPs started from similar, although not identical, positions in 1989 and 1990, they have since evolved in a remarkably diffuse way. Academic research has none the less failed to discuss in a systematic manner the importance of direct and indirect external influences on the programmatic orientation of CSPs. While we do not contest that domestic national opportunity structures play a fundamental role in shaping programmatic change, the contributions to this collection aim to give added value to academic and policy debates by identifying the extent to which external influences have contributed to CSP development.

CSPs and External Influences on Programmatic Change: A Framework for Analysis

One such tool for analysing these questions is the analytical framework developed around ideas of policy transfer and lesson drawing. The generic term 'policy transfer' envelops a host of concepts describing the process of moving policies, programmes, ideas or institutions across time and space. Studies of this temporal and spatial transfer of policy knowledge present us with many varied forms, from voluntary lesson drawing[22] through policy learning[23] to coercive policy pushing.[24] The simplicity and malleability of these concepts has prompted a plethora of analysts to use policy transfer as an analytical framework through which to analyse policy change in areas as diverse as health care, bureaucratic accountability and the willingness to enter institutions such as NATO and the European Union.[25] Diane Stone consequently defines policy transfer as 'a dynamic whereby knowledge about policies, administrative arrangements, or institutions is used across time or space in the development of policies, administrative arrangements and institutions elsewhere'.[26] The best-known and most coherent framework for analysis nevertheless remains that devised by Dolowitz and Marsh, although they clearly encourage other analysts to expand, amend and review their model.[27] In their original review of the policy transfer literature, Dolowitz and Marsh differentiate between transfer that utilizes all available means, both voluntary and coercive, and Richard Rose's description of lesson drawing that emphasizes only the voluntary aspect of transfer and the potential for non-transfer of policy, following prospective evaluation. The European Union provides the most obvious arena for the type of 'friendly' exchange of policy ideas of which Rose writes, as it 'promotes comparison ... so that member states can become aware of what their competitors are doing and decide which elements of foreign programmes they may wish to copy or adapt'.[28] The International Monetary Fund (IMF), on the other hand, is often cited as being one of the most overtly coercive forces on states (and with that on the parties that govern them). As a powerful supranational organization with a determined focus on the economic stability of its member states, it acts as a policy pusher, urging countries to adopt stringent structural adjustment programmes in exchange for loans. Countries — and the parties that lead them — that are going through economically testing times can either take heed of the experiences of others, drawing on accumulated knowledge, or accept the policies imposed by the Fund, given that the consequences of refusal are likely to spawn further economic crises.[29] Dolowitz and Marsh's model, meanwhile, was created principally to promote more focused thinking about links and values existing between the various activities put forward to describe aspects of the policy transfer process (whether voluntary or coercive), and it has acted as a springboard for more detailed, empirically grounded investigations of individual cases of hypothesized policy transfer.

Wade Jacoby has, more recently, built on this framework and convincingly argued that four basic modes of emulation exist. He argues that parties and other actors can actively 'transfer in' policies in a faithful and voluntary fashion (that is, they mimic them precisely). This he simply terms the 'copying' of polices in existence elsewhere. This may be because policy elites see a particular external policy or mode of operation as offering a quick fix to a particular dilemma that they are facing at home. The second form of emulation involves the faithful replication of policy under some form of outside influence — there is a choice available to the party, but party elites may be desperate to find acceptable answers to problems for which they find no particularly palatable solution. This type of emulation is often least successful: the policies adopted may be rushed and adapted *en masse*, and not 'fit' coherently with the policy agenda of the party that is invoking them. If implemented, the policies may fail to take root, and function poorly. Jacoby terms this 'emulation in patches', as the parts of the policy that a party transfers in may be precise, but they are likely to be narrow in scope so as to fulfil distinct and precise sets of criteria. The third method of transfer involves a much more voluntary adoption of external models and approaches, although they may well be modified considerably to take advantage of a party's particular ideological and external setting. Radical reform of a welfare system, for example, will need to take into account the system that is currently in operation, but may not prevent politicians from advocating policies and programmes that have been successful elsewhere. For example, Roland Koch, the conservative Christian Democratic Union (CDU) prime minister of the German state of Hesse, launched a major campaign demanding the curtailment of social benefits much along the lines of the so-called Wisconsin Model – stressing the basic advantages of structuring welfare spending along particular lines while shaping the detailed policy proposals to the German circumstances.[30] Finally, the most coercive and faithful form of transfer occurs when parties find themselves required to meet certain thresholds in terms of policies or programmes that they have no choice but to adopt. These tend to be qualitative, and can frequently include subjective judgments and vague minimum standards that have to be achieved. There is a clear degree of monitoring going on and parties accept this because they think it is imperative that they attain the pot of gold that such compliance will eventually provide. The willingness of a left-leaning communist or socialist party to join the Socialist International (SI) while still attempting to retain much of its communist dogma may prompt an organization such as the SI to set such thresholds.[31]

In order to pinpoint cause and effect in empirical research one is subsequently faced with a series of questions that lead out of such frameworks. Who transfers policy? Why is policy transferred? What gets transferred in the process? From where is policy transferred? What constrains policy transfer? In the case of CSPs, the most obvious objects of emulation were the policies and programmes adopted by parties of the left and/or centre-left in Western Europe. In theory, CSPs were likely to confront their own programmatic failure by first looking for inspiration to the standard operating procedures of other similar, successful actors. If, however, the standard procedures of these actors (that is, the other CSPs) are also compromised by policy failure, as was clearly the case, then policy actors search for other forms of external stimuli. This naturally leads CSPs to look westwards towards social-democratic, socialist or reform-communist parties for inspiration. This search for solutions is oriented by some combination of geographical and ideological proximity, with actors seeking policy solutions that incorporate the values to which they themselves wish to subscribe. Transferring external ideas into policies that are suitable for given local circumstances is a very difficult task for elites, however, and it is clear that a degree of political support for developing and pushing through transferred policies is helpful if it is to be done successfully.[32] By utilizing the concept of policy transfer, it is possible to identify the part self-determined, part externally imposed routes of adaptation taken by CSPs. The contributions to this collection will attempt to provide evidence that will enable us to develop our understanding of who, if anyone, Central European CSPs looked to in their attempts to generate ideological and programmatic legitimacy, and also to estimate how useful the policy-transfer frameworks – as developed by the likes of Dolowitz, Marsh and Jacoby – are in facilitating greater understanding of programmatic change.

Central European CSPs and Programmatic Change

Given the diverse nature of communist successor parties across ECE, it is clearly not possible to analyse the programmatic development of every one of them in this collection. We do not doubt that CSPs in the more eastern and southeastern parts of Europe have undertaken interesting processes of programmatic rejuvenation since 1989, and it is highly likely that they have acted upon pointers from external actors. We none the less concentrate our attention on Central Europe, and more specifically the SLD (Alliance for the Democratic Left) in Poland, the SDL (Party of the Democratic Left) in Slovakia, the PDS (Party of Democratic Socialism) in eastern Germany, and the KSČM (Communist Party of Bohemia and Moravia) in the Czech Republic. These four parties have diverging political and ideological standpoints and are at different stages in their respective reform processes. The SLD, SDL and to a certain extent the PDS have made considerable strides towards what can be defined as West European social-democratic positions, whilst the KSČM lags behind. The Polish SLD comes closest to being what in Western eyes would be termed a 'social-democratic party', while at the other extreme the Czech KSČM has barely departed from the Marxist-Leninism of the pre-1989 era: it remains decidedly anti-European and is reluctant to set out on any path of modernization. The Slovak SDL, before its implosion, was a party that appeared to be adopting social-democratic principles and responding to the challenges of Europeanization, while the PDS is a unique case in itself on account of its metamorphosis into an eastern German regional party. The PDS is in a unique position, as it has to contend with fundamentally differing national and international opportunity structures. The PDS is none the less a useful object of analysis in that it acts as a comparator. It has not been exposed to many of the internal and external influences that the other parties have, yet it has to deal with many of the same ideological and organizational difficulties.

The collection begins with an analysis of how, after 1989, West European actors sought to shape and influence the behaviour of politicians and the institutions where they were – and still are – active. Marcin Zaborowski argues that the role of international factors in post-communist transitions in ECE continues to be underestimated. Just as in analyses of political institutions and political economy, the external dimension is largely ignored in the literature on post-communist party politics. Zaborowski argues that the EU, the institutions of the global capitalist economy and individual politicians from states such as the United States and Germany often came to act as transmitters of transition-related models and ideas. The combination of national opportunity structures and post-communist elites' self-professed embrace of Western ideas served as powerful factors in facilitating the import of foreign institutions and models into the post-communist environment.

William Paterson and James Sloam move the analysis specifically on to the terrain of party politics, as they look at how parties can seek to emulate actors in other institutional contexts. They argue strongly for a qualitative approach to understanding programmatic change, stressing the importance of structural context in influencing the policy directions that party leaders – in Central and Eastern Europe, just as in Western Europe – set out upon. James Sloam then moves on to discuss how West European social-democratic parties, in particular, have acted as a model for transfer, illustrating that geographical proximity to Germany has accorded the German Social Democratic Party (SPD) a particularly significant role. Sloam shows that the French *Parti Socialiste* and the British Labour Party have also acted as tutors, although the institutional reach of the SPD has none the less facilitated it in establishing itself as the first port of call. Michael Dauderstädt then moves on to analyse how the four CSPs in question have come to terms with the plethora of questions that the European Union in particular has asked of them. More specifically, he analyses how they dealt with the issue of whether their countries should seek to join, their attitudes to the principles of European integration, and their positions on individual policy developments such as the common foreign and security policy.

The next four articles deal in detail with programmatic developments within each of the four CSPs under scrutiny here. Piotr Buras analyses the Polish SdRP/SLD, arguing that while local opportunity structures have provided effective barriers to direct transfers from individual social democratic parties, a significant diffusion of social democratic policy concepts has nevertheless taken place. Voluntary lesson drawing is the most prominent form of concrete policy transfer evident and the SdRP/SLD has mixed and matched attractive policies from elsewhere into its own programmatic documents. Buras argues that the party also looked for external inspiration from both the SI and the Party of European Socialists and – contrary to the SLD politicians' claim of following a 'Polish way' of social democracy – there does not appear to be any particularly distinctive Polish model. Vladimír Handl, in his chapter on the Czech KSČM, argues that, much like the SLD, the programmatic development of the Czech Communist Party has been primarily driven by influences that are specific to national politics. Yet, a degree of ideational borrowing from external sources has nevertheless taken place. The strategy of 'leftist retreat' that emerged through the 1990s has its roots in the internal divisions that existed (and continue to exist) within the party. While the KSČM has enjoyed increasing electoral support as a party of radical protest, the internal divisions have resulted in a clear dichotomy in terms of attitudes to prospective external models for programmatic inspiration. In contrast, Vladimír Handl and Vladimír Leška find that the situation within the Slovak SDL was altogether different. New young, dynamic leaders assumed the role of modernizers in the party in the first half of the 1990s before a group of conservative socialists took over in 1996. The two streams developed mutually incompatible attitudes not simply to policy transfer, but to policy development in general. Their contribution argues that fast-track programmatic modernization, along with the internal divisions within the party, was directly influenced by policy transfer from Western social-democratic parties and had a clear effect on the party's eventual implosion. In the final country-specific chapter Dan Hough discusses programmatic developments within the German PDS. The unification of Germany in 1990 left the PDS in an ideological and programmatic vacuum. It found itself in a position where it had to develop programmes and policies from scratch, largely devoid of contact with parties in other countries. In the immediate post-unification period the PDS therefore espoused programmatic positions with the single aim of self-preservation. Only really in the late 1990s – and particularly with its entry into the European Parliament in 1999 – was the PDS's position stable enough to try to realize its internationalist aims of socialist co-operation. Even then, the ideological diversity of the far-left movement across Europe has not been conducive to the creation of detailed policy preferences, even if the PDS – like other far-left parties – is clear about what it does not stand for. The conclusion by William Paterson and James Sloam makes a number of points. It highlights where CSPs have come from (in programmatic terms) and in what direction they are currently heading. Paterson and Sloam argue that, although the sources of policy transfer have been more diffuse than is initially evident, parties have been consistent in seeking to increase internal legitimacy by networking with like-minded actors and developing programmatic standpoints together with them. Some parties have been rather more successful at this, in both electoral and political terms, than others. While pinning down cause and effect is intrinsically difficult, the contributions to this collection make a clear attempt to further our knowledge not just of where CSPs gain policy inspiration from, but also of the mechanisms that all parties invoke in trying to shape policy preferences.

NOTES

1. The research presented in this collection is based upon work for a project on 'Policy Transfer and Programmatic Change in East Central Europe', funded by the Leverhulme Trust (project: F/00094/O).

2. This definition has been used by John T. Ishiyama in his extensive research on communist successor parties: see J.T. Ishiyama, 'Strange Bedfellows: Explaining Political Co-operation between Communist Successor Parties and Nationalists in Eastern Europe', *Nations and Nationalism*, Vol.4, No.1 (1998), p.62. There is now a considerable literature on the electoral performance, political development and ideological self-understanding of communist successor parties; see in particular A.M. Grzymala-Busse, *Redeeming the Communist Past: The Regeneration of Communist Parties in East Central Europe* (Cambridge: Cambridge University Press, 2002); A. Bozóki and J.T. Ishiyama (eds.), *The Communist Successor Parties of Central and Eastern Europe* (Armonk, NY and London: M.E. Sharpe, 2002); J. Leftwich Curry and J. Barth Urban (eds.), *The Left Transformed in Post-Communist Societies: The Cases of East-Central Europe, Russia and Ukraine* (Lanham, MD: Rowman & Littlefield, 2003); J.T. Ishiyama (ed.), *Communist Successor Parties in Post-Communist Politics* (Hauppauge, NY: Nova Science, 1999).
3. The SED used this phrase as a rallying-call to the East German people in the immediate aftermath of the June 1953 uprising and it reappeared periodically until Mikhail Gorbachev's internal restructuring and his policy of openness disillusioned the aging and embattled SED leadership in the late 1980s. The East German SED subsequently proceeded to distance itself from the policies of the CPSU, even banning Soviet-inspired critical magazines and films, in an attempt to preserve its control over an East German society that was growing increasingly vocal in its dissatisfaction with state-socialism.
4. H. Timmerman, 'The CPSU and the System of Communist Parties', in Federal Institute for Soviet and International Studies, *The Soviet Union, 1987–1989: Perestroika in Crisis?* (London: Longman, 1990), pp.254–64; A. Grzymala-Busse, 'The Organizational Strategies of Communist Parties in East Central Europe, 1945–1989', *East European Politics and Societies*, Vol.15, No.3 (2001), pp.421–35. For a particular good analysis of the commitment of Romania's regime to the Leninist model of industrialization as well as its commitment to pursuing national modes of development free from Soviet interference, see C. Chen, 'The Roots of Illiberal Nationalism in Romania: A Historical Institutionalist Analysis of the Leninist Legacy', *East European Politics and Societies*, Vol.17, No.2 (2003), pp.166–201, esp. pp.180–81.
5. See K. Jasiewicz, 'Polish Politics on the Eve of the 1993 Elections', *Communist and Post-Communist Studies*, Vol.26, No.4 (1993), pp.387–411.
6. See H. Kitschelt, 'The Formation of the Party System in East Central Europe', *Politics and Society*, Vol.20, No.1 (1992), pp.7–50.
7. See G. Evans and S. Whitefield, 'Economic Ideology and Political Success: Communist-Successor Parties in the Czech Republic, Slovakia and Hungary Compared', *Party Politics*, Vol.1, No.4 (1995), pp.565–78; B. Racz, 'The Socialist Left Opposition in Post-Communist Hungary', *Europe–Asia Studies*, Vol.45, No.4 (1993), pp.647–70.
8. For detailed analysis on the organizational reforms undertaken by CSPs, see J.T. Ishiyama, 'The Communist Successor Parties and Party Organizational Development in Post-Communist Politics', *Political Research Quarterly*, Vol.51, No.1 (1999), pp.87–112.
9. D.F. Ziblatt, 'The Adaptation of Ex-Communist Parties to Post-Communist East Central Europe: A Comparative Study of the Hungarian and East German Ex-Communist Parties', *Communist and Post-Communist Studies*, Vol.31, No.2 (June 1998), pp.119–37; D. Hough and V. Handl, 'The Post-Communist Left and the European Union: The Czech Communist Party of Bohemia and Moravia and the German Party of Democratic Socialism', *Communist and Post-Communist Studies*, Vol.37, No.4 (2004), pp.313–39 (esp. pp.324–5); J.T. Ishiyama and A. Bozóki, 'Adaptation and Change: Characterizing the Survival Strategies of the Communist Successor Parties', *Journal of Communist Studies and Transition Politics*, Vol.17, No.3 (2001), pp.32–51.
10. See J.T. Ishiyama, 'The Sickle or the Rose? Previous Regime Types and the Evolution of the Ex-Communist Parties in Post-Communist Politics', *Comparative Political Studies*, Vol.30, No.3 (1997), pp.299–330; H. Welsh, 'Political Transition Processes in Central and Eastern Europe', *Comparative Politics*, Vol.26, No.4 (1994), pp.379–91.
11. See J.T. Ishiyama, 'Party Organisation and the Political Success of the Communist Successor Parties', *Social Science Quarterly*, Vol.82, No.4 (2001), pp.846–7.

12. See H. Kitschelt, 'Formation of Party Cleavages in Post-Communist Democracies: Theoretical Propositions', *Party Politics*, Vol.1, No.4 (1995), pp.447–72.
13. See M. Waller, 'Adaptation of the Former Communist Parties of East Central Europe', *Party Politics*, Vol.1, No.4 (1995), pp.473–90; A. Mahr and J. Nagle, 'Resurrection of the Successor Parties and Democratization in East-Central Europe', *Communist and Post-Communist Studies*, Vol.28, No.4 (1995), pp.393–409; I. McAllister and S. White, 'Democracy, Political Parties and Party Formation in Post-Communist Russia', *Party Politics*, Vol.1, No.4 (1995), pp.49–72.
14. See H. Kitschelt, Z. Mansfeldova, R. Markowski and G. Toka, *Post-Communist Party Systems: Competition, Representation and Inter-Party Co-operation* (Cambridge: Cambridge University Press, 1999), pp.62, 63.
15. See A. Ágh, 'The Dual Challenge and the Reform of the Hungarian Socialist Party', *Communist and Post-Communist Studies*, Vol.35, No.3 (2002), pp.269–88; A. Szczerbiak, 'Interests and Values: Polish Parties and their Electorates', *Europe–Asia Studies*, Vol.51, No.8 (1999), pp.1401–32; V. Zubek, 'The Phoenix out of the Ashes: The Rise to Power of Poland's Post-Communist SdRP', *Communist and Post-Communist Studies*, Vol.28, No.3 (1995), pp.275–306; for analysis of the Slovenian ZSLD, see J. Bugajski, *Political Parties of Eastern Europe* (Armonk, NY and London: M.E. Sharpe, 2002), pp.652–3.
16. For discussions of each of these parties, see S. Hanley, 'Towards Breakthrough or Breakdown? The Consolidation of the KSČM as a Neo-Communist Successor Party in the Czech Republic', *Journal of Communist Studies and Transition Politics*, Vol.17, No.3 (2001), pp.96–116; G. Pop Eleches, 'Separated at Birth or Separated by Birth? The Communist Successor Parties in Romania and Hungary', *East European Politics and Societies*, Vol.13, No.1 (1999), pp.117–47; G. Pollo, 'The State of Domestic Politics in Albania', *Südosteuropa Mitteilungen*, Vol.42, Nos.5–6 (2002), pp.6–11; B. Kassayie, 'The Evolution of Social Democracy in Reforming Bulgaria', *Journal of Communist Studies and Transition Politics*, Vol.14, No.3 (1998), pp.109–25; S.D. Roper, 'The Romanian Party System and the Catch-All Party Phenomenon', *East European Quarterly*, Vol.28, No.4 (1994), pp.518–32.
17. See Ishiyama, 'Strange Bedfellows', p.63.
18. J.T. Ishiyama, 'Communist Parties in Transition: Structures, Leaders and Processes of Democratization in Eastern Europe', *Comparative Politics*, Vol.27, No.1 (1995), pp.147–66; Waller, 'Adaptation of the Former Communist Parties of East Central Europe'.
19. A.M. Grzymala-Busse, 'The Programmatic Turnaround of Communist Successor Parties in East Central Europe', *Communist and Post-Communist Studies*, Vol.35, No.1 (2002), pp.51–66; Ishiyama, 'Party Organisation and the Political Success of the Communist Successor Parties'; J.T. Ishiyama, 'Candidate Recruitment, Party Organisation and the Communist Successor Parties', *Europe–Asia Studies*, Vol.52, No.5 (2000), pp.875–96.
20. J. Bielasiak, 'Substance and Process in the Development of Party Systems in East Central Europe', *Communist and Post-Communist Studies*, Vol.30, No.1 (1997), pp.23–44; R. Markowski, 'Political Parties and Ideological Spaces in East-Central Europe', *Communist and Post-Communist Studies*, Vol.30, No.3 (1997), pp.221–54.
21. See the article by William E. Paterson and James Sloam, 'Learning from the West: Policy Transfer and Political Parties', in this collection, pp.37–51.
22. R. Rose, *Lesson-Drawing in Public Policy: A Guide to Learning Across Time and Space* (Chatham, NJ: Chatham House, 1993).
23. P.M. Haas, 'Introduction: Epistemic Communities and International Policy Coordination', *International Organization*, Vol.46, No.1 (1992), pp.1–35.
24. D. Dolowitz and D. Marsh, 'Who Learns What from Whom: A Review of the Policy Transfer Literature', *Political Studies*, Vol.44, No.2 (1996), pp.343–57; D. Dolowitz and D. Marsh, 'Learning from Abroad: The Role of Policy Transfer in Contemporary Policy-Making', *Governance*, Vol.13, No.1 (2000), pp.5–24.
25. See, for example, C. Bennett, 'Understanding Ripple Effects: The Cross National Adoption of Policy Instruments for Bureaucratic Accountability', *Governance*, Vol.10, No.3 (1997), pp.213–33; D. Stone, 'Learning Lessons and Transferring Policy across Time, Space and Disciplines', *Politics*, Vol.19, No.1 (1999), pp.51–9; M. Evans and J. Davies, 'Understanding

Policy Transfer: A Multi-level, Multi-disciplinary Perspective', *Public Administration*, Vol.77, No.2 (1999), pp.361–86; W. Jacoby, *Imitation and Politics* (Ithaca, NY: Cornell University Press, 2000); W. Jacoby, 'Tutors and Pupils: International Organizations, Central European Elites, and Western Models', *Governance*, Vol.14, No.2 (2001), pp.169–200; D. Dolowitz, 'A Policy-Maker's Guide to Policy Transfer', *Political Quarterly*, Vol.74, No.1 (2003), pp.100–108; W. Jacoby, *The Enlargement of the European Union and NATO: Ordering from the Menu in Central Europe* (Cambridge: Cambridge University Press, 2004).

26. Stone, 'Learning Lessons and Transferring Policy', p.51.
27. For further attempts at doing this, see in particular Evans and Davies, 'Understanding Policy Transfer'; Stone, 'Learning Lessons and Transferring Policy'; Jacoby, *The Enlargement of the European Union and NATO*.
28. Rose, *Lesson-Drawing in Public Policy*, p.105.
29. Dolowitz and Marsh, 'Who Learns What from Whom'.
30. *Die Zeit*, 'Die halbe Wahrheit: Roland Koch will Sozialhilfe wie in Wisconsin. Doch die Politik der Amerikaner hat zwiespältige Folgen', at <http://www.zeit.de/2001/33/Wirtschaft/200133_wisconsin.html>, retrieved on 27 Oct. 2004.
31. Jacoby, 'Tutors and Pupils', p.181.
32. Jacoby, *Imitation and Politics*.

Westernizing the East: External Influences in the Post-Communist Transformation of Eastern and Central Europe

MARCIN ZABOROWSKI

Introduction

The role of international factors in post-communist transitions in Eastern and Central Europe (ECE) continues to be underestimated. While it is generally recognized that the origins of these transformations were intimately tied to changes in the international system, and to the removal of the Soviet veto on reform, the subsequent process of democratization and 'marketization' is often claimed to be internally determined.[1] Claus Offe, for example, argues that a lack of significant external pressures is one of most obvious differences between transitions in the post-communist world and those that took place in Cold War Europe and Latin America.[2] The external dimension is also largely ignored in the analysis of post-communist party politics, as with the seminal work of Herbert Kitschelt and his associates or in textbooks on post-communist politics such as those by David Mason.[3]

Marcin Zaborowski is Lecturer in European Politics at Aston University, Birmingham. An early version of this essay was published in *Perspectives*, No.19 (Winter 2002–03). The author would like to thank Vladimír Handl, Dan Hough, James Sloam and Piotr Buras for their useful comments on an earlier draft of the essay.

This article argues that post-communist transitions have indeed been influenced by external actors, most importantly by the EU and other Western international institutions as well as by individual states (in particular the United States and Germany), which often came to act as transmitters of transition-related models and ideas. It is certainly also true that, following the removal of the Soviet veto, the new Central European elites themselves decided to embark on a process of democratization and introducing the market into their economies, and that, whatever external influences there may have been, they have had to be compatible with national opportunity structures. Yet Central Europe's history of being intensely penetrated by foreign powers and the post-communist elites' self-professed embracing of Western ideas served as powerful factors in facilitating the import of foreign institutions and models into the post-communist environment.

ECE was exposed to various kinds of external influence during its post-communist transition. Some of these influences involved the voluntary transfer of ideas, while others were more forceful or even coercive in nature. The purpose of this article is to draw out some of the main features of the interaction between the domestic and external transition drivers and to develop a typology of external influence. The first part discusses the difficulties that are encountered when investigating the role of international factors in ECE transitions. The second discusses the international background of the transitions. The third section looks at the categories of international actors involved in ECE and discusses their influence upon the transition processes. The final section offers some preliminary insights into the interplay between domestic structures and external influences.

The article's key points, using empirical evidence from the Visegrád countries (the Czech Republic, Hungary, Poland and Slovakia), are general enough to be relevant for the whole of former communist Eastern and Central Europe. The external forces discussed here have influenced political and economic activity over the whole of the post-communist area, producing comparable dynamics (though often divergent outcomes) in all the transition countries.

The Pitfalls and Difficulties Ahead

The sheer scale and extent of external influences as well as their often-elusive nature mean that they do not constitute easy research material and are difficult to interpret both empirically and theoretically. There is a growing body of literature dealing with the most obvious manifestations of the phenomenon, which refers to the often-coercive nature of the impact of the EU.[4] However, less coercive international influences on post-communist transformations remain under-researched and under-conceptualized.

There are a number of reasons for this, relating to both the agents of projection and their recipients. For the former, it is apparent that external actors often prefer to exert their influence discreetly, avoiding the risk of being seen as meddling in other states' affairs. Germany, by far the most active EU member state in ECE, has for example been inhibited by historical memory in a region that is deeply influenced by Germany's past domination. Berlin also has to exercise caution *vis-à-vis* its western neighbours, in particular France, which is prone to interpret its 'too active' engagement in Central Europe as threatening the existing balance of power in the EU. But there are also inhibitions on the part of Eastern and Central Europeans themselves who may be unwilling to admit that their reforms are not always domestically inspired. Whilst the post-communist elites in ECE have been predominantly Western-oriented, it is also true that they have operated in the context of nationalizing societies suspicious of any forms of external interference. It is quite significant, for example, that Poland's so-called 'shock therapy' tactics (rapid liberalization of the economy) is known at home as the Balcerowicz plan (named after the first post-communist finance minister), whereas outside Poland it is common knowledge that the reforms were heavily influenced by Jeffrey Sachs from the Chicago Business School.[5]

Finally, and perhaps most importantly, voluntary policy transfer, which is probably most significant among all the different types of influence, is difficult to research as it consists of pinpointing the origins of beliefs and ideas, some of which may be borrowed from more than one source and then processed through national opportunity structures. Poland, for example, when embarking on its territorial reform in 1998, chose the German model in setting up a second tier of local government (the so-called *powiat*), while the French unitary model prevailed in establishing the rules governing the third regional tier.[6]

Overall, the international dimension of democratization in ECE is difficult to conceptualize on account of its highly political nature as well as its complexity and ideational rather than strictly material character. Although it is clear to many observers that the 'international context' is vital for democratization, difficult questions remain as to what exactly the 'international context' is and how it interacts with domestic forces. Geoffrey Pridham argues that the 'international context' is really 'an umbrella term for a variety of different external actors, institutions or conditions'. Consequently, in order to 'unscramble the international context', Pridham categorizes it into: (a) background or situational variables, (b) different external actors, and (c) forms of external influence.[7] The following two sections use these categories as a basic analytical framework, which is developed further with reference to empirical examples.

Background Variables of Post-Communist Transitions

The background variables refer to a given country's position within the international system, its exposure to the global economy, and watershed events outside its borders. An immediate difficulty with such a definition concerns timeframes, which in the case of post-communist transitions is over a decade. Clearly, during the decade and a half since 1989, the international system itself has evolved and its impact on ECE has differed depending on the relative stage of reform in each of the ECE countries. It is therefore essential that the impact of the international environment be seen in a longer-term perspective and against the backdrop of different transition phases across the region.

Geoffrey Pridham suggests that there are three transition phases: (a) inaugural – beginning of the transition; (b) constituent – laying down the foundations of the new liberal-democratic order; and (c) completion – bringing the new system into operation. The experience of the 1990s and the early twenty-first century shows that, while new constitutions have been adopted in ECE, the new systems remain prone to frequent modifications and some of the fundamental democratic institutions such as party systems remain unstable (Hungary and, to a lesser extent, the Czech Republic, being exceptions). Consequently, it is suggested here that it is almost impossible to distinguish between the constituent and completion phases, and the present stage of transition appears to fall somewhere between these poles. The latter two transition phases will therefore be examined as one.

Inaugural Phase

The influence of the West left its mark on ECE politics and economics during the pre-1989 communist period. Beginning in the late 1960s, communist regimes in ECE embarked on economic reforms leading to a limited openness to the West and progressive integration with the global economy.[8] These reforms proved rather patchy and, following Soviet intervention in Czechoslovakia in 1968, Prague – traditionally one of the most progressive state-socialist states – returned to a conservative form of communism. Yet, by the late 1980s most ECE states were increasingly dependent on Western technologies and Western loans. Poland and Hungary, the two most open economies, were in fact heavily indebted to the West by the late 1970s.[9] Hungary struggled to pay back its loans, while Poland defaulted in 1982 and was subsequently denied access to Western technologies. These developments had a considerable influence on the emergence of Solidarity in Poland, which posed a major challenge to communist domination throughout the region.

The Westernizing influence also had its impact on communist elites in ECE. Many younger communists in Poland and Hungary, for example, were convinced that the modernization of their states was dependent upon further integration with the West.[10] It was no coincidence that these individuals, who were often recipients of Western scholarships, were well disposed towards the gradual social-democratization of their parties, as became apparent in the late 1980s.[11] Consequently, in contrast to the Czech and East German parties, which remained more conservative in their outlook,[12] the Polish and Hungarian communists welcomed Gorbachev's reforms, taking them further and effectively co-engineering the start of the transformations.

Clearly the end of communism in ECE would not have been possible without a profound change in the international environment. In this sense, the impact of the international environment on post-communist transitions was of far greater significance than was the case with the Mediterranean and Latin American transitions of the 1970s and 1980s.[13] Essentially, while it is impossible to dissociate post-communist transitions from the demise of Soviet power and the end of bipolarity, the Mediterranean and Latin American transitions occurred against the background of a relatively stable international environment. In addition, the inauguration of transition in one ex-communist state immediately became an 'event' in another, leading to a so-called 'domino effect'.[14] It is difficult, for example, to overestimate the impact of the Polish and Hungarian reforms in the spring and summer of 1989 on the activation of non-communist forces in East Germany and Czechoslovakia and the subsequent collapse of communism in those countries in the autumn of that year.

On the other hand, the role of the international context was, although essential, largely passive during this transition phase. The end of the Cold War 'permitted' political change in ECE, but it was not immediately followed by a large-scale engagement of Western actors interested in shaping new conditions in the area. There was no Marshall Plan for ECE and, whatever US engagement there was after 1989, it was not remotely comparable with its involvement in Western Europe during the late 1940s and early 1950s. This created a certain paradox whereby, at the time when ECE was most open and had the greatest need to import ideas and solutions, little know-how was forthcoming. While this situation would change during the subsequent transition phases, and the interest of the Western actors would increase from the mid-1990s onward, ECE states also became less receptive to foreign ideas.[15]

It is also important to note that, although the West is normally associated with promoting transformations in ECE, in some cases policies and 'events' in neighbouring Western states came to serve the opposite purpose. For example, in Czechoslovakia and Poland, the unification of Germany brought fears of possible German domination in the region, prompting claims that the maintenance of a security alliance with the Soviet Union was desirable.[16]

In the run-up to unification, Bonn failed to confirm the permanence of the Polish–German border as established after the Second World War.[17] As a result, the Polish government slowed down the dissolution of the Warsaw Pact and postponed the planned withdrawal of Soviet troops. In addition, the internal transformation of Mazowiecki's transitional government, which at that stage still included communist ministers in charge of key security services, was delayed. It was only after a joint declaration of the East and West German parliaments confirming the Oder–Neisse border to be permanent (March 1990) that Poland opted for the dissolution of the Warsaw Pact and re-launched negotiations on the withdrawal of Soviet troops. The internal transition was also speeded up after communist ministers left the government and free elections were called for autumn 1990.[18]

Constituent-Completion Phases

The impact of the international system during these transition phases has been considerable, but not in the watershed manner that was the case in the earlier constituent phase. The consolidation of the role of the US, as the only remaining superpower, has certainly strengthened pro-Western attitudes in ECE. The general direction of foreign policies in the region became strongly pro-Western and pro-American – a trend shared by many political forces in ECE including former communist parties (with the notable exception of the Czech and East German communists). In fact, in some of the transatlantic debates the former communist states, particularly the Visegrád Four (but often with the exception of the Czech Republic), chose to side with the US when American positions clashed with those of West Europeans.[19]

Yet, while the post-Cold War unipolarity of the international system contributed to the development of a pro-Western orientation in ECE, its impact on democratic consolidation should not be overestimated. Turkey, for example, has a long tradition of pursuing pro-Western policies, yet its transition to liberal democracy has not been entirely successful. The US retains close links with a number of Middle Eastern countries, and none of them are even remotely democratic or liberal. It is therefore clear that, although the international environment can facilitate internal change (as indeed was the case in 1989), it is not capable of determining the success or failure of domestic transformations. Therefore, Western actors chose not to rely on the facilitating impact of the post-Cold War system alone and developed a more comprehensive strategy towards ECE acting through a variety of methods.

As argued above, ECE has a long tradition of being subject to penetration from external powers. This was the case in the nineteenth century, during the inter-war period, and during the Cold War when ECE states effectively lost their sovereignty. Today's situation is different in that the actors involved have changed, and those who remain active in the region have different objectives and different methods for achieving their ends. Whereas, in the past, external powers wanted to dominate the region in order to strengthen their relative position, today they seek rather to stabilize it in order to protect their external and internal security. Furthermore, the international framework in Europe is marked by the presence of international institutions, which not only constrain their member states' behaviour, but in many respects have replaced them in influencing domestic developments in the region. The three following categories of actors have been active in influencing post-communist transitions:

- *Western international institutions.* As the Council of Europe and NATO have been involved in promoting democratic institutions, the International Monetary Fund and World Bank have influenced the restructuring of ECE economies by attaching conditions to their loans. The impact of the EU on post-communist transitions is both the widest and the deepest since, on the one hand, Brussels has encouraged the broadest range of reforms and, on the other, it has been often closely involved in their implementation.
- *Western governments (in particular the US and Germany).* American interests in the region are part of its post-Cold War global strategy and, as such, are no different from its interests in other parts of the world experiencing forms of transition, such as Turkey, Southeast Asia and the areas formerly belonging to the Soviet Union. By contrast, Germany's interests in ECE are of a particular nature. It is commonly believed in Berlin that the success or failure of post-communist transitions has direct implications for the Federal Republic: first, as a potential source of regional instability; and, second, as a potential source of economic and political opportunities. Consequently, Germany's political, cultural and economic investment in the region has been considerable.[20]
- *Non-governmental actors.* These fall into three categories: (1) know-how agencies (such as USAID); (2) Western political parties, operating sometimes, but not always, through their foundations (for example the Friedrich Ebert Foundation, representing German Social Democrats, or the Westminster Foundation linked to British parties); (3) foreign policy and reconciliation-related foundations, such as the German–Czech Forum or the American Ford Foundation.

These three categories of actors have affected post-communist reforms in a variety of ways and through a variety of methods, ranging from the voluntary transfer of policies and ideas to more coercive ways of shaping the reform agenda in ECE.

Forms of Influence: Conditionality

There are two main ways by which international actors have been able to influence transition processes in ECE: convergence and conditionality.[21] Conditionality is a coercive measure practised by international institutions. Following the decisions of ECE states to apply for membership of the Council of Europe, NATO, the EU and other Western institutions, the latter responded by setting out a number of conditions that had to be fulfilled before these membership applications could be considered. While in most cases the primary reason for setting entry conditions was to preserve internal cohesion of these organizations, they have none the less become directly relevant to the transition processes.

The first Western institution that opened up to Eastern and Central European states was the Council of Europe. Its entry conditions – the conduct of free and fair elections, the rule of law and the protection of minorities (through the adoption of the European Convention on Human Rights) – were fairly general, but they played an important role in influencing the reform agenda during the inaugural stage of transition. The political conditions set by NATO included civilian and democratic control over the armed forces, and they too were significant during the constituent phase of reform. This was particularly the case in Poland, where the military's accountability remained unclear until the adoption of the new Constitution in 1997.[22]

The most clear-cut example of the impact of conditionality is the so-called Copenhagen Criteria set out by the EU in 1993. Unlike in the case of the Council of Europe and NATO, the fulfilment of the EU's criteria did not warrant automatic membership, but merely admission into membership negotiations. The criteria were both very general – 'stable democracy' and a 'functioning market economy' – and specific – 'adherence to the aims of political, economic and monetary union' along with 'capacity to apply the whole body of EU legislation'. In addition, although the EU does not have its own human and minority rights policy, it required of the applicants to demonstrate 'good behaviour' and apply the standards set by the Council of Europe (Convention on Human Rights) and the OSCE (decision of the European Council, 1993).

Following the decisions taken by the EU at the summits in Luxembourg (1997) and later in Helsinki (1999), eight East and Central European states, plus Cyprus and Malta, began their membership negotiations. Consequently, the applicant countries were faced with the enormous task of adopting 80,000 pages of EU law into their legal systems, something that has deeply affected their domestic systems and influenced their transformations. This process is often referred to as Europeanization. The burgeoning debate on Europeanization normally refers to the penetration of EU-level policies, rules and regulations into the domestic areas of member states.[23] More recently, it has been argued that this debate should be extended to the candidate countries, which, like the current members, are increasingly affected by the adoption of the EU's *acquis communautaire* into their domestic legislation.[24] While it is recognized here that the impact of the EU within ECE candidate countries is enormous and growing, it does not seem appropriate to label this process Europeanization, not least because European integration was just an element of the post-1989 call for a 'Return to Europe'.[25] It therefore appears more appropriate to refer to the 'top-down' dynamics between the EU and its current and future members as 'EU-ization'. When defined in this way it is clear that EU-ization represents a form of conditionality and, as such, it has strongly influenced (and in some respects guided) post-communist transitions in ECE.

The interference of the EU in the former domestic policy areas of ECE candidate countries has been truly breathtaking, and ranges from foreign policy issues (for example, introducing visas for neighbouring non-applicant countries) to sanitary standards in agriculture, and setting taxes on cigarettes and alcohol. Practically every single sphere of national life in ECE has to some extent been influenced by the application of the EU's *acquis*. The impact of EU-ization on the shape of political systems in ECE is not always seen as conducive to the promotion of transparency and good governance. For example, the EU has been accused of exporting its 'democratic deficit' by way of prioritizing the executive and forcing upon the candidates the speedy approximation of their legislation with the *acquis* without allowing for proper parliamentary debate.[26] On the other hand, the EU is credited with forcing a change in citizenship laws, ensuring broader political participation that would include resident Russian minorities, for instance in the Baltic states.

In general, it is clear that the EU's conditionality remains a powerful and effective tool that influences transitions in the candidate counties in some crucial policy areas. Nevertheless, the impact of conditionality remains both limited and shallow, and is not able to ensure the regular internalization of EU rules and norms. The most obvious example of conditionality, the Copenhagen Criteria, remains open to a form of interpretation, potentially leading to a politicization of the process. There is also the strong possibility that candidates respond to the EU's conditionality by setting up institutions and rules not because they believe they are good for them, but because they were told to do so. Such a development almost always leads to shallow and patchy implementation of officially accepted rules. In contrast to the shortcomings of conditionality, convergence represents a deeper form of external influence. Convergence lacks the 'sticks' of conditionality, but stresses the role of recipients who accept a certain foreign solution because they see it as being in their best interests. Potential 'exporters' of ideas may have an influence on this process, and it is clear that a number of Western actors – NGOs, political foundations and so forth – have set out to do exactly this.

Convergence and Policy Transfer

Almost as soon as communism collapsed a number of Western agencies opened their offices throughout ECE with the purpose of guiding and aiding political and economic transformations in the region. In contrast to the cases discussed above, these agencies did not have any coercive instruments at their disposal, and their influence counted only as much as their host countries were willing to take their advice. However, in the ideological void that emerged in ECE after the end of communism, and particularly in view of post-communist elites' openness to Western ideas and solutions, it appears that the agencies were well placed to act as transmitters of Western models.

The US and Germany were at the forefront of pioneering this method of projecting the West's influence, although some British, French, Austrian and Swedish agencies have also been active.[27] There has been a clear difference in the way the German and American agencies operated. Reflecting the mistrust of the state prevailing in the US, American agencies targeted the private sector and local governments.[28] USAID, for example, ran a scheme based on placing graduates of American business schools in emerging small and medium-size businesses, with the purpose of spreading American corporate culture. The agencies working with local government structures often organized projects involving the privatization of public utilities.[29] However, since the state continued to be the main actor in shaping post-communist transitions, the focus of American agencies on non-governmental institutions has clearly limited their overall influence in ECE. In addition, beginning in 2000, American agencies have been closing their offices in ECE in line with Washington's assumption that the post-communist transition has now been completed.

In contrast to this, German agencies chose to work with the institutions and structures more closely linked to governments (such as political parties) or at least directly related to the transition processes (such as the media). The best-established and best-funded of these agencies have been the German political foundations – in particular, the Konrad Adenauer Foundation linked to the CDU, the Friedrich Ebert Foundation attached to the SPD, and the liberal, FDP-associated Friedrich Naumann Foundation.[30] Each of these foundations has been engaged in two types of mission: establishing contacts with their kindred parties in ECE and promoting democratic institutions in the areas related to the foundations' specific interests. As far as their political missions are concerned, the foundations used their contacts with their equivalent ECE parties to encourage the emergence of party systems based on liberal-democratic principles and pro-European attitudes. In the second area, there has been a division of labour among the foundations, with the Friedrich Naumann Foundation (FNS) promoting civil society and decentralized government, the Friedrich Ebert Foundation (FES) concentrating on trade unions and independent media, and the Konrad Adenauer Foundation (KAS) promoting local government and the social market economy. All three foundations, but in particular the KAS, have been involved in promoting European integration.[31]

While the German foundations have clearly set out to influence a broad area of transition-related processes, the scope of their influence remains open to question. In contrast to their activity during the Iberian transitions, the foundations were prohibited from financing political parties in ECE, which clearly limited their leverage on the region's politics. The foundations' ability to influence the political landscape in ECE was also impaired by the chronic fluidity of post-communist party systems and the ever-changing constellations of parliamentary parties. In addition, all three foundations experienced difficulties in finding suitable partners.[32] However, in some instances the foundations have had a considerable impact upon political processes in ECE. For example, the FES and FNS acted as interlocutors in the coalition negotiations between the Hungarian socialists and liberals that led to the formation of the government in 1994.[33]

Nevertheless, in general the foundations proved more effective in non-partisan areas of activity. For example, the Polish office of the KAS has financed the Market Research Institute in Gdansk, whose prognoses and reports are generally considered influential in the formulation of government economic policy. The FES has been seen as very effective in promoting independent mass media, particularly during the inaugural phase of transition. In addition, after their rather disappointing experiences with political parties, the foundations have targeted young leaders and potential opinion-shapers who, it appears, are more responsive to the foundations' Westernizing agendas.[34]

But convergence can also take place with little involvement from Western agencies through, for example, the process referred to as the logic of 'appropriateness' – meaning that certain solutions are picked up from the West by ECE countries because they are considered to be 'the right thing to do'. This form of external influence is an entirely voluntary emulation of Western policies and institutions that came to inspire the new post-communist elites while embarking on reforms. This phenomenon needs to be seen in the context of the popular call for 'Return to Europe' – the guiding principle of the post-communist transformations. It is clear that the new elites in ECE admired what they perceived as the West European success in establishing stable political systems and competitive economies. Consequently, they were willing to emulate Western institutions and incorporate them into their own domestic environment. For example, it was due to the logic of 'appropriateness' that liberal-democratic principles found their way into new constitutions throughout the region, and elements of the German electoral system were copied by the Poles, Czechs, Slovaks and Hungarians. The German system of independent central banking (where the Central Bank sets interest rates independently of government) also served as an inspiration in reforming the monetary systems of many ECE countries including Poland, Hungary and the Czech Republic.

Domestic Norms, Institutions and External Influences

In general, it is clear that the 'external dimension' constitutes an important element of post-communist transitions. On the one hand, external agents acted in a variety of ways with the intention of shaping the transformations in ECE in a manner compatible with their own interests. On the other hand, the democratizing states were themselves keen to adopt Western influences. However, the question here remains: how compatible have these influences been with the national opportunities structures in ECE and how effectively did they impinge on the transitions' outcomes? This is clearly an immensely complex question going well beyond the remit of this study. However, some preliminary thoughts on this issue are offered here.

Insights into the logic of conditionality and convergence are offered by the literature on Europeanization and EU-ization, and in particular arguments developed by Tanja Börzel and Thomas Risse.[35] According to Börzel and Risse, two conditions must be in place for EU-ization to occur. First, there must be a degree of 'misfit' between the EU and domestic structures and processes; otherwise, the influence of the EU is unlikely to prompt any change. Second, there must be some domestic facilitating factors, actors and institutions, responding to pressures for adaptation. Börzel and Risse argue that the theoretical perspectives best suited to address these processes are either traditional rational institutionalism or sociological institutionalism, or both.

While rational institutionalism indicates that a 'misfit' between the EU and domestic levels provides some actors with new opportunities (for example it may strengthen the powers of the executive *vis-à-vis* the legislature) and consequently prompt them to act as facilitators of change, the sociological perspective underlines the notions of socialization and collective learning. The rationalist perspective stresses the role of formal domestic institutions – for example, regional governments or central banks – as essential to the furthering or blocking of EU-ization. The sociological argument underlines the role of norm entrepreneurs and informal networks. Norm entrepreneurs are actors and networks – for example, policy experts, NGOs, academics – who claim to possess an authoritative knowledge, and may have a potential interest in changing the normative agenda. 'Informal institutions' refers to collective rules of what constitutes appropriate behaviour and may influence the way domestic institutions respond to EU-ization. For example, the special position enjoyed by the Polish trade unions and the links they have with political parties and individual ministries are often informal though deeply entrenched in the political culture in Poland, hence potentially consequential for the EU-ization process.

There is not necessarily a contradiction here, rather a difference in emphasis between the rationalist and sociological explanations of the domestic impact of the EU. However, the two perspectives differ significantly in their assessment of the relationship between pressures for adaptation and domestic responses to EU-ization. Whilst the rational institutionalists argue that the greater the pressure from Brussels, the greater chance there is of domestic change, the sociological institutionalists argue more or less the exact opposite. In essence, the sociological view is that high pressures to adapt are likely to meet strong domestic resistance as long as the exported norms are not compatible with the pre-existing ones.

As regards the question of convergence or divergence, this study argues that the impact of the EU appears to be very uneven. While there is a far-reaching convergence of policy outcomes, which is often consequential upon member states' compliance with rules and regulations set out by the EU, there is a continuing diversity of means (processes and instruments) employed to achieve this greater homogeneity of results. For example, signing up to EMU led to a convergence of levels of public debt and levels of inflation (convergence of outcome). However, the means through which the states fulfilled the membership criteria differed considerably (divergence of processes). Overall, empirical evidence suggests that convergence of domestic structures and institutions is rather scarce among the member states. The two theories employed in the latter half of this study give some indication of what mechanisms may be responsible for the rather selective nature of convergence and still rather strong divergence of policy processes and institutions amongst member states. The rationalist perspective suggests structural incompatibility and divergence of interests at the level of formal institutions. Sociological institutionalism points to the role of informal institutions, which – being deeply embedded in national identity – are resistant to external pressures and not easily adjustable.

The arguments presented above are useful here in so far as they neatly describe the existing dichotomy within the leading interpretations of the effects of external influences. To some degree this dichotomy is also reflected in this collection, although the nature of the empirical material covered (political ideologies and party politics) is predominantly normative in nature. Consequently, whether by default or design, the arguments in these essays are more often in support of sociological rather than the rational interpretations. As will be often argued here, the first and foremost condition of the effective external influence is that it must be compatible with the norms and domestic conditions already in existence. The studies also stress the role of norm entrepreneurs – the influential individuals within the communist successor parties interested in programmatic innovation and often seeking solutions abroad, alongside more informal policy networks.

Conclusion

The collapse of communism and the generally euphoric attitude in ECE towards all things Western apparently created an ideal opportunity for Western institutions and actors to influence transformation processes in the region. Yet, ECE was not a *tabula rasa*, where Western advisers could experiment with their blueprint solutions. The area experienced 45 years of communist rule, during which time an entire generation developed with no knowledge of the market and little understanding of the rules of democracy. In addition, the stability of the region was threatened by the re-emergence of nationalism and historical disputes between, as well as within, the ECE states. The outbreak of civil war in Yugoslavia and the dissolution of Czechoslovakia were just the most visible perils of these new freedoms in ECE.

It was therefore clear that the multiple (democracy–market–state) post-communist transitions would be more complex than the Mediterranean and Latin American transitions to democracy, where the market institutions had never ceased to exist and the states' territoriality had not been threatened. In other words, there was no precedent for the post-communist type of transitions and consequently the West had no experience of dealing with these kinds of processes. There also was an insufficient will on the part of the Western actors to invest in the region by, for example, offering a Marshall Plan type of aid programme for the former communist states.

None the less, at least in terms of inspiration, the impact of external factors was considerable during the initial transition phase, as demonstrated by the fact that, rather than recalling their pre-communist Constitutions all ECE states chose to build Western-style liberal-democratic regimes. Of these initial systemic reforms the most difficult was the introduction of the market, a task to which the new ECE governments looked towards the West, and in particular to the US, for inspiration. In response, a strategy emerged in the US, specifically from the Chicago Business School, for the introduction of a radical method of reform called 'shock therapy', the essence of which was a rapid price liberalization coupled with privatization and convertibility of currencies.[36]

The subsequent fate of these reforms demonstrated that, for external influences to be effective, they must be compatible with domestic conditions.

Despite the popular appeal the 'shock therapy' held amongst new elites in ECE, the only country where it was implemented, and even then not fully, was Poland. This was because of the apparent preparedness of Polish society – pre-prepared by a decade of economic crisis – to put up with short-term economic difficulties in order to achieve benefits in the long term. Such consent did not exist in Hungary or Czechoslovakia, where economic conditions were markedly better than in Poland.

In terms of other forms of external influences, it was clear that the conditionality imposed by the Council of Europe had beneficial effects upon the position of ethnic and national minorities in the region as well as its democratization. The impact of the Council of Europe coupled with ambitions to join the EU and NATO also encouraged the states in the region to resolve their territorial disputes. During the subsequent transition phases ('constituent' and 'conclusion') the impact of external factors became both more intensive and more sophisticated as Western actors acquired better knowledge of the area. The new Constitutions adopted by the states of the region in the early 1990s (1997 in Poland) borrowed considerably from Western sources and, in particular, from Germany and France. While in Germany's neighbouring countries (principally the Visegrád Four) one can see evidence of this transfer in their Constitutions and parts of their electoral systems, in Romania one sees an adapted French-style division of the executive between the government and a directly elected president.

The whole region has been influenced by the conditionality imposed by Western institutions, the EU in particular. The impact of the subsequent EU-ization represents the deepest penetration into the domestic spheres of ECE states – and not always beneficially for processes of democratization. The rapidly growing Euroscepticism in the applicant and accession states indicates that the pressures exercised by the EU are not always aligned with these domestic environments.

The extent of the impact of foreign agencies, such as the German foundations, is often difficult to conceptualize as they do not have any coercive means at their disposal and are mostly dealing with disseminating particular ideas. Yet it is clear that the foundations have been successful in appealing to the younger generation of opinion-formers, who will come to dominate politics in coming years. Finally, policy transfer by inspiration (or lesson-drawing) is probably the most significant form of external influence in post-communist ECE. External influences in post-communist transition politics represent difficult research material, as both recipients and foreign actors are unwilling to admit that the process is significant or even that it is happening at all. Despite this, it is absolutely imperative for our understanding of transition processes that external influences are firmly incorporated into a comparative analysis. It is the aim of this volume to contribute to this debate.

NOTES

1. See, for example, C. Offe, *Varieties of Transition* (London: Polity, 1996); K. Henderson (ed.), *Back to Europe: Central and Eastern Europe and the European Union* (London: UCL Press, 1999).
2. Offe, *Varieties of Transition*, p.47.
3. H. Kitschelt, Zdenka Mansfeldova, Radoslaw Markowski and Gabor Toka, *Post-Communist Party Systems: Competition, Representation and Inter-Party Competition* (Cambridge: Cambridge University Press, 1999); D. Mason, *Revolution and Transition in East–Central Europe* (Boulder, CO: Westview, 1996).
4. K.H. Goetz (ed.), *Executive Governance in Central and Eastern Europe*, special issue of *Journal of European Public Policy*, Vol.8, No.6 (2001).
5. G. Blazyca, 'The Politics of Economic Transformation', in S. White, J. Batt and P. Lewis (eds.), *Developments in Central and East European Politics 2* (Basingstoke: Macmillan, 1998), pp.191–206.
6. M. Zaborowski, 'Power, Security and the Past: Polish–German Relations in the Context of EU and NATO Enlargements', *German Politics*, Vol.11, No.2 (2002), pp.165–88.
7. G. Pridham, 'The International Dimension of Democratization: Theory, Practice and Inter-Regional Comparisons' in G. Pridham, E. Herring and G. Sanford (eds.), *Building Democracy? The International Dimension of Democratization in Eastern Europe* (Leicester: Leicester University Press, 1994), p.11.
8. G. Schöpflin, *Politics in Eastern Europe* (Oxford: Basil Blackwell, 1993), chs.6–8.
9. J. Batt, *East Central Europe from Reform to Transformation* (London: Pinter/RIIA, 1991), pp.3–42.
10. A.M. Grzymala-Busse, *Redeeming the Communist Past: The Regeneration of Communist Parties in East Central Europe* (Cambridge: Cambridge University Press, 2002).
11. See the articles by Piotr Buras, 'Polish Social Democracy, Policy Transfer and Programmatic Change'; and Vladimír Handl and Vladimír Leška, 'Between Emulation and Adjustment: External Influences on Programmatic Change in the Slovak SDL', in this collection, pp.88–108 and 109–126 respectively.
12. See the articles by Vladimír Handl, 'Choosing Between China and Europe? Virtual Inspiration and Policy Transfer in the Programmatic Development of the Czech Communist Party'; and Dan Hough, 'The Programmatic Development of the Eastern German PDS: Learning What from Whom and Under What Conditions?', in this collection, pp.127–145 and 146–164 respectively.
13. L. Whitehead, 'East–Central Europe in Comparative Perspective', in Pridham *et al., Building Democracy?*, pp.32–59.
14. T. Garton Ash, *The Uses of Adversity: Essays on the Fate of Central Europe* (London: Penguin, 1989).
15. See the articles by James Sloam, 'West European Social Democracy as a Model for Transfer', in this collection, pp.71–87; and Buras, 'Polish Social Democracy, Policy Transfer and Programmatic Change'.
16. A. Sakson, 'Niemcy w Świadomości Polaków', in A. Wolff-Poweska (ed.), *Polacy wobec Niemców: Z Dziejów Kultury Politycznej Polski 1945–1989* (Poznań: Instytut Zachodni, 1993), pp.408–29.
17. K. Malinowski, 'Asymetria Partnerstwa: Polityka Zjednoczonych Niemiec wobec Polski', in Z. Mazur (ed.), *Rola Nowych Niemiec na Arenie Międzynarodowej* (Poznań: Instytut Zachodni, 1996); H. Teltschik, *329 Tage: Innenansichten der Einigung* (Berlin: Siedler Verlag, 1991).
18. M. Zaborowski, 'Polens Westgrenze – Zwischen Rationaler Politik und Historischer Erinnerung', *WeltTrends*, No.23 (Summer 1999), pp.158–73.
19. K. Longhurst and M. Zaborowski, 'America's Protégé in the East? The Emergence of Poland as a Regional Leader', *International Affairs*, Vol.79, No.5 (2003), pp.1009–28.
20. V. Handl and C. Jeffery, 'Germany and Europe after Kohl: Between Social Democracy and Normalization', ESRC-IGS Discussion Paper, 11/1999, Birmingham; A. Hyde-Price, *Germany and The European Order* (Manchester: Manchester University Press, 2001).

21. P. Kubicek, 'European Union Expansion and the Spread of Democratic Norms', unpublished paper delivered at the Arena/Cidel consortium seminar in Avila, Spain, May 2004.
22. A. Michta, *Soldier-Citizen: The Politics of the Polish Army* (Basingstoke: Macmillan, 1997).
23. T. Börzel and T. Risse, 'When Europe Hits Home: Europeanization and Domestic Change', *European Integration Online Papers*, Vol.4, No.15 (2000); C. Radaelli, 'Whither Europeanization? Concept Stretching and Substantive Change', *European Integration Online Papers*, Vol.4, No.8 (2000); C. Knill and D. Lehmkuhl 'How Europe Matters: Different Mechanisms of Europeanization', *European Integration Online Papers*, Vol.3, No.7 (1999).
24. See the chapters by H. Grabbe, and B. Lippert *et al.*, in Goetz (ed.), *Executive Governance in Central and Eastern Europe*.
25. For alternative approaches to Europeanization, see J. Bornemann and N. Fowler, 'Europeanization', *Annual Review of Anthropology*, Vol.26 (1997), pp.487–514; see also M. Zaborowski, *Poland, Germany and Europe* (Manchester: Manchester University Press, 2004).
26. See the chapters by H. Grabbe, and B. Lippert *et al.*, in Goetz (ed.), *Executive Governance in Central and Eastern Europe*.
27. See Sloam, 'West European Social Democracy as a Model for Transfer'; Handl and Leška, 'Between Emulation and Adjustment'.
28. A. Philips, *Power and Influence after the Cold War. Germany and East Central Europe* (London: Rowman & Littlefield, 1999).
29. Information based on the author's contacts with the USAID offices in Warsaw, Poland.
30. Over and above these three Foundations, the CSU-linked Hanns Seidel Foundation has also been active in ECE since 1989, and more recently the PDS-linked Rosa Luxemburg Foundation and the Green Party-related Heinrich Böll Foundation have also looked to spread their ideas through the region.
31. Philips, *Power and Influence after the Cold War*, pp.148–9.
32. Initially after the end of communism the FES was unwilling to co-operate with the former communist parties; Christian Democratic parties, the natural allies for the KAS, did not became significant political forces in the region; the liberal FNS was also inhibited by the weakness of liberal parties in ECE: see Sloam, 'West European Social Democracy as a Model for Transfer'; Buras, 'Polish Social Democracy, Policy Transfer and Programmatic Change'; Handl and Leška, 'Between Emulation and Adjustment'.
33. Philips, *Power and Influence after the Cold War*, p.151.
34. Information based on the author's contacts with the offices of the foundations in Poland.
35. Börzel and Risse, 'When Europe Hits Home'.
36. Blazyca, 'The Politics of Economic Transformation'.

Learning from the West: Policy Transfer and Political Parties

WILLIAM E. PATERSON AND JAMES SLOAM

Introduction

Advances in European integration over the past two decades have increased interest among academics and policy-makers alike in policy transfer and the broader notion of policy learning.[1] Among European governments, 'benchmarking' and 'peer review' are now widely used, notable examples being the introduction of 'employment action plans' and 'economic policy guidelines'. Political parties of the centre-left have similarly sought to learn from each other through bilateral relations and co-operation in the Party of European Socialists (PES).

The dramatic changes that took place in the late 1980s led to a policy vacuum in the transition states of Eastern and Central Europe (ECE), which had no experience of a modern capitalist democracy. The need to adapt was particularly great for the communist successor parties (CSPs), most of which began the search – after comprehensive defeats in the first free

---

William E. Paterson is Professor and Director of the Institute of German Studies, University of Birmingham.
James Sloam is Lecturer in European Studies at King's College London, and an honorary Research Fellow in the Institute of German Studies, University of Birmingham.

elections – for new policy programmes.[2] Although one can identify a number of important external influences on CSP policy, social-democratic party programmes have proved an especially promising source of policies for these parties to emulate.[3] The efforts of social-democratic parties (SDPs) to rewrite their programmes in the early 1990s proved attractive at a rhetorical level, but their lack of political success at the time took the shine off their practical appeal.[4] In the late 1990s, the prominence of SDPs in the governments of Western Europe (seen as a 'social-democratic moment') was accompanied by new programmatic platforms. This was especially true of the British Labour Party, the German Social Democratic Party (SPD) and the French *Parti Socialiste* (PS), which came to power in the three most powerful EU states, and these provide the case studies for this work.

Focusing on the exporter SDPs in Germany, France and the UK, this article will, first, define the concept of policy transfer and explain how it may be used to understand transfer and learning between political parties. Next, the essay will examine the nature of programmes in these political parties through the use of 'policy contexts' that define the opportunity structures for policy making. We will, third, set out an analytical framework for a systematic 'qualitative programmatic analysis' of political parties in a comparative context, demonstrating how transfers might be highlighted through this process.[5] Finally, the study argues that policy transfer, dependent upon 'proximity', is channelled between parties in two main ways: emulation through 'ideational transfer', and the active engagement of the SDPs with their sister parties to the east through 'transfer networks'. These transfers must nevertheless be placed within a complex matrix of opportunity structures, recognizing that SDPs and their programmes are just one external factor in CSP policy making, whose influence might more easily sit within the broader concept of 'policy learning'.

Policy Transfer

Before dealing with the analysis of party programmes, we must explain what we understand by the term 'policy transfer'. Stone defines it as 'a dynamic whereby *knowledge* about policies, administrative arrangements, or institutions is used across time or space in the development of policies, administrative arrangements and institutions elsewhere'.[6] Whereas the previous contribution to this collection looked at the external influences on transition politics in general, this study focuses on transfer from party to party at the voluntary end of the policy transfer continuum, with a view to identifying the transfer that has taken place from West European social democracy to the successor parties of Eastern and Central Europe.[7] Although policy transfer is used as an analytical tool, it is recognized that decision-makers in political parties are influenced by a wide variety of sources that together constitute the opportunity structures (policy contexts) for party programmes.

The first objective in an analysis of policy transfer must be to identify the necessary stages of the transfer process. Mossberger and Wolman argue that there are three essential features involved in policy transfer.[8] The first is 'awareness'. Simply, if a policy is to be transferred the importer must be aware of its existence. The second stage is 'evaluation'. This takes places on the basis of a policy's 'desirability' and 'feasibility'.[9] For a policy to be desirable an 'active search' for policies is not necessary, but there must be some form of policy deficit or uncertainty for a new policy to be attractive. In terms of party-to-party transfer, two main channels of transfer emerge: 'ideational transfer' through inspiration, and more concrete 'transfer networks' (as illustrated below). Diffusion theory tells us that organizations 'emulate' policies 'because the other state provides a timely model which may be seen as the solution to a vexing local political problem'.[10] This is particularly relevant to CSPs in the late 1980s and early 1990s, when the parties had to adapt to new political and economic systems.

Bennett argues, with Mossberger and Wolman, that the process is completed upon 'application' of transfer (in our case, into a CSP programme), but we view this as an unnecessary prerequisite for policy transfer.[11] We argue for a broader interpretation of the existence of policy transfer, and agree with Wolman and Page that, in the final stage of the process, 'policy transfer does require the utilization of knowledge drawn from the experience of others, although it does not require actual adoption'.[12] In other words, the evaluation of policies can be integrated into policy-makers' thought processes, providing reference points for policy formation in a particular area. Transfer may, therefore, take place incidentally over time as a by-product of interaction, as explored in the analysis of transfer networks undertaken later in this collection.[13] In these instances, use of the term 'policy learning' may lead to less confusion.

In empirical research it is often difficult to identify and quantify policy transfer from a particular source, because of the subtle and often unacknowledged nature of the transfers. Furthermore, even where networks exist, transfer may not be easily attributable to a single exporter. It has already been shown that external influences other than party-to-party transfer have impacted greatly on the development of successor parties.[14] When identifying policy transfer between the parties we must therefore be careful to recognize the degree of 'institutional isomorphism' that may be involved[15] – the convergence of party programmes from a single 'point source'.[16] In this regard, accession to the European Union has provided a clear incentive for CSPs to learn from the West.

As was illustrated by Dan Hough in the introduction to this collection of essays, Jacoby argues that the EU along with NATO acted as an 'institutional tutor' for the Eastern accession candidates, 'providing templates, establishing thresholds for membership, and suggesting subsequent adjustments that increase the appeal of policy learning'.[17] This represents the first dimension of 'Europeanization', as policy is 'downloaded' to the national level.[18] The second dimension of Europeanization, explored in the party studies later in this collection, is characterized by parties' attempts to influence the rules of the game through their European policy and 'upload' policy to the EU plane.[19] Our main focus, however, is a third dimension of Europeanization: when political parties learn from sister parties in other countries, 'crossloading' takes place.[20] Because of the diverse set of external and internal influences at work – which together make up the opportunity structures for policy-makers in political parties – the contextualization of political parties and their programmes is the key to understanding programmatic change and policy transfer, and this will be addressed in the following two sections.

Party Programmes and 'Policy Contexts'

To undertake an examination of programmatic change in West European SDPs, it is necessary to ask two questions about the role of programmes in political parties: 'what constitutes a party programme and what is its purpose?' With regard to the first question, the research presented in these studies has concentrated on official party programmes, statutes and election manifestos. Ian Budge and his associates tell us that we can assess official policy through an examination of the party manifesto or election programmes.[21] Yet, as programmes have a different value in different parties, and documents vary in their importance and purpose, we support a broader interpretation of what constitutes a party programme. In the German SPD, for example, programmes are the result of extensive policy reviews undertaken over several years, the purpose of which is to find the best solution for policy challenges for issues of popular concern and as a means of achieving political consensus in the party. For the French PS, programmes have been less about policy solutions than about finding the lowest common denominator for a programme that can hold the disparate leadership figures and possible candidates for the French presidency ('*presidentiables*') together. In France, the presidential and legislative elections, in addition, place different policy priorities at the forefront. In the British Labour Party, official programmes have also been of less of importance than in the SPD, with the exception of the fight over the amendments to Clause IV of the party statute in the early 1990s. For Labour, programmes are produced in the form of manifestos only at election time.

These three parties have developed more hierarchical leadership structures over the course of the 1990s, whether by formal organizational change (Labour) or as a consequence of the need for leadership autonomy in fast-moving media democracies (SPD, PS and Labour). It is therefore also important to study the discourse of the party leadership, which (depending on the level of leadership autonomy in the party) offers the most regular indicator of policy change. The leadership in government enjoys a particularly strong position *vis-à-vis* the party. As a result of the leaders' independent power base and the resources at their disposal, the party as a whole plays a largely reactive role to government policy. The opposition–government paradigm is central to the development of party programmes, also because of the fact that parties in government must pay more attention to the implementation of their policy programmes.[22]

Here we develop a qualitative analysis of party programmes, moving beyond election manifestos and 'basic programmes' that provide only a transient snapshot of party policy once every four or five years, to look at key position papers and statements of a programmatic quality by party leaders, who – in the media politics of today – are paramount in defining the programmatic course of political parties. This is especially the case in a party with a high degree of leadership autonomy such as Labour. We therefore strongly disagree with the assertion of Bara and Budge that the 'manifesto is the only official statement of policy made by the parties' and that leaders' speeches are mere 'expressions of opinion'.[23] Such a narrow definition of programmes is inappropriate for a short-term analysis of political parties as it would, for instance, exclude policy shifts (between elections) such as the German social democrats' radical 'Agenda 2010' reform package set out in 2003.[24] CSP party manifestos, furthermore, have proved to be a less reliable indicator of policy preferences in government than in West European social democracy. Dauderstädt and his associates, in their survey of social democracy in Eastern and Central Europe, explain that there is a

> huge discrepancy between the dominance of culturally and ideologically determined symbolic politics and the socio-economic needs of the electorate in these transforming economies ... Thus, while there may be a clear social-democratic profile in programmatic documents and electoral campaigns, this does not necessarily have any bearing to the actual policies of a party in government.[25]

A further purpose of party programmes is to build electoral alliances and win elections. At the end of the twentieth century, social democracy faced a number of challenges. On the party level, SDPs had to respond to weakening ties with their core supporters due to voter dealignment and a more heterogeneous electorate.[26] While the SPD has had to struggle with competition from the New Left, and the *Parti Socialiste* has faced acute competition from the Communists, Labour has been far less constrained in this sense as it has had – thanks to the winner-takes-all electoral system in the UK – no serious challenger to the left. The success of social democracy at the polls in the late 1990s was characterized by its ability to mobilize broad coalitions of voters, while maintaining support within traditional electoral constituencies, as illustrated by the creation of New Labour, the *Neue Mitte* (new centre) and the *gauche plurielle* (plural left).[27] Although political parties in Western Europe have developed towards an 'electoral–professional' model, with a more top-down leadership issuing policy directives through the 24-hour media, moving to the centre has nevertheless hidden certain risks.[28] All three SDPs have been punished for focusing too much on national rather than institutional concerns, on 'dimensions of competition' instead of 'dimensions of identity'.[29] The peculiarities of the French electoral system, combined with Jospin's attempt to deliver a centrist message (including a denial that his policies were 'socialist'!) led to his humiliating defeat in the first round of the 2002 presidential elections as core PS voters failed to turn out or voted for the far left. François Hollande, First Secretary of the Socialist Party, argued that the subsequent parliamentary elections should be fought on 'simple, concrete objectives' such as the efficacy of public services.[30] The German SPD, furthermore, saw its support implode – in local, regional and European elections – as a result of the Red–Green government's Agenda 2010 reform programme.

The failure to deliver to core supporters when in government was particularly important for SDPs after 1997, leading to efforts to re-emphasize core areas such as 'public services' after poor performances in opinions polls and at regional, national and European elections in the late 1990s and the early twenty-first century.[31] There has therefore been a limit to which parties can escape from their 'genetic model'.[32] Given the socio-economic difficulties for governments in the accession states, noted above, the electoral penalties were severe for CSP governments that failed to deliver, as in the case of the Polish SLD at the 1997 elections.

The different value of party programmes for individual political parties set out above underlines the importance of 'policy contexts' in defining the opportunity structures for party programmes. Policy contexts determine the 'structured context' in which political parties operate – the changing pressures and constraints incumbent upon SDPs and CSPs in their selection of policy alternatives as viewed by the parties themselves.[33] The contexts were analysed, in this collection, on three levels across time and space: the 'institutional' (party), 'national' and 'European' planes. These layers overlapped and altered in their make-up over time, but were distinct in the nature of the pressures and constraints they placed upon party policy. The research looks at the changing programmatic profiles of SDPs and CSPs after 1990, studying the motivations behind policy making on the welfare state, the labour market, the EU and external security – central areas in recent social-democratic programmatic documents. Although not all the contextual data collated for SDPs can be detailed in this essay, a few points should be made. First, as stated above, parties' different and changing circumstances with regard to competition (strategy), levels of leadership autonomy (organization) and relationships with their core supporters (identity) are all crucial. These represent the three essential features of the institutional context. In terms of the national context, policy alternatives must be adapted to both national socio-economic structures (for example, industrial profile, levels of state ownership) and indigenous political systems (for example, government coalitions). The relevance of national contexts can be underlined through reference to public spending. While the Labour Party was the only one of the three SDPs to increase public spending significantly after it came to power,[34] this is rendered relative by the different starting-points in the three countries: in 1997, public spending in the UK was 41 per cent of GDP, compared with 49.3 per cent in Germany and 54.9 per cent in France.[35] What we saw in the late 1990s and the early years of the new century was, therefore, a convergence towards similar socio-economic models. In terms of policy transfer to CSPs in government in Eastern and Central Europe, levels of public spending as well as public indebtedness have been key factors in an evaluation of the feasibility of SDP policies when in government.

The European context has become increasingly relevant for parties and party programmes through the 1990s. The penetration of the EU into erstwhile domains of domestic policy over the course of the decade and into the new century forced social-democratic parties to respond to the challenges of a single market that demands the reduction of state subsidies and a single currency that sets limits to public spending. Despite the similarity of the problems faced, there is still significant space for the adoption of different policies. In other words, SDPs have converged towards a 'corridor' of European values within which social democracy may still have 'several different futures'.[36] The increasing penetration of EU policy into domestic policy domains was mirrored by the increasing interest of political parties in European policy, as they recognized the importance of helping to shape the rules of the game. European integration has some particularly interesting implications for policy convergence and – in some cases – for policy transfer.[37] The pressures of European integration constrain party policy (especially when in government), creating greater interdependence, and promoting the use of similar policy instruments in the pursuit of similar policy goals. For centre-left CSPs in the accession states, this greatly enhanced the attractiveness of ready-made SDP policy platforms,[38] as well as the more general programmes of international socialist organizations (in particular, the Socialist International).

Having looked at the nature of party programmes and underlined the importance of placing these programmes for individual political parties in their context, it is necessary to understand how party programmes might best be analysed. We argue that such an in-depth analysis of party programmes in politics today requires a systematic, qualitative programmatic analysis.

Qualitative Programmatic Analysis

Qualitative programmatic analysis is designed to capture the nuances of programmatic change – in this case, to identify the motivations and opportunity structures for social-democratic policy that provide the background for an examination of policy transfer. The analysis will not utilize a 'content analysis' approach as typified by the work of Budge and his associates, since this does not offer a sufficiently detailed picture of party policy to shed light on the reasoning behind programmatic change over a narrow time period.[39] The methods set out below and in Table 1 offer a systematic qualitative approach, enabling a more detailed analysis of political parties, something that has been conspicuously lacking in the study of party programmes. The four methods proposed to achieve this aims are: a contextual analysis, a programmatic review, discourse analysis and elite interviews (see Table 1).

Programmes must, first, be contextualized to understand and compare parties within divergent institutional and national contexts (see above). A contextual analysis combines a literature review, the examination of archival material and pilot interviews. This builds the foundations for the other methods by helping to identify central policy issues (for the programmatic review), 'key concepts' (for the discourse analysis) and important actors involved in the parties' policy-formation process (for the elite interviews).

TABLE 1
QUALITATIVE PROGRAMMATIC ANALYSIS OF PARTY PROGRAMMES

Contextual Analysis
Detailed examination of contexts for policy making in political parties, using both first- and second-hand sources (e.g. pilot interviews, archive material, literature), on three levels – institutional (party), national, EU/international.

Programmatic Review
Broad range of documents, selected according to the role of programmes in the party and national contexts, and focused upon a limited number of policy areas and major issues (uncovered by the contextual analysis).

(Qualitative) Discourse Analysis
Analysis of the changing meaning of a carefully selected range of 'key concepts'. Changing meaning and prominence of words/terms will reflect developments in party programmes.

Elite Interviews
Semi-structured interviews with central actors in programmatic development of parties to ascertain their own (alleged) motives for policy making.

Second, an analysis of party documents of a 'programmatic quality' must form the backbone of any research into party programmes. The programmatic review (see Table 1) needs to investigate a wide range of documents (as argued above) across the time period covered by the study: election manifestos, party programmes and statutes, leading motions at conferences, individual policy papers and major statements made by the party leadership.[40] With respect to policy learning, this part of the research is integral to establishing what is there to be transferred.

Next, a party's discourse must be contextualized in a qualitative sense, because 'the meaning of words is dependent upon their discursive context'.[41] A qualitative discourse analysis (see Table 1) will examine how common terms are conceptualized within a party, thus shedding light on 'why certain meanings prevail'.[42] The content analysis employed by Budge *et al.* did not seek to examine the changing meaning of these terms.[43] Investigating changes in the usage and meaning of key programmatic concepts (for example, 'social justice'), policy areas (such as 'public services') and policy goals (for instance, 'full employment') provides us with reference points of programmatic convergence from which to investigate policy transfer. Finally, a qualitative programmatic analysis should include elite interviews (see Table 1) with politicians and officials involved in determining party programmes, and with those responsible for contacts with sister parties in an investigation of policy learning or policy transfer. The interviews will reveal, from the perspective of the policy-makers themselves, the detail behind policy change that an institutional analysis of documentation is unlikely to highlight.[44] Actors within the process are able to illustrate why and how changes took place, as well as providing a further check on the contextual data by ascertaining the opportunity structures for policy change from the viewpoint of the main actors.[45]

Although the qualitative approach cannot totally reject the claim of selectivity in its choice of programmatic documents, in the key concepts used for the discourse analysis and the subjects selected for the interviews, the triangulation of methods establishes a sound method (with in-built checks for inconsistencies) for the analysis of party programmes across a limited time period and a limited number of countries. This approach to programmes creates a base from which to conduct an examination of policy transfer, and it is to the channelling of those transfers across time and space that we now turn.

Channelling Transfer

Through the contextualization of party programmes set out above, this study deals with both the structural and agent-centred aspects of policy transfer.[46] While the question of agency is dealt with in depth elsewhere in this collection – in the analysis of SDPs' active engagement with centre-left successor parties – it is appropriate at this stage to look at the main structural aspects of the transfer process.[47] We argue that transfer will take place on the basis of geographical, ideological and cultural proximity.[48] With respect to the influence of West European social democracy on the successor parties of Eastern and Central Europe, the German SPD is likely to be most prominent (of the three parties studied in this article) because of the country's location in Central Europe and its shared experiences with the states of Eastern and Central Europe before and after the fall of the Iron Curtain. Proximity has a number of secondary effects that promote the idea of policy transfer on the basis of greater interdependence mentioned above in relation to the European context, placing pressure on governments (and political parties) to adapt to the economic structures of other states, for example.[49] In short, interdependence and integration encourage policy convergence, so that it is logical for officials to 'desire a reduction in policy incongruence'.[50] Germany, in this respect, has enjoyed by the far the greatest volume of trade with the transition states of Eastern and Central Europe.[51]

In the terms set out by Rose, greater proximity leads to greater desirability – in our case, for CSPs to look to the policies of their closest mainstream equivalents in Germany (the SPD for centre-left parties) – while feasibility will be determined by the contexts in which an individual successor party operates.[52] Another reason why it may have been attractive for CSPs to draw lessons from the policy programmes of their sister parties in the West was their desire to join the European Union. The impact of common European rules, as the accession countries adopted the *acquis communautaire*, was to promote congruence, drawing successor parties to SDP programmes that were already adjusted to these EU norms. The desire to emulate the policies of an individual social-democratic party also stems from that party's success, judged in terms of election victories and policy outcomes in government. The attraction for the poorer countries of Eastern and Central Europe to improve their economic conditions has been especially great: 'to adapt and adopt in one's own country a programme already successful in another, and thus reduce future differences in achievement'.[53] According to Dimaggio and Powell, 'organizations tend to model themselves on similar organizations that they perceive to be more legitimate or successful', and this was especially relevant to CSPs in the early 1990s as they attempted to restore their credibility after the collapse of the old communist regimes.[54] Both legitimacy and success have thus provided powerful motives for successor parties to emulate the policies of West European social democrats. This we call 'ideational transfer' through inspiration.[55] For a policy to be desirable, the importer party must nevertheless be open to new policies in a particular area, where openness is defined by local opportunity structures. Here, there have been critical junctures when successor parties have been most open to or in need of transfer.

Contacts between Western and Eastern sister parties through policy transfer networks, on the other hand, have induced awareness of policies among political actors, who at the same time evaluate their fungibility within a different policy context. The successor party politicians in these networks act as filters for transfer. The networks provide knowledge of policies in other countries, thereby increasing the prospects for emulation across space. Successor parties involved in these networks have gained detailed insights into a broad range of policy alternatives, a key characteristic of what have been termed 'information networks'.[56] Networks allow for the evaluation of the desirability and feasibility of a policy, which is assessed by actors from a potential importer party during the process of engagement and communication. We agree with the concept of policy transfer networks, which Evans and Davies describe as a 'constellation of representatives from epistemic communities' set up to solve certain problems, whereby agents from one organization 'gain access to other organizational networks' and provide 'certain essential skills and knowledge resources' for organizations elsewhere.[57] The networks represent a community of like-minded people, not promoting a single policy through a common strategy as in the advocacy coalition framework,[58] but sharing a set of common assumptions 'in the verity and applicability of particular forms of knowledge' and thereby providing a 'cognitive base' for interaction.[59] In our sense, the trans-party networks both presuppose a high degree of ideological proximity, and encourage greater closeness. Here, international organizations such as the PES and the Socialist International have provided an arena for networking and a source for programmatic membership, to make CSPs appear both modern and legitimate.

Where these trans-national communities have occurred, with the countries studied in this collection, they exist on an informal, *ad hoc* basis through personal contacts that are utilized when information is needed. These are not formal, structured networks, but are based on personal 'friendships' that nevertheless have a functional role.[60] They represent 'thought collectives' – sociological groups with a common style of thinking – and behave like information networks. It is not just the information that is important, however, but also the interactions themselves.[61] They promote dialogue and the search for common ideas (congruence), and influence the ideational framework for policy formation. Here, the transfer of policy does not usually take place in an explicit fashion, but as the result of a more subtle diffusion of policies like the spreading of 'ink-blots'.[62] Thus, transfer through networks is usually incidental (not deliberate and probably not acknowledged).[63] It is important to remember, however, that these channels for policy transfer are truly active only when the importer party is in need of new policies.

Conclusion

This essay has offered a framework for the analysis of party programmes, policy transfer and policy learning between political parties. It has been used to examine the relationship between West European social-democratic parties and the successor parties of Eastern and Central Europe from the perspective of both the exporter and the importer. The framework has also been used to analyse relationships between 'retreatist' successor parties and their sister parties elsewhere in Europe. The analytical work enables us to examine the nature and extent of any learning from the West and to identify likely cases of policy transfer. Policy learning is not just a one-way process from West to East, but the perceived success of Western parties and Western economies relative to Eastern and Central Europe made them attractive sources for new policies within a broader Europeanization process.

We have argued here that only by studying party programmes in depth, and the contexts within which policy making takes place, can we ascertain the existence and (just as importantly) the nature of policy transfer. The qualitative programmatic analysis set out above describes how this may be achieved through a broad analysis of policy contexts, programmatic documents, discourse analysis and elite interviews. Looking at both the exporter and the importer sides allows us, furthermore, to examine the pull and push factors of the transfer process. Importer parties are inspired to adopt and if necessary adapt policies through the perceived success of an exporter party. Learning and transfer, on the other hand, are promoted by the interactions of policy-makers through trans-national transfer networks. Both channels of transfer, as we shall see, have become more probable in the context of European integration through increasing interdependence in both an institutional and an economic sense.

NOTES

1. See, for example, R. Rose, *Lesson-Drawing in Public Policy: A Guide to Learning across Times and Space* (Chatham, NJ: Chatham House, 1993); D. Dolowitz and D. Marsh, 'Who Learns What from Whom: A Review of the Policy Transfer Literature', *Political Studies*, Vol.44, No.2 (1996), pp.343–57; C. Bennett, 'Understanding Ripple Effects: The Cross-National Adoption of Policy Instruments for Bureaucratic Accountability', *Governance*, Vol.10, No.3 (1997), pp.213–31; D. Stone, 'Learning Lessons and Transferring Policy across Time, Space and Disciplines', *Politics*, Vol.19, No.1 (1999), pp.51–9; M. Evans and J. Davies, 'Understanding Policy Transfer: A Multi-Level, Multi-Disciplinary Perspective', *Public Administration*, Vol.77, No.2 (1999), pp.361–85; E. Page, 'Future Governance and the Literature on Policy Transfer and Lesson Drawing', prepared for the ESRC Future Governance Workshop on Policy Transfer, available at <http://www.hull.ac.uk/futgov>, accessed 1 Nov. 2004; K. Mossberger and H. Wolman, 'Policy Transfer as a Form of Prospective Policy Evaluation', Future Governance Paper 2, available at <http://www.hull.ac.uk/futgov>, accessed 1 Nov. 2004; W. Jacoby, 'Tutors and Pupils: International Organizations, Central European Elites, and Western Models', *Governance*, Vol.14, No.2 (2001), pp.169–200; H. Wolman and E. Page, 'Policy Diffusion Among Local Governments: An

Information-Theory Approach', *Governance*, Vol.15, No.4 (2002), pp.477–501; S. Padgett, 'Between Synthesis and Emulation: EU Policy Transfer in the Power Sector', *Journal of European Public Policy*, Vol.10, No.2 (2003), pp.227–45.
2. See Rose, *Lesson-Drawing in Public Policy*.
3. See G. Pridham, 'Uneasy Democratizations: Pariah Regimes, Political Conditionality and Reborn Transitions in Central and Eastern Europe', *Democratization*, Vol.8, No.4 (2001), pp.65–94; M. Zaborowski, 'Westernizing the East: External Influences in the Post-Communist Transformation of Eastern and Central Europe', in the present collection, pp.20–36.
4. See R. Gillespie and W.E. Paterson (eds.), *Rethinking Social Democracy in Western Europe* (London: Frank Cass, 1993).
5. This approach is used here and – in greater depth – elsewhere in this collection to evaluate SDPs as a model for the CSPs of Eastern and Central Europe since 1990; see in particular the articles by J. Sloam, 'West European Social Democracy as a Model for Transfer'; P. Buras, 'Polish Social Democracy, Policy Transfer and Programmatic Change'; and V. Handl and V. Leška, 'Between Emulation and Adjustment: External Influences on Programmatic Change in the Slovak SDL', in the present collection, respectively pp.71–87, 88–108 and 109–126.
6. Stone, 'Learning Lessons and Transferring Policy', p.51 (original emphasis).
7. For analysis of external influences, see Zaborowski, 'Westernizing the East'. For more on the policy transfer continuum, see D. Dolowitz, and D. Marsh, 'Learning from Abroad: The Role of Policy Transfer in Contemporary Policy Making', *Governance*, Vol.13, No.1 (2001), pp.5–24.
8. Mossberger and Wolman, 'Policy Transfer as a Form of Prospective Policy Evaluation', pp.2–4.
9. Rose, *Lesson-Drawing in Public Policy*.
10. R. Eyestone, 'Confusion, Diffusion, and Innovation', *American Political Science Review*, Vol.71, No.2 (1977), p.441.
11. C. Bennett, 'How States Utilise Foreign Evidence', *Journal of Public Policy*, Vol.11, No.1 (1991), pp.31–54; Mossberger and Wolman, 'Policy Transfer as a Form of Prospective Policy Evaluation'.
12. Wolman and Page, 'Policy Diffusion Among Local Governments', p.480.
13. See Sloam, 'West European Social Democracy as a Model for Transfer'.
14. See Zaborowski, 'Westernizing the East'.
15. For an explanation of institutional isomorphism, see P. Dimaggio and W. Powell, 'The Iron Cage Revisited: Institutional Isomorphism and Collective Rationality in Organizational Fields', *American Sociological Review*, Vol.48, No.1 (1983), pp.147–60; C.M. Radaelli 'Policy Transfer in the European Union: Institutional Isomorphism as a Source of Legitimacy', *Governance*, Vol.13, No.1 (2000), pp.25–43.
16. J. Walker, 'Innovation in State Politics', in H. Jacobs and K. Vines (eds.), *Politics in the American States* (Boston, MA: Little, Brown, 1971), pp.377–8.
17. W. Jacoby, 'Tutors and Pupils: International Organizations, Central European Elites, and Western European Models', *Governance*, Vol.14, No.2 (2001), pp.169–200, at p.171. The possibility of institutional isomorphism is borne in mind in the country case studies later in this collection. That offer a broader analysis of the external influences on CSPs than this essay on party-to-party transfer. Where 'influence' is clearly identifiable but 'policy transfer' is not, 'policy learning' is generally referred to.
18. See R. Ladrech, 'Europeanization and Political Parties: Towards a Framework for Analysis', Keele European Parties Research Unit Working Paper, No.7, Keele University, 2003. The idea of 'Europeanization' refers more correctly to 'EU-ization' – the process of adaptation to increasing European integration. See also S. Bulmer, D. Dolowitz, P. Humphreys and S. Padgett, 'Electricity and Communications: Fit for the European Union?', in K. Dyson and K. Goetz (eds.), *Germany in Europe* (Oxford: Oxford University Press, 2003), pp.251–69.
19. See Ladrech, 'Europeanization and Political Parties'; Bulmer *et al.*, 'Electricity and Communications'.
20. I. Bache and A. Marshall, 'Europeanization and Domestic Change: A Governance Approach to Institutional Adaptation in Britain', available at <http://www.qub.ac.uk/schools/SchoolofPoliticsInternationalStudies/FileStore/EuropeanizationFiles/Filetoupload,5456,en.pdf>.

21. I. Budge, Hans-Dieter Klingemann, Andrea Volkens, Judith Bara and Eric Tanenbaum, *Mapping Policy Preferences: Estimates for Parties, Electors, and Governments 1945–1998* (Oxford: Oxford University Press, 2001).
22. See W.E. Paterson, 'Political Parties and the Making of Foreign Policy', *Review of International Studies*, Vol.7, No.1 (1981), pp.227–35; J. Sloam, *The European Policy of the German Social Democrats: Interpreting a Changing World* (Basingstoke: Palgrave, 2004).
23. J. Bara and I. Budge, 'Party Policy and Ideology: Still New Labour?', *Parliamentary Affairs*, Vol.54, No.4 (2001), p.591.
24. The SPD's *Agenda 2010* proposed a wide range of significant reforms for the German welfare state, labour market and tax system, and was launched by the party leadership in 2003 (shortly after the 2002 federal elections), but bore little relation to the treatment of these policy areas in the election campaign and manifesto.
25. M. Dauderstädt, A. Gerrits and G.G. Markus, *How Social Democrats, After the Collapse of Communism, Face the Task of Constructing Capitalism* (Bonn: Friedrich Ebert Stiftung, 1999), pp.60–61.
26. See K. Lawson and P. Merkl (eds.), *When Parties Fail* (Princeton, NJ: Princeton University Press, 1988); R. Inglehart, *Silent Revolution: Changing Values and Political Styles Among Western Publics* (Princeton, NJ: Princeton University Press, 1977); A. Giddens, *Modernity and Self-Identity: Self and Society in the Late Modern Age* (Cambridge: Polity, 1991).
27. The *gauche plurielle* was a leftist alliance including the Greens, Communists and other smaller groups.
28. A. Panebianco, *Political Parties: Organization and Power* (Cambridge: Cambridge University Press, 1982).
29. G. Sani and G. Sartori, 'Polarization, Fragmentation and Competition in Western Democracies', in H. Daalder and P. Mair (eds.), *Western European Party Systems: Continuity and Change* (London: Sage, 1983), pp.307–40.
30. François Hollande, cited in *Le Monde*, 6 Aug. 2002, available at <http://www.lemonde.fr/web/recherche_breve/1,13-0,37-768020,0.html>.
31. See Labour Party, 2001, *Ambitions for Britain*, at <http://www.labour.org.uk/manifesto>; Parti Socialiste, 2002, *Choisissons le progres–en avant le gauche*, at <http://www.psinfo.net>; SPD, 2002, *Erneuerung und Zusammenhalt – Wir in Deutschland*, SPD-Vorstand, at <http://www.spd.de/servlet/PB/show/1019292/Regierungsprogramm%20der%20SPD.rtf>.
32. Panebianco, *Political Parties*.
33. See C. Hay, 'Structure and Agency', in D. Marsh and G. Stoker (eds.), *Theories and Methods in Political Science* (London: Macmillan, 1995), pp.189–206.
34. The Labour Party nevertheless left its major increases in public spending until its second term (beginning in 2001), after the public debt had been reduced from 60.8 per cent to 50.4 per cent of GDP: OECD, 2004, *Economic Outlook No.75*, Annexes, at <http://www.oecd.org/document/61/0,2340,en_2649_33733_2483901_1_1_1_1,00.html> accessed 1 July 2004.
35. Ibid.
36. W.E. Paterson and A.H. Thomas, *The Future of Social Democracy* (Oxford: Clarendon, 1986), p.16.
37. Labour Party, *Ambitions for Britain*; SPD, *Erneuerung und Zusammenhalt*; PS, *Choisissons le progress*.
38. See Sloam, 'West European Social Democracy as a Model for Transfer'.
39. See Budge *et al.*, *Mapping Policy Preferences*.
40. The choice of documents may be open to the charge of selectivity when compared with the consistent use of election manifestos across time. Yet, as programmes have a different value in different parties and reflect alternative configurations of opinion within the party structure (explored in a contextual analysis), a more open approach to what constitutes a programme is required.
41. T. Diez, *Die EU Lesen: Diskursive Knotenpunkte in der britischen Europadebatte* (Opladen: Leske und Budrich, 1999), p.610.

42. A. Hoffman and V. Knowles, 'Germany and the Reshaping of Europe: Identifying Interests – The Role of Discourse Analysis', ESRC–IGS Discussion Paper Series, 99/9, University of Birmingham, 1999, pp.33–4.
43. Budge *et al.*, *Mapping Policy Preferences*.
44. W. Grant, 'Elite Interviewing: A Practical Guide', Institute for German Studies Discussion Paper, 2000/11, University of Birmingham, 2000.
45. Although interviewees may not acknowledge the broader framework for policy making (as they may be 'locked into path dependency' – that is, have only one policy alternative – from their own perspectives), attempts should be made to bring the various layers of policy context (actors and structures) into the discussions.
46. Dolowitz and Marsh, 'Learning from Abroad'; Bennett, 'Understanding Ripple Effects'; Evans and Davies, 'Understanding Policy Transfer'; Jacoby, 'Tutors and Pupils'.
47. See Sloam, 'West European Social Democracy as a Model for Transfer'.
48. For similar arguments, see Rose, *Lesson-Drawing in Public Policy*; and Padgett, 'Between Synthesis and Emulation'.
49. Dolowitz and Marsh, 'Learning from Abroad', claim that such 'interdependence' leads to indirect coercive transfer.
50. S. Eyre and M. Lodge, 'National Tunes and a European Melody? Competition Law Reform in the UK and Germany', *Journal of European Public Policy*, Vol.7, No.1 (2000), pp.63–79, at p.64.
51. See Sloam, 'West European Social Democracy as a Model for Transfer'.
52. See Rose, *Lesson-Drawing in Public Policy*. Communist 'retreatist' parties have been drawn towards the German Party of Democratic Socialism (PDS) for similar reasons: see D. Hough and V. Handl, 'The (Post-) Communist Left and the European Union: The Czech KSČM and the German PDS', *Communist and Post-Communist Studies*, Vol.37, No.3 (2004), pp. 333–6. See also Buras, 'Polish Social Democracy, Policy Transfer and Programmatic Change'; Handl and Leška, 'Between Emulation and Adjustment'; V. Handl, 'Choosing Between China and Europe? Virtual Inspiration and Policy Transfer in the Programmatic Development of the Czech Communist Party'; and D. Hough, 'The Programmatic Development of the Eastern German PDS: Learning What from Whom and Under What Conditions?', in the present collection, respectively pp.127–145 and 146–164.
53. See Rose, *Lesson-Drawing in Public Policy*, p.5.
54. Dimaggio and Powell, 'The Iron Cage Revisited', pp.150–52.
55. See Sloam, 'West European Social Democracy as a Model for Transfer'.
56. Wolman and Page, 'Policy Diffusion Among Local Governments'.
57. Evans and Davies, 'Understanding Policy Transfer', pp.374–6. The networks described in this volume are far from rigid, which makes sense of a focus on interactions between key actors (the 'hubs' of these networks) as reference points for the research.
58. P. Sabatier and H. Jenkins-Smith (eds.), *Policy Change and Learning: An Advocacy Coalition Approach* (Boulder, CO: Westview, 1993), pp.16–20.
59. P. Haas (ed.), *Knowledge, Power, and International Policy Coordination* (Columbia, SC: University of South Carolina Press, 1999), p.3.
60. Interviews in 2003 with a number of officials and politicians from the three social-democratic parties and the Party of European Socialists confirmed the informal and *ad hoc* nature of these networks.
61. Haas, *Knowledge, Power, and International Policy Coordination*, p.4; Virginia Gray claims that interaction increases the likelihood of the diffusion of policies: see V. Gray, 'Innovation in the States: A Diffusion Study', *American Political Science Review*, Vol.67, No.4 (1973), pp.1174–85.
62. J. Walker, 'The Diffusion of Innovation Among the American States', *American Political Science Review*, Vol.63, No.3 (1969), pp.880–99. Interaction in these networks is similar to the concept of 'normative isomorphism', where trans-organizational networks provide arenas through which 'new models diffuse rapidly': see Dimaggio and Powell, 'The Iron Cage Revisited', pp.150–52.
63. See Handl and Leška, 'Between Emulation and Adjustment'.

The Communist Successor Parties of Eastern and Central Europe and European Integration

MICHAEL DAUDERSTÄDT

Introduction

For most of the Cold War period relations between the communist countries of Eastern and Central Europe (ECE) and the European Union (EU) were next to non-existent. The Soviet Union and the Soviet-dominated regional integration bodies of Comecon and the Warsaw Pact actively discouraged co-operation with the EU. This freeze thawed in the second half of the 1980s when the Soviet Union under Mikhail Gorbachev loosened its grip on ECE. The ruling communist parties slowly started to move towards a rapprochement with the countries of the EU; Poland, Czechoslovakia and Hungary eventually signed trade and co-operation agreements in 1988–89.

Michael Dauderstädt is Head of the International Policy Analysis Unit, Friedrich Ebert Foundation, Bonn, Germany.

In 1989 internal dynamics took over in forcing the pace of change. In the Polish elections in June, the communists lost virtually every seat that they contested to the buoyant Solidarity Movement. In the autumn, the communist governments of the GDR and Czechoslovakia collapsed in the face of widespread public demonstrations. In Hungary the communists conceded free elections during Round Table talks that resulted in their defeat in March 1990. By mid-1990, the former ruling parties were in opposition in all Central European countries and were, for the most part, redesigning themselves in a much more social-democratic mould by changing their names, re-registering members, adopting new programmes and resolving conflicts over what they claimed to be party assets. The major exception to that general trend was the Communist Party of Bohemia and Moravia (KSČM), which remained communist not only in name but also in many other respects such as its membership and programmatic orientation. In Slovakia, the communists chose at an early stage to follow the general trend, becoming the Party of the Democratic Left (SDL). However, an orthodox faction continued to exist under the name of the Communist Party of Slovakia (KSS), which succeeded in entering parliament in 2002 just as the SDL was in the process of collapsing.[1]

The new programmes of the reformist successor parties incorporated the major elements of the multifaceted transition process from party dictatorship to democracy, away from a planned and towards a social market economy, and from being part of the Eastern bloc to becoming integrated into the open, European and increasingly global economy. In six of the eight former accession countries a further transition took place, namely the building of a new sovereign nation-state. The respective national communist parties supported this transition between 1990 and 1993, leading to the disintegration of the Soviet Union, Czechoslovakia and Yugoslavia.

Transformation and Integration: Party Competition in the New Member States

The successor parties thus became part of the general political consensus in the transition countries – with the partial exception, again, of the Czech KSČM. That consensus included the so-called 'return to Europe', which was narrowly understood as joining the European Union. The transition countries began to adapt their social, economic and political systems to the criteria set out by the European Union for prospective members. More specifically, this entailed the introduction of democratic structures, the rule of law, a functioning market economy and the adoption of community rules, standards and policies – in short, an acceptance of the *acquis communautaire*. This dynamic ensured that accession preparations continued apace, with a threefold transformation of the communist system plus a partial reversal of the fourth transition (nation building), with nation-states giving up some of their newly-won sovereignty.

This difficult process of adaptation required a social consensus in the post-communist accession countries which had to be maintained in the face of costs and disappointments that at first were disregarded, but later became palpable (see Table 1). Although the frustrated electorates in Eastern and Central Europe punished and voted out almost every government after only one term in office, the transfer of power prompted only minor corrections to the policy of reform, system transformation and preparations for accession.

In the case of left-wing parties this was particularly striking, since transformation was basically a liberal project for the introduction of capitalism. In the case of the Polish and Hungarian former communists, a pro-capitalist attitude was less surprising as the 'red managers', who had acquired former state-owned enterprises during a sometimes dubious privatization process, now had a vested interest in the maintenance of the new capitalist system. The parties of the left were also prompted – as were the parties of the right that led most ECE states in the early 1990s – to give their view on the 'new' values and requirements of the EU. They needed to elaborate positions on the EU in party programmes and party manifestos, as did left-wing parties who were still committed to communist objectives.[2] The multiparty consensus none the less remained intact, as is illustrated by the fact that the applications for membership were filed by governments of both liberal-conservative and left-wing orientation. Little changed in terms of this fundamental multiparty consensus even during the long negotiation phase up to the conclusion of the accession agreements (see Tables 2 and 3).

Positions on European integration unfold along both of the axes that typically structure electoral competition: first, the socio-economic axis

TABLE 1
SUPPORT FOR EU ACCESSION IN THE THEN CANDIDATE COUNTRIES
(AS A PERCENTAGE OF ALL RESPONSES)

	1993	1996	1997	1998	2001	2002	2003 Referendum % of votes cast	2003 Referendum % of electorate
Estonia	79	76	29	35	33	39	67	43
Poland	80	93	70	63	51	61	77	46
Czech Republic	84	79	43	49	46	50	77	43
Hungary	83	80	47	56	60	77	84	39
Slovenia	92	79	47	57	41	62	90	54
Latvia	78	80	34	40	33	54	67	49
Lithuania	88	86	35	40	41	53	91	58
Slovakia	84	88	46	62	59	69	92	48

Source: Eurobarometer and <http://www.mdr.de/eu/aktuell/938582.html>.

TABLE 2
PARTY POLITICAL ORIENTATION OF GOVERNMENTS AT THE TIME OF APPLICATION FOR EU MEMBERSHIP

Country	Date of application	Ruling coalition	Political orientation
Czech Republic	23 January 1996	ODS + ODA + KDU–CSL	Centre-right
Estonia	24 November 1995	EK + EME + others	Centre
Hungary	31 March 1994	MDF + KDNP + FKgP	Centre-right
Latvia	13 October 1995	LC, DPS, LZS	Centre-right
Lithuania	8 December 1995	LDDP	Left
Poland	5 April 1994	SLD + PSL	Left
Slovakia	27 June 1995	HZDS	Populist
Slovenia	10 June 1996	LDS + SKD	Centre-right

Source: Nick Crook, Michael Dauderstädt and André Gerrits, *Social Democracy in Central and Eastern Europe* (Amsterdam: FES, 2002), p.20.

where left-wing parties stand for stronger market regulation and wealth redistribution; and, second, the politics of identity axis where left-wing parties generally oppose authoritarian-nationalist projects.[3] Doubts about the prevailing pro-European consensus could stem from fears concerning its distribution effects (considerable in the case of Polish farmers and orthodox communists, for example) or its consequences for the survival of national values (considerable among, for example, the religious right in Poland). In terms of economic interests and the protection of national industries and issues of wealth distribution, however, the left can hope to regain some of the declining influence of the nation-state at the European level. This is particularly true when one remembers the ever-deepening processes of European integration and economic globalization that are taking place.[4] A further motive influencing positions taken towards European integration is the type of capitalism that each of the parties has to deal with (be it Rhineland capitalist, social market economies or more free market neo-liberal varieties).[5]

TABLE 3
PARTY POLITICAL ORIENTATION OF GOVERNMENTS AT THE CONCLUSION OF THE ACCESSION AGREEMENT, END OF 2002, COPENHAGEN

Country	Ruling coalition	Political orientation
Czech Republic	CSSD + KDU-CSL + US-DEU	Centre-left
Estonia	EK + ER	Centre-right
Hungary	MSzP + SZDSZ	Centre-left
Latvia	JP + LPP + ZZS + TB/LNNK	Centre-right
Lithuania	LSDP	Left
Poland	SLD + UP + PSL	Left
Slovakia	SDKU + SMK + KDH + ANO	Centre-right
Slovenia	LDS + ZLSD + SLS + SKD + DeSUS	Centre-left

In this context, left-wing parties strive to protect the social components of the market economy, while liberals seek to avoid the feared return of elements of a planned economy. If one looks at the course and outcome of the accession negotiations, it becomes clear from the host of conflicting demands and transition regulations agreed that the structures and interests of the former accession countries are far from congruent, and very considerable differences have emerged.[6]

Linked with this are ideas concerning the future development of the integration project. This has two dimensions: first, the relationship between national sovereignty and supranational European governance; and, second, the extension of 'positive integration' or, more specifically, the control and regulation of trans-national markets which emerged as a result of 'negative integration'. The Eurosceptical attitude of the former Czech prime minister and now state president Václav Klaus of the liberal-conservative Civic Democratic Party (ODS) was founded on his economic-liberal rejection, for example, of the Common Agricultural Policy,[7] as well as his desire to defend Czech sovereignty from attacks by 'Brussels bureaucrats'. The Czech and German successor parties complain about the lack of strong economic governance at the European level, which should, they assert, protect workers and the environment, and provide for social justice. Figure 1 depicts this situation.

In Figure 1, the shaded circle represents the political positions permissible within the framework of the *acquis* and the Copenhagen Criteria. It leans towards market-liberal orientations, since the EU is at present characterized more by market integration than by supranational market control and redistribution. Before the Amsterdam Treaty, the position of the EU circle was even more inclined in this direction. Some parties have exemplary positions that are either fully EU-compatible (for example those of the Hungarian Socialist Party, MSzP), while others have more ambiguous stances that place them in potential conflict with European positions. These parties include the Hungarian *Fidesz*, the Czech ODS, Vladimír Mečiar's HZDS in Slovakia, the Czech communists, and the Estonian Centre Party, EK (which, before the Estonian referendum, called on voters to reject accession). Some lie well outside the EU consensus, the most notable of which is Andrzej Lepper's *Samoobrona* in Poland.

The extent to which parties attempt to enhance their profile with a European policy position, and particularly with a stance on EU accession, also depends on the importance of this issue in the society and politics of their country. A big party will not go out on a limb explicitly to oppose a broad national consensus in favour of integration (see Table 1), while in a more sceptical environment this can certainly be an option (as was the case, for example, in Estonia). Also important here is whether the parties in question form part of the government or not.

FIGURE 1
ACCESSION COUNTRY POLITICAL PARTIES IN THE EUROPEAN POLITICAL FIELD

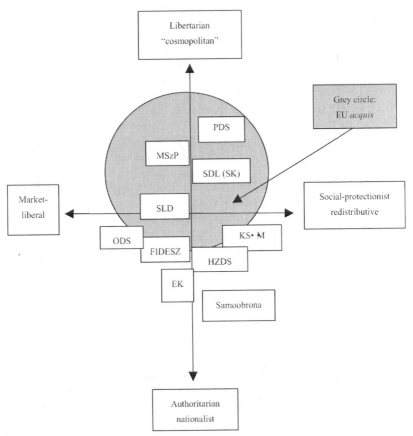

In this respect Eastern and Central Europe is not particularly different from the 15 member states of the old EU. The question of European integration plays a relatively minor role in shaping and moulding electoral competition. No important and electorally significant party is against EU membership or accession. Even in countries where the population is relatively Eurosceptical, such as the UK, Sweden and Denmark, or the Baltic states among the accession countries (see Table 1), the big parties are not totally against membership, but rather reject particular policies (for example, the single currency) or the further restriction of national sovereignty. Although the advocates of accession achieved satisfactory – indeed, often considerable – majorities in their referendums, turnouts were frequently very low. The 'yes' vote, as a proportion of all those entitled to vote, exceeded 50 per cent only in Lithuania and Slovenia (see Table 1).

The European Policies of Selected Successor Parties

In order to gain a closer understanding of how communist successor parties deal with questions of European integration, it is necessary to look at the policies, as well as statements and (if available) programmes, of the successor parties concerned (in this case Poland, Slovakia, the Czech Republic and the GDR). Those investigated here are the successor parties of the former state-socialist parties whose character is now mostly social-democratic: the SLD in Poland, the SDL in Slovakia and the MSzP in Hungary. The KSČM in the Czech Republic represents something of an exception, since it retains the word 'Communist' in its name and is committed to corresponding aims.[8] The German Party of Democratic Socialism (PDS), the successor party of the Socialist Unity Party (SED), represents another special case as it became part of the party system of a unified Germany, which has always been a member state of the EU. In the following sections, I analyse the programmatic positions of the parties listed above, and the extent to which they are embedded in the party system of their respective country and, in particular, their European policy positions.

The Polish 'Union of the Democratic Left'

The Union of the Democratic Left (*Sojusz Lewicy Demokratycznej* – SLD) is the social-democratic successor of the old state-socialist party. The SLD was founded before the parliamentary elections in 1992. It consists of some 30 groupings, led by the Social Democracy of the Republic of Poland (*Socjaldemokracja Rzeczypospolitej Polskiej* – SdRP).[9] The SLD no longer describes itself as openly left-wing and clearly distances itself, particularly in terms of economics, from the objectives of its socialist predecessors.[10] The SLD has even been criticized as 'crypto-liberal' by its current coalition partner, the Union of Labour (UP), which – on account of its trade union past (in Solidarity) – possesses stronger social-protectionist orientations.[11]

The SLD won the national election in 1993 and the government that it led (together with the Polish Peasant Party – PSL) submitted the Polish accession application in 1994. During its 1993–97 term of office, and also since 2001, it has decisively driven the Polish reform and EU preparation process. The SLD Prime Minister, Józef Oleksy (1995–96), sat as representative of the parliament in the European Convention. During the accession negotiations, the party found it much more straightforward to reach agreement with the EU than did its conservative predecessor because, unlike the centre-right coalition, it did not have to take account of strong Eurosceptical forces within its own camp.[12] In the Polish party system, however, the SLD has taken on – just as the weak liberal right has done – pro-European positions, while a large part of the religious right and rural parties range from sceptical to positively anti-European. Indeed, the Alliance called on its supporters before the referendum to vote for accession.[13]

In the EU Accession referendum on 7 and 8 June 2003, 77.45 per cent of Poles who voted did so in favour of accession to the European Union and 22.55 per cent against; the turnout was 58.85 per cent.[14] Before the referendum four of the parties represented in parliament backed accession – the SLD, the PSL, the Citizens' Platform (*Platforma Obywatelska* – PO) and Law and Justice (*Prawo i Sprawiedliwość* – PiS). Among the opponents of accession were the two national-conservative parties, the Polish League of Families (*Liga Polskich Rodzin* – LPR) and the Self-Defence of the Republic of Poland (*Samoobrona Rzeczypospolitej Polskiej*).[15]

Our understanding of the SLD's European policy stance is mostly based on statements by the Polish foreign minister, Włodzimierz Cimoszewicz (SLD), and the president of the Sejm's European Committee, Józef Oleksy (SLD). These statements concentrate primarily on national security and the EU's policy towards all its eastern neighbours. Although they emphasize the significance of the EU as a community with shared values, this – both quantitatively and qualitatively in SLD rhetoric – plays a comparatively minor role as both politicians have focused their attention much more on external policies. Only during the convention on the future of Europe were they forced to develop their positions further on the internal structure and policies of the EU.

Four 'institutions of security' in particular are associated with the security aspect of the party's European policy: the US, NATO, and the EU's common foreign and security policy (CFSP) and security and defence policy (ESDP). Foreign minister Cimoszewicz makes it clear that maintaining Poland's security is the principal goal of Polish foreign policy and that the guaranteeing of this security is directly linked to NATO membership. He also supports the development of the CFSP and the ESDP, while emphasizing that one aim of this development should be support for the US. By this he means that Europe should not become 'stronger' for its own sake or as a counterweight to the US, but rather it should be a stronger partner of the US as Europe's security depends upon America and transatlantic co-operation.[16] For this reason a European security and defence identity should be kept within NATO structures and not detached from the alliance.[17] Cimoszewicz makes it clear that Poland is striving to become the main partner, not of other European countries, but of the United States:

> Through co-operation and dialogue with the USA we will strive to exert adequate influence on decisions concerning the policy of NATO

towards the states of Central and Eastern Europe, especially on issues regarding the further enlargement of the Alliance and its partnership with Russia. In this way we would like to consolidate the image of Poland as the main partner of the United States in the region and one of the most important partners of the USA in Europe.[18]

This verbal confirmation of Polish solidarity was shortly followed by action when Prime Minister Leszek Miller (SLD), with seven other European leaders, signed a letter entitled 'Europe and America must stand united', supporting the US position on Iraq.[19]

The second main emphasis of Polish European policy is the relationship with the non-EU-accession countries of Eastern Europe. For all the importance which Poland attaches to its relationship with the West, it has a strong interest in not shutting out 'the East' and once more having to endure a divided continent. Asked what it meant when the former president of the European Commission, Romano Prodi, mentioned on a number of occasions that Poland was important for the EU in its relations with countries to its East, Cimoszewicz replied:

> We attach particular importance to building a civic society – a fundamental guarantee that all democratic tendencies last ... Poland's task will consist in explaining, motivating and directing our European partners to define the policy toward Eastern Europe exactly in this fashion.[20]

There are no developed ideas concerning the future structure or 'finality' of the EU in the statements of SLD members. Only the president of the Sejm's European Committee, Józef Oleksy (SLD), has anything to say on that subject within the framework of a debate on the future of Europe. Here too, however, he only vaguely endorses a federal system, while the details will be discussed only after accession.[21] The SLD-led Polish government strongly supported the inclusion of the Charter of Fundamental Rights in the Constitution,[22] while Cimoszewicz (SLD) strongly defended the idea of including a reference to God (sought by conservative Polish representatives).[23]

The Czech Republic's Neo-Communists (KSČM)

The neo-communist Communist Party of Bohemia and Moravia (*Komunistická strana Čech a Moravy* – KSČM) did not undergo substantial reforms after 1989, although it does now accept the democratic system within which it now finds itself. Within the Czech party system, it occupied positions on the far left, while the centre-left was colonized by the Social Democrats (ČSSD), a group with long-standing historical roots in the country. Indeed, the Czech Republic is the only post-communist polity where historical social democrats rather than reformed successor parties won elections and formed a government.

The KSČM emerged from the most recent election in 2002 with 18.51 per cent of the vote, making it the third-strongest party after the Social Democrats with 30.2 per cent of the vote, and the conservative Civic Democratic Party (ODS) with 24.47 per cent. The KSČM was none the less the only Czech party that actually increased its share of the vote. In the referendum on EU accession on 13 and 14 June 2003 the Czech people returned a clear majority in favour: 77.3 per cent of the voters said yes to the EU on a turnout of 55.2 per cent.[24] The share of yes votes by party was above 80 per cent for all major parties except for the KSČM, where only 37 per cent of supporters voted for accession.[25] In the European election of 2004, the KSČM benefited from its opposition role and won six of the 24 Czech seats in the European Parliament.

The KSČM advocates European integration but is strongly opposed to the EU in its current form.[26] The KSČM expressly emphasizes that the Czech Republic's future does not lie in isolation; that integration, both economic and political, is of central importance; and that the development of this integration will lead to both greater economic efficiency and cultural enrichment.[27] At the same time, it takes the view that the European Union is not capable of handling this development in the right way:

> However, [the KSČM] does not overlook the harsh pressures in the present European Union, which are aimed at restricting social certainties, or the mushrooming bureaucracy and increasing profits of the biggest transnational monopolies, made at the expense of wide sections of the population. We reject the EU in its current form.[28]

Although the Czech communists believe that the project of economic and political integration needs to be fundamentally restructured, the KSČM does accept the need and value of the Social Charter, EU environmental policy and aid programmes for regional development.[29] However, the party rejects the European Central Bank in its present form.[30] One area which, according to the KSČM, should not be integrated into the EU – and definitely not into NATO – is security and defence policy. The Czech communists regard the OSCE as an alternative which could constitute 'a realistic and efficient structure of European security'.[31] 'It [the KSČM] emphatically rejected NATO membership and promoted the Organization for Security and Co-operation in Europe (OSCE) as an alternative'.[32] The KSČM pleads consistently against the further 'Americanization' of the European continent and for the creation of an alternative to the EU, for a 'common project for a socialist Europe'.[33] In so far as the common European security and defence policy

(ESDP) serves the purpose of developing an independent European policy separate from the American line, the KSČM supports it.[34]

In terms of a referendum on EU accession, it was mainly the Communists who came out strongly in support of the people being given the opportunity to decide. In the course of the national debate on EU accession the KSČM's stances became increasingly clear, and it ended up by calling for a rejection of Czech accession.[35] In the *International Herald Tribune* the KSČM president was quoted as saying 'people can expect to be disillusioned. The conditions we negotiated for our country are bad',[36] while deputy leader Václav Exner expressed himself in similar fashion at a press conference at KSČM party headquarters:

> We continue to take the view that the accession conditions negotiated by the Czech government, like the accession conditions negotiated by the new member states in general, are unfavourable. The outcome of the referendum has done nothing to change that.[37]

The Slovak 'Party of the Democratic Left'

The Party of the Democratic Left (SDL) was one of the most vigorous earlier reformers among the various successor parties in Eastern and Central Europe. Its position in the Slovak party system was determined by the unique polarization of the Slovak polity between the long-dominant Movement for a Democratic Slovakia (HZDS), led by the authoritarian populist, Vladimír Mečiar, and all other parties. The HZDS remained the strongest party at the 2002 election. Mečiar, with his nationalist-authoritarian rhetoric, had long blocked further EU integration. As a result, Slovakia was not included in the Luxembourg group of first candidates in 1997. In 1998, however, a broad democratic coalition managed to remove Mečiar (as had previously been achieved in 1994, but only temporarily). The SDL was prominently represented in both victorious anti-Mečiar coalitions in 1994 and 1998. Although the SDL possessed a number of portfolios in the cabinet, the most prominent of this was clearly the finance ministry, where Brigita Schmögnerová drew much criticism for her reform-oriented austerity measures. Internal party conflicts eventually led to Schmögnerová's resignation in 2002, and ultimately to electoral defeat.

The SDL's share of the vote in 2002 fell from over 13 per cent to 1.4 per cent, and it is no longer represented in parliament. The Slovak left is now deeply divided and weak, not least because its electoral potential was for a long time drawn off by the HZDS. In parliament the left is now represented by the orthodox communists (KSS) and a new party, *Smer* (Direction). In the European elections of 2004, the SDL won one seat (for its vice-chairman

Vladimír Manka) in an electoral coalition with *Smer*, which won three of the 14 Slovak seats.

At the referendum on 16 and 17 May 2003 the Slovaks showed that they were, to some extent, tired of voting: only 52 per cent of the electorate – a mere two per cent above the minimum 50 per cent threshold required for the vote to be valid – found their way to the polling booths, although they came out surprisingly strongly in favour of accession, 92.5 per cent of voters backing it.[38] According to surveys, the Slovak people associate the EU with prosperity, and hope to find a solution to their economic and social problems through EU accession.[39]

The SDL was always one of the driving forces behind Slovakia's EU accession. At the first meeting of the National Convention on the Future of Europe both Jozef Migaš, at that time speaker of the parliament and SDL party chairman, and Peter Weiss, at that time chairman of the parliament's foreign policy committee (and SDL founding chairman), made important speeches. Migaš was in favour of a Europe of citizens, federal structures and a strengthening of the European parliament. Weiss underlined the political significance of European unification and of the European social model and called for the incorporation of the charter of human rights into the European Constitution.[40] After having left the Slovak government, Brigita Schmögnerová wrote a book on the European social model, calling for a 'third way' between traditional redistribution and neo-liberal dismantling of the welfare state.

In terms of the role of the EU Commission, the SDL called for the direct election of the EU president, and supported an increase in the commission's power to initiate legislation. It favoured a reduction in the number of commissioners in order to improve internal efficiency. As regards the council of ministers, the SDL supported its transformation into a chamber of nations. The SDL opposed an additional chamber of national parliaments since institutionally it would represent a retrograde step. The SDL wanted to strengthen the European parliament's co-decision-making rights, and it supported the introduction of a European Constitution that would contain fundamental rights and a division of powers between the institutions. The charter of fundamental rights should, so it was asserted, also be incorporated into the Constitution and this should be binding, and clearly reflect the importance of maintaining the European social model. The Union should none the less know its limits and remember that it exists to facilitate member states and citizens, as well as to defend the multicultural character of the European continent.[41]

The emphasis placed on the European social model by the SDL reflects domestic political cleavages. The conservative–liberal government enacted one of the most liberal reform programmes among all new member states and the SDL hoped to use European integration as a way to protect as much as possible of the Slovak welfare state.

The manifestos that the SDL produced for the European elections demanded 'a strong and social Europe'. That implied a further deepening of political and economic integration in order to meet the expectations of the citizens regarding an effective union while avoiding a European 'super-state'. The SLD wanted stronger co-ordination of the EU's economic and social policies, including more democratic control of the European Central Bank. The freedom of movement of labour should not, so it was said, be constrained to states within the EU. Regional policy needed to be strengthened so that it focused on investment in infrastructure and the promotion of rural tourism. The Common Agricultural Policy would need to be reformed, in order to create more jobs in rural areas and more ecological, agricultural production. All citizens should have access to free public services, and in particular education including (in the long term) access to the internet. In the area of foreign policy, the SDL favoured a common foreign policy of the EU independent from NATO. This independence should not, however, endanger the transatlantic relationship, although quite how this would work in practice was never made clear. The SDL supported further enlargements of the EU, applying the same criteria and conditions Slovakia had to face during its candidacy.[42]

The German Party of Democratic Socialism

The Party of Democratic Socialism (*Partei des Demokratischen Sozialismus* – PDS) is the successor party of the Socialist Unity Party of Germany (*Sozialistische Einheitspartei Deutschlands* – SED), the ruling party of the German Democratic Republic (GDR). The GDR ceased to exist when it acceded to the FRG in October 1990, concurrently joining the European Union. The PDS has remained for the most part a regional party with relatively strong support in the five eastern *Länder* and Berlin, where it benefits from grievances that have arisen from the consequences of unification, such as de-industrialization, widespread unemployment and rising socio-economic inequality. In the western *Länder* it tries to occupy the role of a radical left-wing party: a position that a number of minor communist parties and the Green Party have fought for over a number of years. At the federal level the PDS has never won much more than five per cent of the vote, frequently relying on direct mandates in eastern Berlin constituencies to enter parliament. Within the German party landscape, the PDS is often seen as a protest party that does not offer a feasible policy alternative, but asks for radical reform – if not a fundamental change – of the system. That attitude applies to its European policy just as it does to other areas.

As a party of an existing EU member state, the PDS participated in several European elections and won seats in the European parliament in 1999 and 2004. In 2004, it benefited from the weakness of (and the voters' disgruntlement with) the ruling SPD, acquiring seven of the 99 German seats. In the European parliament it is a member of the umbrella United European Left/Nordic Green Left (GUE/NGL) group that encompasses, among others, the United Left of Spain, the Communist Party of France, Communist Refoundation of Italy, the Communist Party of Portugal, the Communist Party of Greece, *Synaspismos* of Greece, the Left Party (VP) of Sweden, the Left Alliance (*Vas*) of Finland, and the Socialist People's Party (SF) of Denmark.[43] In many regards, the PDS has developed its European policy much more than the successor parties in the former accession countries. This is not surprising given its much deeper involvement in European politics.

Its European policy focuses primarily on economic and social areas.[44] The PDS's positions derive from its ideological heritage as a leftist party and from its position in the German party system. Above all, it seeks a strong state that is not scared to intervene in social and economic affairs and particularly in the battle against unemployment and social injustice. Since it sees the viability of these policies as being endangered by the forces of globalization, the PDS favours a strong European social model. On the other hand, it is well aware of the fact that market integration within the EU reinforces the very same competitive pressures that often lead to more inequality and unemployment. It criticizes, in particular, the stability and growth pact because of its stability bias, which prevents national Keynesian policies of demand management and redistribution that could be used to counteract the effects of globalization and integration.

Since the PDS is to a large extent a regional party, representing a relatively poor part of Germany, it seeks to protect the flow of EU regional aid into the new *Länder*. Thus it supports continuing assistance for poor regions in the old EU-15 that will suffer on account of the EU's enlargement. The concomitant lowering of the EU average income may end the eligibility of much of eastern Germany for the EU's regional funds, since their per capita income will no longer be below 75 per cent of the EU average.

The PDS favours a pacifist CFSP with a strong emphasis on multilateralism and 'soft power'.[45] It rejects US policy towards Iraq but goes beyond that: it did not support NATO intervention against Serbia, and does not want a military role for the EU at all. Instead, it wants to expand and strengthen European efforts in the fields of human rights policy, development co-operation and a more just world order.[46]

Conclusion: Co-operation and Conflict in the Enlarged European Union

In terms of electoral competition within the former accession countries' political systems, the successor parties have adopted very different attitudes towards European integration. The Slovak and Polish successor parties were strong advocates of accession and of the ongoing integration process. Opponents that base their political platforms on nationalist grounds are usually to be found overwhelmingly on the right, although the orthodox Czech (and Slovakian) communists combine arguments about sovereignty with left-wing ideological positions (primarily against international capital and imperialism). However, in the latter field, the orthodox communists do admit that only a united Europe would have a chance of going its own way, as this is something that is no longer practical for individual countries. The social objective of all left-wing forces is to preserve a European welfare state model in the face of the forces of economic globalization. Neither the German PDS nor the Czech KSČM is against European integration as such, but they do favour a social (or socialist) Europe with a much stronger emphasis on protecting the interests of European citizens.

The evolving European policy of the successor parties in the new member states cannot be understood without taking into account the intensive dialogue and networking with their West European sister parties. West European parties, particularly social-democratic ones, in the old member states have tried to steer their partners in the accession countries towards compatible development paths. For this purpose, particularly within the framework of the Socialist International (SI) or the Party of European Socialists (PES), the European Forum for Democracy and Solidarity has been useful, co-ordinating with foundations close to national political parties (such as the Friedrich Ebert Foundation, the Alfred Mozer Foundation, the Karl Renner Institute, the Olof Palme Centre and the Jean Jaurès Foundation). The radical left, through bodies such as the PDS-affiliated Rosa Luxemburg Foundation, also sought to network with its European partners, even if this was difficult because of some of their inherent Euroscepticism (the KSČM being the best case in point).

The successor parties are now likely to become rapidly embedded in their respective party families. As early as 1995, the Slovak SDL and the Polish SLD were granted observer status by the Party of European Socialists (together with four other leftist parties of Eastern and Central Europe). At the PES congress in 1999 in Milan, the 12 observer parties from Eastern and Central Europe became associate members.[47] In May 2003, the presidency of the PES decided to grant full membership to six parties, among them the Polish SLD, while the weak and fragmented Slovak SDL remained an associate member. A similar process took place within the Confederal Group of the European United Left/ Nordic Green Left (GUE/NGL), which accepted the German PDS first as an associate member and as a full member from 1999. In 2003, as part of the accession process, seven parties joined the group, with parties from Cyprus, the Czech Republic, Latvia and Slovakia becoming observers. Among the three new Czech observers, the KSČM is by far the most significant.

The attempt to generate political and institutional co-operation and integration has brought about some verbal harmonization but it has not been able to prevent major conflicts, in particular in the area of foreign policy. The leader of the Polish SLD was one of those Central and East European statesmen who signed the 'letter of eight' which sided with the US and the UK against Germany and France over the Iraq War. If one looks at the foreign policy standpoints of individual parties more closely one may discern a clear dividing line between – roughly speaking – 'Atlanticists' and 'Europeans'. The first place the security issue in the foreground and emphasize the need for American engagement on European soil, and the integration of European security structures in NATO. In this group we find above all the Polish SLD. It is interesting that two communist successor parties, the SLD and the LSDP, are among the Atlanticist 'hardliners', having fully distanced themselves from their earlier aims and ideals.

On the other 'European' side one can find the Czech ČSSD and also a successor party, the Hungarian MSzP. Their party programmes are markedly different from those of the other parties. Both give political integration considerable emphasis and advocate the reinforcement of supranational structures with the European Union – even, in the case of the MSzP, at the expense of national sovereignty. The second point of emphasis in their EU agenda is that of European identity, to which the Czechs and the Hungarians apparently feel more strongly bound than do the Poles or the parties in the Baltic states. The Czech KSČM is an exception as it is in favour of deeper European integration but is opposed to the EU in its present form, and is the only successor party to declare its loyalty to communist ideas emanating from its past as a state party.

These conflicts over foreign policy will be complemented and superseded by further conflicts regarding the core business of the European Union: institutional and constitutional questions (voting weights and so on), the budget and the reform of major spending policies such as the common agricultural policy, regional policy and economic and monetary union.[48] Thus, the attitudes of the post-communist parties in Eastern and Central Europe reflect the conflicts that the old EU-15 has had to cope with, and these conflicts are likely to continue not just because of the scale of the EU's enlargement, but also because of the heterogeneity of the parties involved.

NOTES

1. For a general overview on the development of the post-communist successor parties after 1989, see J.T. Ishiyama (ed.), *Communist Successor Parties in Post-Communist Politics* (Hauppauge, NY: Nova Science, 1999); A.M. Grzymala-Busse, *Redeeming the Communist Past: The Regeneration of Communist Parties in East Central Europe* (Cambridge: Cambridge University Press, 2002); A. Bozóki and J.T. Ishiyama (eds.), *The Communist Successor Parties of Central and Eastern Europe* (Armonk, NY: M.E. Sharpe, 2002); J.L.

Curry and J.B. Urban (eds.), *The Left Transformed in Post-Communist Societies: The Cases of East–Central Europe, Russia and Ukraine* (Lanham, MD: Rowman & Littlefield, 2003).
2. See N. Crook, M. Dauderstädt and A. Gerrits, *Social Democracy in Central and Eastern Europe* (Amsterdam: FES, 2002), p.22; J. Sloam, *Policy Transfer and Programmatic Change in Communist Successor Parties in East–Central Europe* (Birmingham: University of Birmingham, Institute for German Studies, 2003), available at <http://www.igs.bham.ac.uk/research/Policytransferweb.pdf>, accessed 3 July 2003; P. Taggart and A. Szczerbiak, 'Parties, Positions and Europe: Euroscepticism in the EU Candidate States of Central and Eastern Europe', Working Paper No.46, Sussex European Institute, 2001, pp.11–12.
3. See H. Kitschelt, Z. Mansfeldova, R. Markowski and G. Tóka, *Post-Communist Party Systems: Competition, Representation, and Inter-Party Co-operation* (Cambridge: Cambridge University Press, 1999).
4. See G. Marks and C.J. Wilson, 'The Past in the Present: A Cleavage Theory of Party Response to European Integration', *British Journal of Political Science*, Vol.30, No.3 (2000), pp.433–59.
5. See P.A. Hall and D.W. Soskice (eds.), *Varieties of Capitalism: The Institutional Foundations of Comparative Advantage* (Oxford: Oxford University Press, 2001).
6. See M. Dauderstädt, 'Interessen und Hindernisse bei der EU-Osterweiterung. Die Rolle des "acquis communautaire"', in *Politikinformation Osteuropa 98* (Bonn: FES, 2002).
7. It was the common agricultural policy that caused Václav Klaus to demand in Davos that the EU revise its policy rather than force the then candidate countries to adopt it, at which EU Commissioner van den Broek made his famous remark that it was the Czech Republic that wanted to join the EU, not the opposite.
8. On terminology, see M. Dauderstädt, A. Gerrits and G. Markus, 'Three Roots of Social Democracy in Post-Communist Societies', in M. Dauderstädt, A. Gerrits and G. Markus, *Troubled Transition. Social Democracy in East–Central Europe* (Amsterdam: FES, 1999), p.69ff; G. Meyer, 'Demokratie und Marktwirtschaft – ohne soziales Netz? Parteien, Wählerverhalten und politische Kultur. Konflikte und Konjunkturen der Macht: Das Beispiel der Sozialdemokraten', in Landeszentrale für politische Bildung Baden-Württemberg (ed.), *Der Bürger im Staat*, No.3 (1997), p.2; Kitschelt et al., *Post-Communist Party Systems*, p.16.
9. See K. Ziemer and C.-Y. Matthes, 'Das politische System Polens', in W. Ismayr (ed.), *Die politischen Systeme Osteuropas* (Opladen: Leske und Budrich, 2002), pp.215–16; D. Bingen, 'Die "Sozialdemokratie der Republik Polen" (SdRP) in der "Demokratischen Linksallianz" (SLD)', in G. Hirscher (ed.), *Kommunistische und postkommunistische Parteien in Osteuropa: Ausgewählte Fallstudien* (Munich: Hanns Seidel Stiftung, 2002), pp.70–71.
10. See K.-O. Lang, 'Polens Demokratische Linksallianz – eine post-postkommunistische Partei? Vom Bündnis SLD zur Partei SLD', *Aktuelle Analysen des Bundesinstituts für ostwissenschaftliche und internationale Studien 4* (Cologne: Bundesinstitut für ostwissenschaftliche und internationale Studien, 2000), p.3.
11. See J. Bugajski, *Political Parties of Eastern Europe: A Guide to Politics in the Post-Communist Era* (London: Centre for Strategic and International Studies, 2002), p.172.
12. See N. von Redecker, 'Polen', in W. Weidenfeld and W. Wessels (eds.), *Jahrbuch der Europäischen Integration* (Berlin and Bonn: Europa-Union Verlag, 2002), p.421.
13. According to Mildenberger, populist anti-Western voices within the leadership occasionally make themselves heard: see M. Mildenberger, 'Der Europäische Integrationsprozess aus Sicht der Beitrittskandidaten Polen, Tschechien und Slowakei', *DGAP-Jahrbuch 2000* (Munich: R. Oldenbourg-Verlag, 2001), p.187.
14. See <http://www.chancen-erweitern.gv.at/default.pxml?lang = de&kap = 186>; accessed 20 Aug. 2004.
15. See H. Tewes, *Polen vor dem Referendum* (Bonn: KAS, 2003), available at <http://www.kas.de/publikationen/2003/1925_dokument.html>; accessed 15 July 2003.
16. See W. Cimoszewicz, 'Future of the Common Foreign and Security Policy', lecture by the minister of foreign affairs of the Republic of Poland Włodzimierz Cimoszewicz, Friedrich-Ebert-Foundation Berlin, 12 March 2003, available at <http://www.msz.gov.pl/start.php>; accessed 3 July 2003.

17. See W. Cimoszewicz, presentation at the 16th Session of the Sejm on 14 March 2002; available at <http://ww.polandembassy.org/Policy/p4-1.htm>; accessed 16 July 2003.
18. Ibid.
19. See J.M. Aznar, J.-M.D. Barroso, S. Berlusconi, T. Blair, P. Medgyessy, L. Miller and A.F. Rasmussen, 'Europe and America must stand united', statement of 30 Jan. 2003, available at <http://www.kprm.gov.pl/english/1433_5777.htm>; accessed 16 July 2003.
20. Foreign Minister Włodzimierz Cimoszewicz interviewed by *Warsaw Voice*, May 2003, available on <http://www.msz.gov.pl/start.php>; accessed 3 July 2003.
21. See Center for International Relations, 'The Future of Europe in the Opinion of Polish Politicians', transcript of a debate, *Reports & Analyses*, No.1 (2002).
22. See C. Franck and D. Pyszna-Nigge (eds.), *Positions of 10 Central and Eastern European Countries on EU Institutional Reforms: Analytical Survey in the Framework of the CEEC-DEBATE Project* (Louvain-la-Neuve and Brussels: Université Catholique de Louvain, 2003), at <http://europa.eu.int/futurum/documents/other/oth010603_3_en.pdf>, p.70; accessed 20 Aug. 2004.
23. Ibid., p.80.
24. See 'Schweik zieht in die Welt hinaus', *Frankfurter Rundschau*, 16 June 2003, available at <http://www.fr-aktuell.de/ressorts/nachrichten_und_politik/international/?cnt = 231869>; accessed 20 June 2003.
25. See K. Larischová, *Zum Ausgang des EU-Referendums in der Tschechischen Republik* (Prague: Friedrich Ebert Foundation, 18 June 2003), p.3.
26. See *Communist Party of Bohemia and Moravia: Political Programme*, available at <http://www.kscm.cz/news_detail.asp?menu = 1&necId2 = 321&necId = 321&newId = 492>; accessed 18 June 2003.
27. See D. Hough and V. Handl, 'The (Post-)Communist Left and the European Union: The Czech KSCM and the German PDS', *Communist and Post-Communist Studies*, Vol.37, No.3 (2004), pp.319–39.
28. See *Communist Party of Bohemia and Moravia: Political Programme*.
29. See V. Handl, *Die Tschechische Kommunistische Partei: Orthodoxes Fossil oder erfolgreiche neo-kommunistische Protestpartei?*, Analysen der Friedrich-Ebert-Stiftung, Politikinformation Osteuropa, No.105, Oct. 2002 (Bonn: FES, 2002), p.12.
30. See Lang, 'Polens Demokratische Linksallianz', p.29.
31. From the report of the Central Committee of the KSCM on party activities since the 4th party congress, cited in V. Handl, *Die Tschechische Kommunistische Partei*, p.12.
32. See *Communist Party of Bohemia and Moravia: Political Programme*.
33. Ibid.
34. See Lang, 'Polens Demokratische Linksallianz', p.29.
35. See Larischová, *Zum Ausgang des EU-Referendums in der Tschechischen Republik*, p.3.
36. M. Grebeníček, cited in 'Czech Voters Say "Yes" to EU', *International Herald Tribune*, available at <http://www.iht.com/cgi-bin/generic.cgi?template = articleprint.tmplh&ArticleId = 99560>; accessed 16 June 2003.
37. See G. Schubert, 'Das kommunistische "Nein" zur EU und die Haltung der Partei nach dem Referendum', available at <http://www.radio.cz/de/artikel/42176>; accessed 16 July 2004.
38. See <http://www.eureferendum.sk>; accessed 28 July 2003.
39. See C. Thanei, *Wahlen zum slowakischen Parlament: Regierungsmehrheit für die Mitte-Rechts-Parteien*, KAS-Auslandsinformation, No.10 (Bonn: KAS, 2002), p.99.
40. See V. Bilčík, 'Slovakia's Future of Europe Debate', *Slovak Foreign Policy Affairs*, Vol.3, No.1 (2002), pp.14–31.
41. Ibid., synoptic table, p.26.
42. See <http://www.sdl.sk/euromanifest.htm>; accessed 24 Aug. 2004.
43. See D. Hough, 'The Programmatic Development of the Eastern German PDS: Learning What from Whom and Under What Conditions?', in the present collection, pp.144–164, for further information on how the PDS has interacted with these organizations.
44. See also ibid.

45. See PDS, *Alternativen sind machbar: Für ein soziales, demokratisches und friedliches Europa! PDS-Wahlprogramm für die Wahlen zum Europäischen Parlament am 13. Juni 2004*, available at <http://www.pds-pirmasens.de/PDS_Europa-Politik/pds_europa-politik.html>; accessed 16 July 2004.
46. See PDS, *Europa mit Programm*, available at <http://www.sozialisten.de/wahlen2004/wahlprogramm/langfassung/index.htm>; accessed 24 Aug. 2004.
47. S. Hix and U. Lesse, *Shaping a Vision: A History of the Party of European Socialists, 1957–2002* (Brussels: Party of European Socialists, 2002).
48. M. Dauderstädt, *Conflicting Distributive Interests in a Deepening and Widening Europe: A Challenge to the Emerging Europolity* (Bonn: FES, Reihe Europäische Politik, 2004).

West European Social Democracy as a Model for Transfer

JAMES SLOAM

Introduction

This essay examines the extent to which the British Labour Party, the German Social Democrats (SPD) and the French *Parti Socialiste* (PS) have provided a model for policy transfer for the communist successor parties (CSPs) of Eastern and Central Europe (ECE). In analysing West European social democracy as a model for emulation, the essay will explain how and why transfer takes place within a broader process of 'policy learning'. It will assess the opportunity structures for policy transfer from the perspectives of the Western exporter parties.[1] The two channels explored represent the push and pull factors of policy transfer: 'ideational transfer' (the attractiveness of West European social-democratic ideas as a model) and the transfer of policies through interaction in concrete 'transfer networks'.[2] It will thus respond to David Dolowitz's complaint that 'relatively few existing studies identify the process directly', by looking at both how and why the transfer of ideas and

---

James Sloam is Lecturer in European Studies at King's College London, and an honorary Research Fellow in the Institute of German Studies, University of Birmingham.

policies takes place.[3] The study tests the hypothesis that policy transfer is dependent upon geographical, ideological and cultural proximity between exporter and importer parties set out earlier in this collection.[4] While the three West European social-democratic parties (SDPs) identified above have been chosen as a model for the successor parties of ECE because of their ideological proximity, the study will focus particularly on the German SPD in view of its geographical and cultural proximity.

The essay will, first, explain the extent to which West European social democracy has provided a 'model for emulation', looking at why individual SDPs and their policies may appear attractive, why transfer is desirable and what there is to be transferred. It will argue that greater proximity leads to a more substantive policy transfer because it relates not just to the desirability but also to the feasibility of transfer taking place across different socioeconomic and institutional settings. Next, attention will turn to an analysis of transfer networks. This section will explore SDP positions towards the eastern enlargement of the EU, which reflected their degree of enthusiasm for engagement with their sister parties to the east. It will also examine how SDPs have engaged in bilateral terms, but also on the international plane, before moving on to look at the policy goals that lay behind this interaction. Finally, the essay will illustrate the relative intensity of SDP networking with eastern colleagues by giving an overview of the resources devoted to these activities. The study concludes that the German Social Democrats have, in general, exerted the most influence on the centre-left successor parties, but that this has been the product of a subtle diffusion of policy through interactions as CSPs have tried to adapt to the norms of the European Union.

A Model for Emulation?

This section looks at the degree to which West European social-democratic parties have presented a model for emulation for the successor parties of Eastern and Central Europe. Studies by Richard Rose, and by Mark Evans and Jonathan Davies, both offer detailed frameworks suitable for analysing hypothesized processes of transfer – yet transfer does not, in practice, fit into such a structured format.[5] These frameworks, furthermore, describe how transfer takes place in a very general way, lumping together the two channels for transfer set out in this essay. Here, we focus on causal factors: why transfer takes place. Transfer from one party to another in a second country is inevitably voluntary in nature, so the motivations behind the transfer become doubly important. In assessing the attraction of Labour, the SPD and the PS and their policies for CSPs, we turn first to the 'pull' dimension of policy transfer.

There must, as stated above, be a defined need (no matter whether it be implicit or explicit) for new policies if transfer is to take place, and this is clearly the case for ideational transfer.[6] Here, the policy context of the successor party is of paramount importance. Importer parties assess the success of a policy both in political terms (potential exporter parties' electoral performance and the general appeal of their policy programmes) and in terms of policy implementation, especially if the party is in government. While the motivations for transfer may emanate from inspiration and through desirability in political terms, the feasibility of policy transfer, in both a party and a public policy perspective, is dependent upon proximity.

Political Appeal

Electoral performance is a central determinant in policy transfer. The electoral success of the three SDPs examined in this study was very limited in the early 1990s. Although the PS was in government until 1993, the party was already breaking apart at the seams as a result of political in-fighting and economic problems, and between 1990 and 1993 the PS nominated three different prime ministers.[7] The parties, as a group, became more attractive in terms of political success after they entered government in the late 1990s. New Labour, in particular, became an appealing electoral model for CSP elites because of its top-down leadership structures and glossy communications system. In terms of the appeal of successful parties, charismatic national leaders and effective electoral programmes in the late 1990s and the early years of the new century, the greatest incentives for ideational transfer came from the Labour Party, followed by the SPD and then the *Parti Socialiste*. For CSPs who wanted to appear 'Western' and 'modern' it is hard to think of more attractive role models.[8]

Furthermore, it was transparently more enticing to CSP leaders such as Leszek Miller (former leader of the Polish social democrats – the SLD) to be seen with the government heads of other countries, such as Chancellor Schröder and Tony Blair, rather than merely the leaders of Western sister parties. It is worthwhile noting, however, a considerable case of irony in the fact that when the successor parties were most in need of transfer to adapt to the new capitalist environment in the early 1990s, the Western SDPs were not a particularly attractive model for emulation. At this stage, the vaguer programmes of the Socialist International (SI) and the emergent Party of European Socialists (PES) proved most attractive to centre-left CSPs. By the time the social-democratic moment arrived in the late 1990s – with SDPs in power in the UK, France, Germany and most of the EU – the need for transfer was considerably diminished.[9]

While the three SDPs were succeeding in electoral terms in the late 1990s, they also constructed cohesive, media-friendly policy programmes. The SDPs had responded to a changing political and socio-economic environment through programmatic renewal. Levels of welfare provision across the EU, for example, were being challenged by ageing populations (and the increasing cost of pensions and healthcare). Added to this were the limits placed on public spending by the EU's single market programme and the single currency. The recipes devised in Britain, Germany and France were embodied by the Third Way, the *Neue Mitte* and *réalisme de gauche*, respectively.[10] These new programmes sought to find syntheses between the dualism of party programmes and the reality of modern governance.[11]

The nature of these programmes can be captured by the parties' positions on welfare spending. New Labour, on the one hand, no longer sees welfare as a means of redistribution to achieve greater equality of outcomes (contrary to the party's position in the 1980s). The passive nature of entitlements is seen as leading to dependency on the state.[12] The welfare state is a means for countering social exclusion and to provide the opportunity of work or training ('Welfare to Work'). The benefits system should thus be 'structured around work',[13] through a system of incentives and penalties. Incentives concentrate on support for low-paid work (for example, tax credits and low tax rates), and the linkage of 'opportunity' to 'responsibility' has taken the form of cuts in benefits for those not accepting work.[14] The *Parti Socialiste* sees the welfare state within the broader sense of *l'état providence*, which emphasizes the role of the state in shaping individuals' destinies.[15] Welfare provides for both redistribution of wealth and equality of opportunity. Furthermore, responsibility is deemed to pertain to the state rather than the individual, with individuals enjoying rights to social security. The question of whether welfare should be used for redistribution remains a controversial topic within the German SPD. The position adopted by the most fervent advocates of the *Neue Mitte* that welfare should work as a 'trampoline' rather than a 'safety net' was initially unsustainable within the party.[16] These ideas were nevertheless given concrete form in the Red–Green Government's Blairite 'Agenda 2010' programme, propagating a reform of the welfare state, labour market and tax system, launched in 2003.[17]

The political appeal of successful parties and policy programmes for the centre-left successor parties of Eastern and Central Europe has often had much more to do with desirability than with feasibility. Although these policy proposals might be brought into CSP programmes to make them look more attractive to voters, the feasibility of policies has determined whether they were implemented when these importer parties were in government. This is particularly relevant with respect to the vastly different socio-economic circumstances of these ECE states. For example, the pressures on public spending in Poland, the Czech Republic and Slovakia since the mid-to-late 1990s have been far more severe than in the case of Western Europe. In Slovakia, the most dramatic example, public expenditure was 65.4 per cent of GDP in 1997, increasing public indebtedness at an unsustainable rate (from 28.3 per cent in 1997 to 45 per cent by 2000).[18] This example demonstrates the importance of the policy contexts of the importer parties, and also the superficial nature of transfer through political appeal. In this collection, for instance, Vladimír Handl and Vladimír Leška write of the limited applicability of Third Way approaches for the Party of the Democratic Left (SDL) in the Slovakian context – despite the efforts of some its former pro-Western leadership to promote these new concepts in the party. As and when centre-left CSPs have sought to emphasize the alleviation of poverty, the more *dirigiste* French concept of what modern social democracy should look like has had more symbolic value than the Blairite Third Way.

Proximity

A second and deeper pull factor is proximity, which is seen as the central causal factor behind policy transfer. This concept is less voluntary than the inspirational reasons for emulation described in the previous paragraphs. With greater proximity, so this essay contends, comes greater interdependence. According to Robert Keohane and Joseph Nye, where interdependence exists, programmes – rather than running parallel to each other – interact.[19] With greater interdependence, policies are likely to be more feasible. Interdependence as a consequence of proximity promotes interaction and the congruence of policy where fungibility exists. If one country depends upon another for its primary market, for instance, policy transfer may easily occur. Germany has always been the dominant state in terms of trade with East–Central Europe, dominating the tables for both EU (about 50 per cent of ECE–EU trade) and OECD countries in 1995 with a trade volume of well over €40 billion.[20] Proximity can also affect the potential for policy transfer in a less direct fashion. Because of the SPD's greater geographical proximity to the successor parties than Labour or the PS, it has, for instance, sought to engage more with its sister parties in Eastern and Central Europe and champion the cause of the eastern accession countries in the EU (see below).

Geographical proximity favours Germany with regard to transfer to Eastern and Central Europe given its location in Central Europe. Interviewees from the three SDPs, the Party of European Socialists and the EU enlargement directorate have pointed out that ECE is simply in Germany's sphere of influence. A key figure in the SPD's foreign policy team in the 1990s argued that 'for geographical and historical reasons, neither of the other parties [Labour or the PS] were as engaged or as accepted, or made anywhere near as much effort as the SPD' in these countries. Britain and France, it was stated, simply have other, more important, spheres of influence – such as the Commonwealth and North Africa, respectively. The importance of geographical proximity is highlighted by the fact that, as other interviewees have emphasized, the German

Christian Democrats were just as engaged as the SPD in Eastern and Central Europe, if not more so.

Cultural proximity was also an important factor in determining the potential for transfer. In the early 1990s, many ECE states were suspicious of German intentions, but were won over by its level of involvement and commitment. Several of these countries (among them Poland) had a cultural affinity with France, but were 'very disappointed by the French reaction after 1989', as typified by the reluctance to support their accession to the EU.[21] The close ties between Germany and Eastern and Central Europe further related to the common use of the German language in the late 1980s and early 1990s and – more potently – a Central European perspective that led to the adoption of constitutional forms similar to Germany (for example, proportional representation and a constitutional court). Germany, furthermore, felt indebted to its eastern neighbours for the part they played in the lifting of the Iron Curtain and the reunification of Germany, and through 'historical memory' as a result of Germany's role in the Second World War.[22] Despite the positive steps taken in the relationship between Germany and its eastern neighbours after 1989, some tensions and suspicions remain.[23] The ECE states' concerns about their powerful neighbour, given Germany's clear prioritization of relations with France over the EU Constitution and the US-led invasion of Iraq in 2003 and 2004, have nevertheless led to a recent deterioration of the relationship.

Ideological proximity, while making the SPD a much likelier source of policy transfer to CSPs than its Christian Democrat counterpart, does not on its own make the party a more probable source of transfer than its Western sister parties. Ideological proximity is extremely important, however, in the sense that the chances for transfer are highly dependent on the ideological position of the importer party. The potential for policy transfer for all SDPs to the reformed Polish SLD was thus infinitely greater than to the largely unreformed Czech KSČM.

Transfer Networks

There is no doubt that ideational transfer motivated by inspiration, and made more feasible by some form of proximity, is an attractive channel for policy transfer. Equally, transfer can take place through a concrete engagement between importer and exporter parties – the push factor of policy transfer. Cross-party networks are promoted by a small, close-knit circle of experts generally involved with foreign policy in individual social-democratic parties. The international secretaries of the SDPs, for example, know one another well and interact on this basis. In the early 1990s, when contacts with sister parties in ECE were first being established, these were the people who actively sought to develop networks of communication, and they remain the first port of call for inter-party dialogue. The transfer networks allow interaction, consisting of communication and dialogue, over policy areas that are relevant to both parties. In the early 1990s, these contacts quite naturally revolved round the question of EU accession and of the centre-left CSPs joining the Party of European Socialists. The size of the networks increased somewhat as these successor parties were integrated into the European family over the course of the 1990s and into the new century, when they grew to include experts and politicians specializing in most areas of EU policy. Interviewees have argued that, in these types of informal trans-national communities, transfer is most likely to be the product of socialization. In this essay it is argued that transfer networks and the intensity of contacts between the parties enhance the prospects for policy transfer, whether it be deliberate and acknowledged or unintentional and unacknowledged (incidental). Engagement correlates with two preconditions for transfer – awareness and evaluation – thereby increasing the chances of efficient and successful emulation.

Eastern Enlargement of the EU

Geographical, cultural and ideological closeness has increased the potential for policy transfer since 1989. Levels of engagement have reflected the degrees of support for eastern enlargement of the EU. From the German perspective, with Eastern and Central Europe on its very doorstep and the existence of a strong cultural affinity between Germany and ECE, the SPD supported ECE applications to join the EU at an early stage. As the SPD executive committee put it in 1990, 'only if the new Central and Eastern European democracies can be joined to the economic and ecological development of Western Europe, will it be possible to prevent new social dislocation, new mass migration from the East to the West and the return to dictatorship'.[24] There was no real mention of Eastern and Central Europe in *Parti Socialiste* documents throughout the 1990s, as the French socialists were sceptical about a widening of the union that would shift the balance of power towards Central Europe and Germany: 'we should enlarge Europe without diluting it', and it must 'not be used as an excuse for dismantling common policies (agricultural policy, regional funds)'.[25] Labour, sharing much of the British caution about deeper EU integration, could, for the opposite reasons, support 'creating the conditions in which, at the appropriate time, the new democracies of Central and Eastern Europe can join the Community', but only as a brief aside from its policy guidelines on European integration.[26] Outside the election manifestos, the SPD was the only party that consistently took positions on eastern enlargement. As one key official in the EU enlargement directorate put it, 'there was until very recently really no Labour or PS, UK or

French, interest in the enlargement process, certainly not compared to the interest of the SPD'. The SPD, even so, had to think more practically about eastern enlargement once in government, and began to attach conditions to the process – as illustrated by the transition periods proposed (and achieved) for the free movement of workers from ECE after accession, and the concerns raised over the cost of enlargement *vis-à-vis* German payments to the EU budget. While the PS in government remained quiet on an issue that was controversial in the party and the country at large, Labour stated in clear but brief terms that 'enlargement will benefit Britain economically and politically'.[27]

Engagement

In line with the SPD's strong support for enlargement, it sought contacts and established links with its sister parties in Eastern and Central Europe to a far greater extent than the Labour Party or *Parti Socialiste*. Even the SPD, however, was reluctant to seek contacts with these successor parties in the late 1980s and early 1990s when the new political landscapes in ECE were far from clear-cut, and it was unclear which parties would take the social-democratic path. The party, furthermore, was hindered by two factors in its relations with Eastern and Central Europe in the early 1990s: first, the SPD's *Ostpolitik* had focused on ties with the former communist regimes (at the price of alienating former dissidents after regime change); second, the SPD leadership after Brandt was little interested in these countries.

The shock of reunification and regime change across Eastern and Central Europe slowly changed the party's apathetic approach. From the early 1990s onwards, the SPD's foreign policy groups – following on from the work carried out by their political foundation, the Friedrich Ebert Foundation (see below) – began to establish links with these political parties. A major figure in SPD foreign policy at that time stated that he had 'very intensive contacts' with the SPD's East European sister parties through the 1990s, and they became 'more intense' as time went by. For example, he had close ties to Peter Weiss, then chairman of the Slovakian SDL, with whom he could 'just pick up the phone' and speak about any matter. In the early and mid-1990s, Labour and the PS had barely any contact with these parties.[28] One Labour politician involved in European politics admitted that the party had 'no real contact with its sister parties in Eastern and Central Europe before 1997 and its entry into government – it didn't have either the resources or the will'. A key official in the enlargement directorate stated that 'in comparison, there was no interest at all from the UK and France – the PS did not want to even discuss eastern enlargement until [Pierre] Moscovici became foreign minister in 1999'.

The only other social-democratic party that has been consistently mentioned in connection with the enlargement issue is the Austrian Social Democratic Party (SPÖ), which was second behind the SPD in its attempts to establish contacts with sister parties in ECE. The engagement of the smaller Austrian party gives further weight to the hypothesis that geographical proximity is of genuine significance. While geographical proximity – for the most part – increased the probability of transfer taking place, this is not to say that such closeness did not produce its tensions. For the SPD, 'national issues' were important in relations with its sister parties: for example, an SPD politician conceded that 'relations with the Czech Social Democrats became very frosty after the remarks of [Miloš] Zeman [former prime minister and party leader]' over the question of the Sudeten Germans. The intensity of SDP–CSP contacts, furthermore, has depended upon the location of the successor party. The German SPD, according to a key figure in the party's foreign policy establishment, focused its energies on 'establishing contacts, in particular, with [new] social democrats in Poland, Hungary, the Czech Republic and Slovakia [Germany's neighbours to the east]'. Ideological proximity was even more important in connection with the successor parties, and this has depended largely on the existence of historic social-democratic parties. In the Czech case, for example, Western SDPs quite naturally allied themselves with the Social Democratic Party rather than the largely unreformed communists (KSČM). In Germany, the Party of Democratic Socialism had little opportunity to enter the social-democratic mainstream as an independent party after unification because of the existence of the SPD. In Slovakia, the movement of the SDL to the left in the late 1990s stifled relations with Western SDPs, whereas – after some initial confusion about the orientations of the Polish successor party – the German Social Democrats were glad to recognize the SLD as a sister party.

It is accepted that contacts between Western SDPs and centre-left successor parties have increased over the course of the 1990s and since the turn of the century. As illustrated above, the SPD's contacts with its sister parties in the East began in the early 1990s and steadily increased in intensity. A key moment came for all three social-democratic parties when their ECE sister parties were accepted as associate members of the Party of European Socialists. Once the accession negotiations with the candidate countries got under way, it was clear that these parties would soon become equal partners in view of their parallel accession into the PES's decision-making structures in 2001. For the SPD, contacts intensified further, led by the work of the party in government. A key actor in the SPD international section argued in 2003, drawing on the example of the Polish SLD, that relations with the successor parties in the PES were now 'of the same type and intensity as with the Western parties', which has meant greater discussion of domestic policy issues. A common working group was, in addition, set up with the SLD in 1999. SPD government officials have emphasized the increased levels of co-operation with their sister parties in ECE, reiterating the point that 'relations with social-democratic parties in the PES are all the same now, whether they are from Western or Eastern Europe', and that they now seek to promote policy co-operation in specific policy areas with these parties (even if these are often 'trumped' by party politics in the national context, as in the case of SPD relations with the Polish SLD over EU institutional reform).

The Labour Party in power initiated a 'step-change' in government and party relations with Britain's European neighbours, and the links with Eastern and Central Europe took off after 1999 as contacts were channelled through the vastly superior resources of government. Labour's international section was subsumed into the work of the government, as illustrated by the incorporation of international policy work into the party's policy unit.[29] Evidence of this was provided by a meeting between Tony Blair and Leszek Miller and the subsequent joint paper in November 2001, which – among other things – set up a common Labour–SLD working group. Contacts were nevertheless strongly led by relations between the two governments, from the office of the minister for Europe. The aim in these contacts was very much to 'spread the word of New Labour', and to develop 'policy coalitions' in specific policy areas in the European parliament and the European Council after EU enlargement in 2004.[30] Since 1998, party-to-party interaction has also been pursued in relation to ECE, as illustrated by the EU Accession Forum – set up 'to assist sister parties campaigning for the forthcoming Referendums ... [and] to develop exchanges between Labour MEPs on policy issues and training workshops for prospective candidates for the 2004 elections'.[31] The *Parti Socialiste*, on the other hand, continues to be reluctant to concentrate its limited international relations resources in Eastern and Central Europe. Its engagement has proceeded in a haphazard fashion, and the interest of the international section of the party in ECE was only – temporarily – sparked through the involvement of Pierre Moscovici as secretary for international affairs after the party's 2002 election defeat.

The International Plane

The international socialist and social-democratic organizations – the Socialist International and the Party of European Socialists – were of fundamental importance to centre-left CSPs, particularly in the early years of transition. Association with (and eventually membership of) the SI and PES crucially offered these parties national legitimacy (given their association with the former communist regimes), and the chance to appear both 'modern' and 'Western' (by showing their affiliation with sister parties in affluent Western Europe). Membership of these organizations was therefore a primary goal. The SI and PES were important both as a source of programmatic inspiration (promoting ideational transfer) and as forums for interactions (promoting transfer networks) which encouraged the diffusion of West European social-democratic values in Eastern Europe.

In programmatic terms, the Socialist International played a key role in influencing the early programmes of CSPs. Vladimír Handl and Vladimír Leška, and Piotr Buras, emphasize elsewhere in this collection the role of SI and PES programmes, which acted as 'templates' in the construction of early programmatic documents in the Slovak and Polish CSPs. This strategy also enabled the CSPs to sidestep suspicions at home of adopting policies from a sister party in a different country. The process of adapting to the membership criteria of the SI and PES further encouraged them to adopt and adapt many common social-democratic values and policies. The relationship between these organizations and the CSPs was, in a sense, similar to that of priest and penitent.[32] Membership was granted to CSPs in return for a certain degree of repentance (for their communist past) and penitence took the form of programmatic change and the acceptance of some fundamental social-democratic tenets. Accepting these general values had the further bonus of feasibility, unlike the detailed emulation of individual party policies.

These international organizations also played an important role as forums for interaction with other social-democratic parties. The process of accession to the Party of European Socialists was especially relevant in terms of the establishment of transfer networks. The Party of European Socialists became a central arena for interaction with the social-democratic-oriented parties of ECE after 1999. From the early 1990s, the PES had sought to encourage interaction with Eastern sister parties, albeit with very limited resources. The sister parties were given observer status from 1995 onwards (before this date most of the work was left to the PES's European Forum for Democracy and Solidarity), but the parties were not yet included in the PES decision-making bureau. Although recognition by the PES was a very important event for the social-democratic successor parties in terms of legitimization, SPD and PES officials involved with contacts to Eastern and Central Europe concur that, at that time, the networking was led by the work of individual SDPs, such as the German SPD. The PES provided a much better structure for co-operation after 1999, when the parties from the accession states acquired associate status and entered the organization and became more involved in policy discussions. This was especially important for the international departments of SDPs with their small budgets. The real change in the quality of relations came in May 2001 (appropriately at the PES's Berlin congress) when the Eastern parties were integrated into the PES's internal decision-making machinery with a view to the forthcoming accessions in 2004. Within the PES, it was the Germans, who – of the major countries – played the key role: one PES official commented in 2003 that on enlargement issues he 'would never dream of setting out a position without the prior agreement of the Germans and the Austrians'. The Socialist Group in the European parliament, on the other hand, established contacts in Eastern and Central Europe quite late, taking on the role for 'training' prospective MEPs from the moderate left after 2000.[33]

Policy Goals

If contacts and interaction are to precede policy transfer, it is clearly necessary to examine the aims of the exporter parties and the issues that have actually been discussed with the importer parties. The SPD, in its engagement with sister parties in ECE, has claimed that it was much more interested in general interaction than in trying to exert influence directly over policy. This was especially the case in the early 1990s as these parties tried to adapt to new capitalist democracies. Several interviewees have pointed out that, after all, the SPD was naturally much closer in its policy programme to the Christian Democrats in Germany than it was to those of its sister parties to the east. SPD representatives argue that 'there is no intentional attempt to influence policies', and interaction has been more about 'democratization' than 'imparting social-democratic views'.[34] Nevertheless, although there may be no intention on the part of the exporter party to transfer its policies, transfer can – as stated above – take place incidentally through interaction. At that time, the main goal of the SPD was to help the parties in their adjustments to a modern capitalist democracy, and ease their path into the Party of European Socialists, which was the reformist CSPs' 'top goal' – the SPD wanted to act as the 'advocate of these parties for their entry into the PES and to help in their adjustment to the rules of the EU'.[35] According to its own representatives, the Labour Party, on the other hand, was 'extremely late' in supporting CSPs with reformist tendencies, and did not establish formal links with the Polish SLD, for example, until 1998.[36] The *Parti Socialiste* was similarly unengaged in Eastern and Central Europe at that time.

After 2001, and the formal acceptance of the ECE parties into the PES, the SPD has sought to engage with these parties over its goals for Europe, and domestic policy within the European Union. Although the influence of the SPD was in general stronger than that of Labour or the PS, the picture was differentiated according to policy area (for example, 'in security the Poles are much closer to the US and the UK and in CAP to the French').[37] Given the new status of ECE social-democratic sister parties in the PES, Western SDPs sought to engage in dialogue and find common solutions in policy areas that went beyond foreign policy and into the domestic policy domain. From the perspective of the Labour Party, interaction was clearly policy-driven in terms of its particular attitude to the goals of the Lisbon agenda.[38] A further aim for West European SDPs in these interactions was to build up majorities for their positions in the European parliament after enlargement.

From the perspective of the PES secretariat, the transfer of policy was not something they thought a great deal about as their policy platforms were already vague and imprecise, working on the lowest common denominator for member parties. The PES nevertheless acted as an arena through which centre-left successor parties were influenced by their Western sister parties as they were brought into the European fold – for example, the 'Warsaw declaration' sponsored by the Polish SLD – providing positions on a whole range of European issues. As European integration has penetrated ever more into former areas of domestic policy, the positions of social-democratic successor parties as potential members of the union are highly likely to be influenced by their sister parties in adapting to the EU. Another reason why the acceptance of ECE sister parties as full partners in the PES was such an important step for SDP–CSP relations was that the networks were now no longer reserved, in the Western parties, to a small group of individuals concerned with foreign policy. This change in status was a spur to interaction over the whole spectrum of EU policies on both a bilateral and a multilateral basis. Although policy learning and a diffuse 'social democratization' has occurred in this environment, identifying the source of the learning or specific transfers has become more complicated.

Resources

Resources are key to the West European SDPs' engagement in Eastern and Central Europe as they are to networks in general.[39] Here, the German Social Democrats have enjoyed a clear advantage over Labour and the *Parti Socialiste* – an advantage that was particularly evident when all parties were outside government. Throughout the 1990s the SPD possessed an international section composed of several full-time officials and researchers with a high level of focus on ECE to promote interaction with their sister parties. The party was further assisted by the work of the parliamentary *Fraktion* and its foreign policy working group. The international contacts of the Labour Party, on the other hand, have been co-ordinated by one international officer with support from between two and four full-time staff. The PS has equally devoted a scant amount of resources and manpower to its international operations, which – like Labour – has been particularly telling outside government. Both the PS and Labour, furthermore, have a greater focus on their traditional, national spheres of influence – North Africa and the Commonwealth respectively. The PES has been able to afford only one or two officials to work on Eastern and Central Europe since the early 1990s.

In terms of resources, political foundations have been extremely important as they provided the main channel of support for the social-democratic successor parties, particularly in the early years of the young democracies when Western SDPs were cautious about establishing links with former communist parties. The Friedrich Ebert Stiftung (FES) – linked to the German SPD – has undoubtedly been the most important individual foundation.[40] An SPD politician, central to the party's foreign policy team in the 1990s, confirmed (in an interview in 2003) that the FES played an indispensable role in paving the way for the party's contacts in Eastern and Central Europe. In comparison to the FES, Labour and the PS (respectively through the Westminster Foundation and the *Fondation Jean Jaurès*, both founded in 1992) had meagre resources, which were not nearly as focused on ECE.[41] The resources of the Western SDPs are not only important with respect to their engagement with their sister parties to the East, but also with regard to attracting potential importer parties through funding, information and expertise. A member of the international section of the SPD, for example, stated in 2003 that he did not even need to contact sister parties in Eastern and Central Europe – they contacted him as a potential source of information and financial support.

Networks are, therefore, clearly very important in creating concrete channels through which policy transfer may take place. The informal networks described above increase the probability of this taking place, despite the numerous obstacles that exist in transferring policy across space to such different contexts.[42] The research published elsewhere in this collection nevertheless shows that the external influences on policy are varied and diffuse, so that transfer through party-to-party networks has more to do with the transfer of policy ideas (entering the framework for reference of policy making in the importer party) than specific policies. Here, policy transfer can be more easily understood by the concept of policy learning within a broader Europeanization process.

Conclusion

In conclusion, it is possible to say that West European social-democratic thought has provided an attractive model for centre-left successor parties in Eastern and Central Europe, presenting a source from which to adopt and adapt policies as well as a framework of reference for a wide range of policy alternatives. In terms of ideational transfer, the perceived electoral success of the SDPs and their policies is crucial, although the promotion of policy learning also takes place through interactions in transfer networks. Identifying the source of transfer, particularly with regard to transfer networks, has proved difficult given the large range of domestic and external influences on CSP policy. A picture of the motivations for programmatic change can nevertheless be drawn through the use of a qualitative programmatic analysis (as has been mapped out by Paterson and Sloam in this collection), which sheds light on the relative influence of specific policy actors.

In determining the source of the transfer for political parties geographical location, cultural affinity and ideological closeness are of key importance in prompting transfer to take place. For these reasons, the SPD has had the greatest overall influence on the centre-left successor parties in ECE. This is particularly so when this influence is compared with that of its sister parties in the UK and France. The SPD has been greatly aided by its superior resources and commitment to international co-operation. This hypothesis is further supported by the strong impact of the Austrian SPÖ. The context of the importer party is none the less still fundamental in dictating the openness of the channels for transfer and the receptiveness to policies and policy experiences from the West. Despite the CSPs' decreasing need of policies from the West, the existence of transfer networks – in addition to the Europeanization of SDPs and CSPs in the light of European integration and EU enlargement – has encouraged the convergence of policy through policy transfer and more general policy learning in the new Europe.

NOTES

This study is based on research carried out for a Leverhulme-funded project (F/00094/O) on 'Policy Transfer and Programmatic Change in the Communist Successor Parties of East–Central Europe'.

1. The present study explores policy transfer from the perspective of the exporter party, complementing the analyses of CSPs elsewhere in this collection, which analyse transfer from the point of view of the importer party.
2. M. Evans and J. Davies, 'Understanding Policy Transfer: A Multi-Level, Multi-Disciplinary Perspective', *Public Administration*, Vol.77, No.2 (1999), pp.361–85; H. Wolman and E. Page, 'Policy Diffusion among Local Governments: An Information-Theory Approach', *Governance*, Vol.15, No.4 (2002), pp.477–501. A number of studies have looked at why policies are adopted by importer parties – see, for example, R. Rose, *Lesson-Drawing in Public Policy: A Guide to Learning across Times and Space* (Chatham, NJ: Chatham House, 1993) – and other works focus on the intentional aspects of policy transfer for exporter parties – see, for example, W. Jacoby, 'Tutors and Pupils: International Organizations, Central European Elites, and Western Models', *Governance*, Vol.14, No.2 (2001), pp.169–200. This essay focuses on the exporter side of the transfer process.
3. D. Dolowitz, 'Introduction', *Governance*, Vol.13, No.1 (2000), pp.1–4, at p.2.
4. See the article by William E. Paterson and James Sloam, 'Learning from the West: Policy Transfer and Political Parties', in this collection, pp.37–51.
5. Rose, *Lesson-Drawing*; Evans and Davies, 'Understanding Policy Transfer'.
6. See Paterson and Sloam, 'Learning from the West'.
7. President Mitterrand was considered to be 'above politics' and not really representative of the PS during the cohabitation of 1993–95, and his ill health also forced him to remain something of a peripheral figure; in terms of electoral success, the PS was unable to hold the government and the presidency simultaneously after 1993.
8. In 2001 one former member of the Polish Politburo revealed in conversation that 'Giddens is the only author who is translated into Polish and whom the SLD leaders such as Miller read'.
9. Furthermore, in the late 1990s several of the successor parties were in government, and therefore had greater knowledge resources of their own. They also had to pay more attention to the implementation of policy in their very different socio-economic circumstances (national contexts).

10. A. Giddens, *The Third Way: The Renewal of Social Democracy* (Cambridge: Polity, 1998); A. Gamble and T. Wright (eds.), *The New Social Democracy* (Oxford: Basil Blackwell, 1999); F. Walter, *Die SPD: Vom Proletariat zum Neue Mitte* (Berlin: Alexander Fest Verlag, 2002); J. Sloam, *The European Policy of the German Social Democrats: Interpreting a Changing World* (Basingstoke: Palgrave, 2005); W.E. Paterson and J. Sloam, 'Gerhard Schröder and the Unlikely Victory of the German Social Democrats', in D. Conradt, Gerald R. Kleinfeld and Christian Søe (eds.), *A Precarious Victory: Schröder and the German Election of 2002* (Oxford: Berghahn, 2005); B. Clift, 'The Jospin Way', *Political Quarterly*, Vol.72, No.2 (2001), pp.170–79.
11. T. Meyer, 'Soziale Demokratie statt demokratischer Sozialismus: Alte SPD und neue Realität: Ketzereien eines bekennenden Sozialdemokraten', *Frankfurter Rundschau*, 18 Sept. 2003.
12. Giddens, *The Third Way.*
13. Labour Party, *Ambitions for Britain* (London: Labour Party, 2001); see also <http://www.labour.org.uk/manifesto>, accessed 18 Nov. 2004.
14. T. Blair, *The Third Way: New Politics for the New Century*, Fabian Society Pamphlet 588 (London: Fabian Society, 1998).
15. L. Jospin, *Modern Socialism*, Fabian Society Pamphlet 592 (London: Fabian Society, 1999).
16. The *Neue Mitte* economic liberal wing of the SPD came into the ascendancy after the resignation of Oskar Lafontaine as finance minister and party chairman in March 1999: see B. Hombach, *The Politics of the New Centre* (Oxford: Basil Blackwell, 2000).
17. Chancellor Gerhard Schröder was a strong proponent of this reform agenda, arguing that Germany must 'modernize or die': see 'Modernise or Die', *Guardian*, 8 July 2003, available at <http://www.guardian.co.uk/globalization/story/0,7369,993469,00.html>, accessed 18 Nov. 2004.
18. OECD, *Economic Outlook No.75*, Annexes, 2004, available at <http://www.oecd.org/document/61/0,2340,en_2649_33733_2483901_1_1_1_1,00.html>, accessed 1 July 2004.
19. R. Keohane and J. Nye, *Power and Interdependence*, 2nd edn. (Glenview, IL: Scott, Foresman, 1989), p.8.
20. €40,000 million. See Sloam, *The European Policy of the German Social Democrats.*
21. Interview in 2003 with an official in the secretariat of the Party of European Socialists.
22. One SPD politician, strongly identified with the German reunification process, emphasized in 2003 the point that 'people from Eastern Germany have felt the need to engage with these parties and countries much more keenly'.
23. These continuing tensions, furthermore, have made CSP politicians reluctant to admit to any German influence on their policy programmes.
24. SPD, *Der Neue Weg: ökologisch, sozial, wirtschaftlich stark* (Bonn: SPD-Vorstand, 1990), p.23.
25. Parti Socialiste, *Changeons d'avenir* (Paris: Parti Socialiste, 1997), available at <http://www.psinfo.net/elections/legislatives/1997/changeons0.html>, accessed 18 Nov. 2004; Parti Socialiste, *Un Vote Clair Pour Une France Plus Juste* (1995), available at <www.psinfo.net/elections/president/1995/programme/html>.
26. Labour Party, *It's Time to Get Britain Working Again* (London: Labour Party, 1992).
27. Labour Party, *Britain in the World* (London: Labour Party, 2001), p.10. Labour, like the SPD, also began to attach conditions to eastern enlargement when in government, although only last-minute measures when accession became imminent. An example of this was the attempt to place restrictions, in spring 2004, on the entitlement of citizens from the accession states to receive welfare benefits in the UK.
28. See the article by V. Handl and V. Leška, 'Between Emulation and Adjustment: External Influences on Programmatic Change in the Slovak SDL', in this collection, pp.109–126.
29. The subordination of the Labour Party's international section to government activities was further illustrated by the fact that the person responsible for international contacts in the Number 10 Policy Unit subsequently became international secretary of the party. The foreign policy section of the Labour Party website in 2004, in addition, had links to the relevant government department, but none to the international section of the party itself.
30. Interview in 2003 with Labour Party politician who is heavily involved in European politics.

31. Labour Party, *Labour Party International*, Vol.1 (London: Labour Party, 2003).
32. W. Jacoby, 'Priest and Penitent: The EU as a Force in the Domestic Politics of Eastern Europe', *East European Constitutional Review*, Vol.8, Nos.1–2 (1999), pp.62–7.
33. Interview in 2003 with a Labour MEP.
34. Interview in 2003 with a representative of the SPD's international section.
35. Interview in 2003 with an official from the SPD's foreign policy establishment.
36. Interview in 2003 with a Labour MEP.
37. Interview in 2003 with a senior figure in the EU enlargement directorate.
38. Interview in 2003 with a Labour MEP.
39. Evans and Davies, 'Understanding Policy Transfer'; D. Marsh and M. Smith, 'Understanding Policy Networks: Towards a Dialectical Approach', *Political Studies*, Vol.48, No.1 (2000), pp.4–21.
40. With an annual budget of over €110 million and a long tradition of international activity (over 50 per cent of the budget is devoted to international co-operation), the FES had established offices in all the countries of Eastern and Central Europe by the mid-1990s.
41. The Westminster Foundation was nevertheless central to Labour Party work on Eastern and Central Europe outside government, as it funded two of the three permanent staff working in the international office. All of its €3 million funding, furthermore, went towards international activities. While international co-operation is a 'central goal' of the *Fondation Jean Jaurès* (attached to the *Parti Socialiste*), its €2.3 million budget is only partly devoted to external operations. The one advantage that these two foundations had in terms of the diffusion of ideas and policies over the FES is their ability to co-operate directly with their sister parties (they are allowed to offer assistance and support for political activities).
42. Transfer networks do not, however, represent a one-way flow of information. The engagement of importer parties is also a key to their successful operation. The willingness of the Polish SLD to interact with its sister parties on both a bilateral and a multilateral basis, for example, led to the instances of co-operation with the SPD and Labour mentioned above, as well as to the party hosting important Socialist International and PES meetings in 1999 and 2002.

Polish Social Democracy, Policy Transfer and Programmatic Change

PIOTR BURAS

Introduction

The vast majority of the delegates to the final congress of the Polish United Workers' Party (PZPR) in January 1990 opted to dissolve Poland's former ruling party and establish the Social Democracy of the Republic of Poland (SdRP) in its place. Only a small group refrained from joining the new party, opting instead to form a new, completely independent, competitor organization. While the latter soon disappeared from the political scene, the SdRP underwent a remarkable development in terms of its electoral performance. With 11 per cent of the votes in the 1991 parliamentary election, 20 per cent in 1997 and 40 per cent in 2001, it became not only the most successful but also the most stable political force in the Polish Third Republic. Up until 1999 the SdRP remained the most powerful part of a broad electoral coalition entitled the Alliance of the Democratic Left (SLD). In that year the SdRP underwent a process of internal consolidation and formally dissolved itself,

---

Piotr Buras, political scientist and journalist, is with the Willy-Brandt Centre at the University of Wrocław.

reappearing under the name of the alliance of which it had been the most significant part – the SLD. Despite a landslide victory in 2001 – when it failed to gain an absolute majority of seats in parliament by only the slimmest of margins – the SLD imploded a mere two-and-a-half years later. Internal unity proved impossible to maintain as corruption scandals, poor performance in the opinion polls (the party was registering figures of about ten per cent in 2004) and internal dissent over ideological issues forced ever more serious divisions between different groups of members. In March 2004 a group of SLD parliamentarians broke away from the rapidly disintegrating SLD to establish Social Democracy of Poland (SdPl). The success story of the SdRP/SLD as a communist successor party as defined by Dan Hough in the introduction to this collection therefore came to an end.[1]

This article examines the programmatic development of the SdRP and SLD since 1990, placing particular importance on the external influences on this process. The Polish social democrats paid much attention to establishing international contacts in the early 1990s for a number of reasons. First and most importantly, its isolation from other Polish parties (on account of its communist past) in the immediate post-1990 period prompted it to treat relations with the Western social-democratic parties (SDPs) as a channel of external legitimization. Second, international recognition and contacts with leading social-democratic politicians in Western Europe were seen as ways of gaining legitimacy with respect to the SdRP's leaders' own political biographies (in short, they hoped it would act as a compensation for their complicity in the communist period). Third, the SdRP explicitly sought to be recognized as a modern European party, and intensifying relations with Western counterparts appeared to be a natural aim. Fourth, it also looked for programmatic inspiration, as it had to construct a social-democratic identity upon the ruins of a collapsed communist system and a compromised Marxist ideology. Not surprisingly, the development of a legitimate and popular party programme could therefore be significantly influenced by the emulation of values and policy concepts from West European social-democratic parties.

As James Sloam argues in this collection, the opportunity structures for policy transfer are largely defined by the policy contexts in which the potential importer parties operate. The first part of this article will therefore start by outlining the nature of party competition in the Polish political system, discussing the level of leadership autonomy in the SdRP/SLD and defining the party's identity in terms of its programme and the beliefs of its core supporters (the 'institutional context'). Then, the national socio-economic conditions after 1989 will be addressed as the background for the party's programmatic provisions in the areas of the welfare state and labour market policy (the national context). Finally, the influences on programmatic development, emanating from the party's international contacts and the process of European integration, will be analysed (the international context). The second part of the article examines the significance of voluntary 'policy transfer', 'lesson drawing' and 'emulation' in shaping SdRP/SLD programmes. These developments will be analysed through five brief case studies: welfare policy, labour market policy, European policy, security policy and ideas of a Third Way. The article will conclude by evaluating how and to what extent the SdRP/SLD has learnt from the West. It argues that, despite potential incentives for transfer from West European social democrats, local opportunity structures have provided effective barriers to explicit transfers from individual parties. A more subtle diffusion of policy nevertheless took place, as the SdRP/SLD adopted a number of policy concepts common to social-democratic parties in Western Europe.

Policy Contexts

Institutional Context

Since the process of policy transfer is usually centralized and elite-driven, the role of the leadership and its level of autonomy in determining the party's strategic options is particularly important when looking at programmatic change. The SdRP/SLD leadership has enjoyed a considerable level of autonomy for a number of reasons, distinguishing it from the member-heavy and grass-roots-dependent traditional social-democratic mass parties of Western Europe.[2] First, the SdRP was isolated by most of the other Polish parties that were not active within the SLD, and it was subsequently ignored as a potential coalition partner more or less regardless of its programmatic declarations. This isolation – based upon a communist–anticommunist cleavage – considerably strengthened the position of the party leadership *vis-à-vis* the party membership. In view of the acute danger of political marginalization, the main party line tended not to be questioned by the rank and file, and internal coherence became the party's principal *raison d'être*.[3] Second, for most of the time there was an overlap of elites between the party leadership and the leadership of its parliamentary caucus. Third, the power of the party leadership was also increased by the peculiarities of SdRP's position in a broader electoral alliance – the SLD (until 1999) – which led to a strengthening of the leadership role beyond the 'official' level of autonomy that was set out in the party rules.[4]

The character of the party changed over time. While the SdRP resembled a cadre party, with a relatively small membership (about 60,000) and a strong sense of solidarity among its members, the SLD was more like a modern catch-all party with strong vertical dependency and centralized decision-making processes. It broadened its membership base (up to 120,000) and replaced the old party structures with new ones created by representatives of the party leadership. Consequently, neither the SdRP nor the SLD had to cope with the organizational problems of parties such as the German Social Democratic Party (SPD). Of course, this is not to say that tension did not exist between the leadership and the rank and file. The dissatisfaction of members in the middle levels of the party was a relatively late phenomenon, however, caused by their lack of influence on government policy after 2001, as well as their lack of a share in the division of material benefits. The party leadership was also reproached for abandoning traditional socialist policy positions and pushing the party towards what was loosely termed 'liberalization'.

Up until very recently (2004), party competition in Poland was determined by cleavage structures that were specific to the Polish environment. Voting in Poland is neither interest-driven nor related to particular social structures. The deep cultural and political divisions in Polish society crystallized during the election of 1989 (principally between supporters of the post-communist PZPR and those of Solidarity), and these blocs remain the key to understanding electoral behaviour in Poland in the 15 years since the end of communism (even if the parties within them have changed). In terms of the SdRP electorate, traditional characteristics such as level of education, profession, age and geography have not structured party support. These variables played a secondary role, since the main political cleavage was formed by attitudes to the communist past and the Catholic Church, and were less dependent upon socio-economic variables. Analyses show that the SdRP/SLD has been constantly able to mobilize voters in all social groups.[5] The composition of the SdRP/SLD voter base subsequently cut across social strata.

The nature of the SdRP's support base clearly provided a socio-political framework for understanding the party's programmatic development. The programmatic profile of the SdRP was greatly shaped by issues such as abortion, state–church relations and attitudes to the past. Secularism, along with the defence of the old regime, was its most significant 'core belief', very clearly determining the party's public image.[6] Both addressed anti-clericalism and nostalgia for the pre-1989 period. Economic and social issues (traditional social-democratic areas) were far less useful in mobilizing popular support. Interestingly, the

> SdRP held stances that were far more secular than the Polish voters ... at the same time, given the intrusion of the Church into public life in 1990–2, retaining secularism gained the party votes. The Polish party was thus able not only to retain its core support, but to gain a broader electorate in 1993.[7]

Leftist values were thereafter associated mainly with secularism, women's rights, defence of sexual minorities, anti-clericalism and rejection of any form of 'de-communization'. Intriguingly, the party did not hesitate to raise these issues again in public debate when it found itself in the deepest crisis in its history in 2003–04.[8] Since the SLD electorate was dissatisfied with plans to cut social expenditure drastically (in order to prevent a collapse of the public finances), renewing the battle for the liberalization of the abortion law seemed to be a means of last resort to keep voters' support.

Polish Social Democracy has had the image of a 'pragmatic' party, and the 'primacy of voters over members' has distinguished the SdRP from the traditional member-heavy mass parties of Western Europe.[9] The party has not been inclined to engage in long and exhausting programmatic debates; its programme has been designed to maximize votes rather than to reflect the party's ideological and programmatic diversity. Consequently, the drafting of programmes became centralized and the programmes themselves remarkably flexible, further distinguishing the party from traditional West European social-democratic parties. The first programme was written in 1990 by a small group of party experts, and although party members were given the right to make amendments, they were not permitted to change any provisions on economic and social policy. In 1999, the SLD programme was written by Andrzej Celiński and Lech Nikolski without any real debate. To a certain extent, this enabled the party to adopt a pro-reform stance on economic issues and accept the capitalist system.[10]

The formation of one party, the SLD, through the merger of the SdRP and other smaller organizations, marked a further retreat from any interest in programmatic issues. If the SdRP did not make an effort to work out a coherent political conception of social democracy, this is even truer of the SLD. While the former consisted – all deficiencies notwithstanding – of people committed to a certain set of social-democratic values, the SLD was established as a mere machine to win elections and it became a 'trade union of party activists'.[11] Management tasks – organization of the local party structures and broadening the membership base – counted for more than sharing common values and policy goals.[12] The result of this priority structure was that the party lacked the means to generate sophisticated programmatic proposals and neglected relations with broader academic and cultural circles.[13]

National Context

While the appeal of the programmes and policy proposals of centre-left parties in Western Europe was unquestionable given the deficit in the SdRP's own ideological identity, their practical usefulness was determined by the Polish national context. The transformation from a command economy to a market system created problems and tensions that differed greatly from those prevalent in Western Europe. Nevertheless, it was the German concept of the 'social market economy' that enjoyed much attention in the initial phase of Polish transformation and was seen as the most successful combination of a 'hard' capitalist economy and a welfare state. While German ordo-liberals (economic liberals who favoured order) were critical of excessive social spending and supported entrepreneurship (as the creator of public wealth), the redistributive elements of the German system prevailed in Polish interpretations.[14] Huge expectations with regard to the regulative role of the state (providing social security) were the result of both the legacy of the communist era and the deterioration of the living standards of large segments of society in the years after 1989.

In fact, there is not a specific Polish model of the welfare state that fits into the typology set out by Esping-Andersen.[15] Like other countries in Eastern and Central Europe, Poland had to cope with an acute crisis in public finances, which set limits to any reform of the welfare state. The state budget deficit as a proportion of GDP grew rapidly after 1989: in 1990 it was 0.4 per cent, in 1991 3.8 per cent, and in 1992 6.1 per cent.[16] To a large extent, this stemmed from the rapid increase in social expenditure in the first years of transition (from 31.5 per cent in 1991 to 35.4 per cent in 1994) – a common trend in ECE caused by the rapid accumulation of new social problems and old problems that were becoming more acute. However, the situation was most severe in Poland and one of its partners in rapid reform, Hungary. Frequent changes in government prompted Poland's policy makers to take defensive positions on social spending, pensions, education, the health service and other social benefits. The economic reforms that Polish elites instigated in the early 1990s naturally prompted those affected to call for the state to protect their interests, and successive governments found themselves divided between the need to protect levels of social welfare and the need to carry on processes of socio-economic reform. Another social problem which was a particular burden to public finances and a challenge for all governments (but the leftist ones in particular) was unemployment. The unemployment rate grew in the first years of transition to 16.4 per cent (1993), before decreasing to 10.3 per cent in 1997. However, the improvement in the labour market was not durable. In subsequent years unemployment grew steadily – to approximately 20 per cent in 2003. Again, national influences shaped national policies and – as will be illustrated below – placed barriers on attempts to transfer in policies from elsewhere.

International Context

As was indicated above, the SdRP sought to use international contacts and international recognition mainly for the purposes of legitimizing its own position in domestic party politics. This opened channels for policy transfer, as membership of international organizations such as the Socialist International (SI) and the Party of European Socialists (PES) placed a number of conditions upon applicant parties and proved to be a powerful incentive for programmatic adjustment. The redefinition of foreign policy strategy (especially with regard to NATO and the EU) also involved external actors and pressures and opened up the SdRP to further outside influences. The programmatic development of the SdRP/SLD thus offers examples of both lesson drawing and policy inspiration, on the one hand, and programmatic convergence (with other European social-democratic parties) on the other. This evolution can be divided into several phases, each of which has a different motivation at its core, and these, in turn, have promoted different channels of policy transfer.

Initially, the reformist circles of the PZPR maintained close contacts to the German SPD – both before and immediately after 1989. Mieczysław F. Rakowski, the last party leader, pointed to Herbert Wehner as his 'intellectual father' and stressed that relations with the SPD leaders greatly moulded his political thinking.[17] The SPD and PZPR established, as early as the 1970s, joint working groups that offered a platform for the exchange of views and the tightening of informal links between the party elites.[18] The PZPR's increasing international activity in the aftermath of the Helsinki process subsequently opened it to non-communist thinking. Even if it was not reflected in party documents at that time, its impact on the ideological evolution of the party elite was unquestionable – even though, with the creation of the SdRP, there was a considerable turnover in party leaders.

The new generation of mid-level activists that took control of the SdRP in the immediate post-1990 period consisted of people that were not involved in the PZPR's internal debates before 1989. They nonetheless profited from the increasing ideological openness of the party. Those who constituted the Movement of 8 July (*Ruch 8 Lipca*) – a loose grouping of academics that played an important role in the founding period of the SdRP – had pursued careers in the institutions informally associated with the party (such as the Institute for Research on Marxism and Leninism) or universities.[19] Many of them (such as Danuta Waniek or Kazimierz Kik) worked as analysts on left-wing movements in Western Europe. According to Waniek, it was not only professional interest that made these contacts attractive, but also ideological proximity with the values represented by the social democrats of Western Europe.[20] The programmatic declaration adopted at the founding congress of the SdRP invoked the concept of 'democratic socialism', drawing very clearly on the ideas of Willy Brandt.[21] The attractiveness of West European left-wing ideology was enormous at that time given the failings of the 'domestic socialist experience' in the form of Polish communism. On the other hand, the poor electoral performance of social-democratic parties across Western Europe was a disincentive for the SdRP, as these parties struggled (frequently in vain) to garner enough popular votes to enter government.

The SdRP's application for membership of the Socialist International, and its determination to overcome a lack of legitimization by establishing formal contacts with sister parties in Western Europe, also opened up new channels for programmatic inspiration. Initially, West European social-democratic actors did not see the SdRP emerging as the main party on the left in Poland, since a broad left-leaning alliance was expected to emerge out of the Solidarity movement.[22] Even the German SPD seemed to underestimate the electoral potential of the ex-communists and was more inclined to build up contacts with the other party on the left – the Labour Union (*Unia Pracy* – UP). Only after the SdRP gained more than 20 per cent of the vote in 1993 and entered the governing coalition was the SPD encouraged to forge closer ties with the Polish ex-communists.[23] The SdRP was invited to – and attended – SPD conferences from 1993 onwards, but it was only in 1996 that the party was given full-member status of the Socialist International. The fact that the SdRP entered this institutionalized social-democratic network accounted for substantial change in the party's position. The activities in Poland of the German Friedrich Ebert Foundation (FES), associated with the SPD, played a significant role in fostering good relations between the parties. Although its Warsaw office was opened as early as 1990, the FES refrained from closer contacts with the party (following SPD policy), choosing to concentrate on disseminating social-democratic ideas on social and economic policy to broader circles of left-wing elites. The FES was not keen to be associated with only one political alternative – not least because of the historical background of the Polish left – and it refused to give financial support to the SdRP's own political foundation (the Kelles Krauz Foundation). Instead, the FES focused on socio-economic programmes and invested in education and research, while concomitantly also providing assistance in forging international contacts with left-wing parties and in training their young cadres. The direct influence of the FES in programmatic terms has been very limited, however.

More significant potential for policy transfer existed in the late 1990s, after the SdRP's defeat in the 1997 parliamentary elections and the creation of the SLD in 1999. The formation of the SLD represented a critical juncture in the Polish left's programmatic development, given in particular the electoral successes of the British Labour Party (1997) and the SPD (1998). The publication of the Schröder–Blair paper in 1999 coincided with the formation of the SLD and the creation of its programmatic commission. The SLD appeared to be impressed by the successful electoral strategies of West European social-democratic parties, with their move to the centre of the political spectrum and their departure from more traditional socialist ideas. Leszek Miller admitted that he believed in the efficiency of this 'method of winning elections given the actual level of economic development, the social structure and the nature of social conscience'.[24] It was one of the few moments when the FES also attempted to inspire programmatic debate within the Polish centre-left.[25]

Last, but certainly not least, a new channel for external influence was opened by the process of Polish accession to the European Union. The significance of the issue of European integration increased substantively for the SLD with the opening of formal negotiations in 1999. Moreover, since the SLD (as with other parties in ECE) was increasingly required to present its own views on the future of Europe, it arrived at another critical juncture where external inspiration was welcomed. The SLD, for example, fully subscribed to the programmatic documents presented by the Party of European Socialists, and the PES is considered by SLD politicians to be the most important forum for inter-party relations on the European level.[26] The SLD hosted the conference of the Council of the Party of European Socialists in Warsaw in November 2002.

Policy Preferences

Welfare Policy

The construction of a 'social state' has always been the party's stated goal.[27] This concept, which was clearly copied from the German SPD (*Sozialstaat*), was the party's vehicle for expressing its commitment to the notion of social justice. The key elements of this 'social state' were to be an emphasis on caring for the 'poorest and weakest' and implementing a broad range of public services that would ensure citizens were well looked after in times of need. In the early programmes, the 'development of the mass production of cheap products' and 'control of prices of products and basic services for the poorest people' were strongly advocated as a form of aid for the worst-off.[28] In later documents, 'minimum social standards' were identified as the appropriate means for limiting poverty and these were described as a 'human right' in the 1997 election manifesto. From 1993 to 1999, declarations of support for the poorest were not usually given a prominent place in party programmes. The re-emergence of the chapter on the 'rights of the weakest' in the election manifesto of the SLD–UP coalition in 2001 can be interpreted as a result of both a critical evaluation of the socio-economic situation (in the aftermath of the reforms launched by the centre-right government, 1997–2001) and the influence of the SLD's more radical leftist coalition partner, the Labour Union.

The 'representation of the social groups and citizens who do not enjoy, for various reasons, equal opportunities to take advantage of economic growth and self-development' remained the party's goal in the programmes of 1997 and 1999, marking a shift of focus from the concept of '(social) security' to 'equality of opportunity'.[29] This was not just a change in terminology. 'Equality of opportunity' stresses the importance of individual action, while 'social security' prioritizes state action. It is a very clear sign of an increasing programmatic convergence with the part of the West European social democracy subscribing to central aspects of Third Way ideology.

Generally in the area of welfare policy, the SdRP/SLD has made an effort to combine liberal concepts for the reform of public services (inherited from the communist system) with clearly social-democratic strategies for alleviating poverty. It addressed the weakest groups in society through programmes relying on budgetary resources (for example, subsidies for school equipment and school canteens in 2001), while at the same time agreeing to a step-by-step departure from mere redistribution – to investment in employment as the way to get people out of poverty (see below).

However, when in power (1993–97), the SdRP/SLD failed to implement any substantial reform of the country's social and economic structures. It clearly benefited from the painful reforms undertaken by the first democratic (post-Solidarity) governments between 1989 and 1993, and came to office only after the economic situation had started to improve. It was only then that the necessary reforms of the welfare state (and particularly the pension system and the health service – the so-called second stage of transformation) could be carried out. Instead, the SdRP/SLD used the success of transformation and faster economic growth to serve its electoral base by, for example, raising pensions to 39 per cent of the average wage level.[30] The only substantial change under the SdRP/SLD government was a tax increase.[31] In fact, the disproportionality between the powerful position of the party in the Polish political system and its participation in the transformation is striking, as none of the most far-reaching and substantial reforms were realized by the SdRP/SLD.[32]

Labour Market Policy

Increasing levels of unemployment through the post-1989 period were seen by former communists – trumpeting the achievement of virtual full employment in the pre-1989 era – as a pretext to criticize the transformation path of the liberal governments. The fight against unemployment has subsequently been one of the central tasks on the social-democratic agenda throughout the whole post-communist period. Since 'work' is an 'inherent human right',[33] and 'the right to work means liberty from degradation, poverty and famine', unemployment is not seen as being consistent with a social-democratic vision of society.[34] The concept of *powszechność pracy* (general access to work), used by the party in its programmatic documents, is very close to the one of 'full employment' promoted by most SDPs in Western Europe.[35] The meaning of *powszechność pracy* in practice is not entirely clear, however, since the party has not envisaged the reduction of unemployment to zero. It has mostly talked about reducing unemployment and preventing it from reaching mass levels.

The SdRP has always advocated an active labour market policy. In the early party documents the emphasis was placed on state programmes and action to fight unemployment. It hoped to avoid mass unemployment through high public expenditure in the form of subsidies, government commissions and support for state-owned enterprises, and also better management of the available workforce. According to the party's socio-economic programme of 1990 the state should 'prevent the collapse of enterprises that faced temporary difficulties for external reasons'.[35] Public investment to create new jobs as well as increase economic demand (even at the cost of inflation) remained the focus of SdRP labour market policy until the late 1990s. The 'Strategy for Poland', a comprehensive economic policy programme launched by SdRP Finance Minister Grzegorz Kołodko in 1994, claimed to make the jump from 'passive policy ... to active policy, whose intention is to stimulate the process of creating new jobs'.[37] The programme envisaged the strengthening of investment in public infrastructure (housing, transport, telecommunications, energy) and also a preference for labour-intensive industries in regions of high structural unemployment. Characteristically, the concept relied predominantly on public expenditure and investment in the public sector, with tax incentives and changes in the implementation and organization of policy seen only as secondary solutions.

A substantial change came only in the late 1990s with a shift of focus from public expenditure to a comprehensive strategy that included reform of the labour law, support for private employers, and a clear prioritization of 'education' as a primary area for investment. It is worth noting that this reorientation of party employment policy coincided with the electoral success of New Labour and Gerhard Schröder's *Neue Mitte*, which promulgated similar tools for labour market policy. The harbinger of the new labour market policy was the alternative programme presented by the opposition SdRP in April 1999. Exceeding the mere demand for more public expenditure, it emphasized the need for 'integration of the reform of general and professional education [and training] with the requirements of the labour market'.[38]

This programme was developed after the party came to power in 2001. The centre of the new strategy was the 'First Job' programme, which constituted the core of the government's general economic concept, 'Entrepreneurship–Development–Work'. These ideas very much resembled the key concepts of the Third Way, focusing on tax cuts, labour market flexibility and support for those willing to employ young job-seekers. An adviser to the finance minister admitted that the 'First Job' programme 'is not our original idea but the new social contract developed by New Labour'.[39] In contrast to previous concepts of employment policy as well as with those applied by, for example, the French Socialist government, the new SLD strategy aimed to create jobs primarily in the private sector by reducing the labour costs of small-to-medium enterprises (SMEs) – for example, support for the health insurance of employees from the state budget. It also promoted self-employment and the establishment of private firms, as well as providing benefits for non-salaried workers (mostly young people gaining experience in the non-profit sector and public administration). These job-seeker provisions were accompanied by the 'entrepreneurship above all' programme, the aim of which was 'to abolish the formal barriers to the creation of new enterprises, to facilitate the activity of the existing enterprises as well as to increase employment'.[40] From the point of view of employment policy, it was the reform of the labour law that was the key to this concept. The liberalization aimed to reduce labour costs, making redundancies easier and working hours more flexible. The expansion of unemployment benefits and pre-pension benefits should, it was also argued, be stopped because they 'contribute to the professional exclusion of people'.[41] The advocacy of the system of incentives to work reflected a clear shift in the party towards programmatic modernization along the lines of modern Western SDPs (and especially the British Labour Party).

European Policy

The immediate acceptance of the idea of Polish accession to the EU was indispensable in the process of social democratization in the former communist party. Both the intensity of references to European integration and their connection with various aspects of domestic policies have increased markedly since 1990.[42] Initially, the electoral coalition (SLD) only vaguely supported Polish 'accession to the pan-European integration process from the Atlantic to the Urals' and strongly opposed 'connecting it only with the EEC'.[43] At the same time, however, the prioritization of the EC was cautiously accepted by the 1991 party programme.[44]

Nevertheless, with the passage of time, when speaking of the 'European economic centre' or 'European economic integration', the SdRP attributed more and more competences to the EC/EU. From 1997 onwards, focus was given to its role in solving social and economic problems. The EU's activities in fighting unemployment, protecting the environment and fighting crime were warmly greeted.[45] The party also announced that it would 'strive for the realization of the goals of the European Social Charter'.[46] It has clearly subscribed to the idea of a 'social Europe', which has been the central pillar of its concept of the EU. As early as 1997, in a declaration at its third party congress, the SdRP pointed out that, in an integrated Europe, it would strive for the 'reduction and elimination of unemployment', the 'development of educational opportunities' and the 'development of economic programmes that would protect the environment'.[47] The concept of a 'social Europe' was also advocated in the SLD manifesto of 1999,[48] and was one of the key issues for the party in the debate on the future of Europe. The party's spokesperson in the parliamentary debate on the European Convention underlined that 'for our party, social justice, building a Europe based on values, protection of labour and of the poor, and protection of the unemployed are values of particular importance'.[49]

The concentration on the social dimension of European integration was clearly a result of the Europeanization process, which opened the party up to external influences (if not necessarily specific policies) from Western social democracy. While core social-democratic ideas and values were incorporated into party programmes in the early 1990s, the concept of Europe was also 'social-democratized' along West European lines (mainly in accordance with the PES programmes). However, the concept of a 'social Europe' has remained the only visible example of successful emulation. The SLD declined to take a position on the issue of *finalité politique* of the EU with the excuse that it could evoke unnecessary problems in the negotiation process. Thus, the party leader Leszek Miller's support for building a 'European federation' should be seen as the expression of his pro-European views rather than as a clear-cut vision of Europe in the manner of – for example – Joschka Fischer's speech at the Humboldt University.[50]

The importance of the joint letter published by Miller and Tony Blair in 2001 should not be overestimated as an example of a programmatic convergence between the SLD and Labour.[51] While this letter advocated the strengthening of the European Council by giving it more power to set the EU's strategic agenda, another document signed by Miller and Czech Prime Minister Zeman provided for the opposite: the strengthening of the community method as the best protection for the interests of the new member states. 'This goal, it seems, can be achieved by the extension of the qualified majority voting', argued SLD Foreign Minister Cimoszewicz.[52] This ambiguity led one an analyst to conclude that 'when one reads that article [by Miller and Blair] and the article written by Miller with Zeman, one has the impression that they were written by different people'.[53]

The limits to policy transfer in European policy were twofold. On the one hand, the reason lay in the SLD and its lack of interest in programmatic development. In contrast to their Western counterparts, Polish social democrats did not publish any documents sketching out their concept of Europe. Consequently, the party did not look for any conceptual feedback in this area. On the other hand, the visions of Europe are largely dominated by the national perspectives of all EU member states. While the PES documents, which the SLD was keen to emulate, are quite precise with regard to the idea of 'social Europe', they do not elaborate any concrete vision of the institutional framework of the EU since it has proved not to be a matter of consensus on the European left.

External Security

The evolution of the SdRP's position on security policy emanated from a mistrust of any stronger affiliation with transatlantic defence and security structures towards its acceptance as a pillar of Poland's *raison d'être*. Building a new 'collective security system in Europe', which the SdRP strongly advocated, was seen as the only way out of the geopolitical vacuum that Poland found itself in after the end of the Cold War and the dissolution of the Warsaw Pact (1991).[54] Accession to NATO was clearly 'ruled out'.[55] The distanced attitude towards NATO was officially explained by its dubious role as a 'military pact in a sort of vacuum', and an alliance that will have 'to think about its own future': 'Europe will only really be safe when all the countries of our continent feel safe'.[56] NATO was perceived as a 'minority alliance', which would – by definition – be unable to fulfil this task.[57] In the party programme of 1993 NATO was not mentioned at all.[58] Among the three European security organizations that survived the Cold War (NATO, WEU, CSCE), the CSCE (later OSCE) remained the organization in which the SdRP party elite had most interest until 1993.[59] The party believed it could be the framework for a new collective security system; co-operation with NATO and the WEU was seen as possible, but not as an end in itself.[60]

The period 1993–97, when the party was in power, was the turning point in its security strategy. By January 1994, party leader Aleksander Kwaśniewski declared in the Sejm that 'full NATO membership is the main goal of our policy'.[61] Interestingly, he also added that this was the case 'despite the fact that we will join a new NATO, different from the one we know'.[62] It must be remembered that, even as late as the 1993 electoral party programme, a 'change in the character of NATO' (which should cease to be a military pact rooted in the era of confrontation) was considered to be the precondition for Polish accession.[63] However, the controversy about NATO membership re-emerged in 1997 in the debate on the new party programme. It was only against a strong opposition from the party rank and file that the leadership managed to push through a paragraph supporting Polish accession.[64]

Polish NATO accession (1999) coincided with the outbreak of the Kosovo war, which opened a new chapter in the history of the alliance. At the same time, the question of European security and defence emerged, and the conclusions of the EU's Helsinki summit set a schedule for the development of European capacities in this area. Since then, the major challenge for the government as well as the political parties (among them the SdRP) has no longer been the choice among various institutions but rather adaptation to the changing security environment. The SdRP fully subscribed to the government's support for NATO intervention in Kosovo, pointing to the helplessness of the OSCE.[65] However, there were also serious doubts about the legality of the intervention within the SdRP parliamentary caucus.

The SdRP's external security policy strategy has been formulated and developed under strong influence from the 'national context'. There has not been much space for the 'policy transfer' in this area since it was the geopolitical situation, national historical peculiarities and foreign policy constraints that predominantly structured the Polish debate on foreign and security policy after 1989. However, some traces of policy convergence with Western social democracy – most notably the German SPD – can be observed in this policy area. The distanced attitude to NATO and the preference for the CSCE in the early 1990s confirm this opinion. Also, the eventual acceptance of the transatlantic alliance as the central pillar of security policy came almost simultaneously in both parties.

The Third Way

The SLD approached the concept of the Third Way with a large amount of scepticism.[66] The leaders of Polish social democracy were keen to point to the stance of the French Socialists as proof of the lack of consensus about the Third Way as the only possible definition of modern social democracy. Leszek Miller cited the views of Pierre Mauroy, the chairman of the Socialist International, that 'the concept of the Third Way was actual in the bipolar world': 'I agree with Pierre Mauroy. I think that today we should ask not about a "Third Way" but about what face of capitalism we can approve of, what level of state interventionism we accept, what kind of social security concepts we envisage and on what scale'.[67] There is little evidence of an in-depth analysis of Giddens's or Blair's concepts in the SLD. Their critics referred to the misunderstanding evoked by the term 'Third Way' itself rather than to any specific policy concepts outlined by its authors.

There were also, however, better founded critical opinions of the employability of the Third Way concept in the Polish case. Andrzej Celiński, chairman of the SLD programme commission, argued that:

> Polish political and economic life develops under specific circumstances. We have an incomparably more difficult situation as far as social stratification and specific problems connected with the transformation of the economic system are concerned. In a state which bears such a big burden of restructuring ... the role of the budget must be much bigger than in those countries which do not need to make such an effort.[68]

This is why the SLD advocated the idea of a 'big budget' to meet the enormous social needs as well to finance large investments in infrastructure. Tax cuts and large reductions in social spending were thus inconceivable.[69] He also pointed to the limitations of policy transfer: 'A mechanical transfer of programmes from one economic and cultural area to another seems to me rather pointless. It is fair enough, that we share the same values'. Consequently, Celiński refused to include the term 'Third Way' in the new programme of the SLD, although he admitted that 'he was tempted to do it'.[70]

Włodzimierz Cimoszewicz, a prominent SLD member of the Sejm, also referred to the French example to support his sceptical position on the concept of the 'Third Way'. In line with Celiński's point, he argued that, in Poland, 'the active role of the state in the economy is indispensable, and the range of social policy must take into account the level of poverty as well as the need to alleviate inequalities in society'.[71] The policy concepts and goals proposed by Giddens seemed inappropriate in the Polish case owing to the 'specific experiences and the state of public finances which limit freedom of movement'.[72]

While statements by party officials explicitly dismissed the Third Way as not applicable in the context of the Polish transformation process, the appeal of some of its language and concepts was much stronger than Polish social democrats were willing to admit. Celiński, for example, elaborated the need for 'the state to conduct the policy of establishing opportunities, especially through education ... [so that] as few people as possible feel excluded from society'.[73] The concept of 'inclusion' – central to the Third Way ideology – was also echoed in the SLD's 1999 programmatic manifesto, where the party warned that Poland was 'becoming a society of inherited poverty ... with increasing numbers of people excluded from the benefits of growth and social progress' (in earlier documents the party referred to the traditional social-democratic 'target groups' – 'the poorest and weakest'). The shift of focus in the party programme towards education and SMEs was also a sign that the developments in West European social democracy did not pass unnoticed in Poland. Yet, the SLD adopted Jospin's slogan for modern social democracy: 'Yes to the market economy, no to the market society'.

Conclusions: Learning from the West?

Despite potential incentives (the search for a new identity, close contacts to SDPs in Western Europe) as well as good organizational preconditions (leadership autonomy in the SdRP/SLD), policy transfer between the SDPs and the Polish Social Democracy was more limited than might be expected. Research has shown that, with regard to political parties, it is the transfer of ideas and values rather than policy concepts that is likely to take place. To be sure, the SdRP clearly and deliberately adopted a large body of social-democratic ideology in its first programmatic documents (the social state, democratic socialism, a social Europe and so on). For a number of reasons, however, it was far less keen on directly emulating specific policy concepts or ideas.

First, the SdRP/SLD is an even less ideological party than its counterparts in Western Europe. The party programme has been far less important than in the SPD, or even the Labour Party. It has not had any tradition of programmatic debate and its pragmatism merely relates to the political challenges it faces. Party leaders have stressed that programmes should follow reality. The party has not been trained in debating ideological issues or policies. This is the main reason why it is less interested in, or open to, specific policies. Second, the adoption of the social-democratic identity by a section of the PZPR was, to a large extent, an instrumental step to adapt to the new political situation in which there was no space for communists. What was needed was a social-democratic label and programme based on social-democratic ideas, but the party was not interested in filling it with more detailed content. Third, the same motivation (struggle for legitimization) informed the party's relations with the West European SDPs. Admission to the SI or PES was much more about external recognition than about 'learning from the West'. Fourth, the programmatic identity of the SdRP/SLD was formed by a totally different political cleavage from that in the Western democracies. Consequently, political and ideological values (secularism, attitude to the communist past) formed the identity of the Polish party and the profile of its supporters, while traditional SDPs are the products of the socio-economic cleavage. Fifth, the different models of the welfare state in Poland and Western Europe set limits to the transfer of concrete policy concepts and solutions.

Of course, there is some evidence of a significant and increasing convergence of SLD and West European SDP programmes in terms of both general ideology and – to a lesser extent – social and economic policy. Although the Polish party denied any fascination with the Third Way, its own programmes show some distinct traces of its perhaps unconscious adaptation. Labour market policy (see above) is the best illustration of this development. However, this convergence may also be seen as a result of the pragmatization and liberalization of the whole social-democratic movement across Europe (and thus also a departure from one part of the social-democratic identity) rather than of the process of an actual emulation of specific policy concepts – a diffusion of policy given similar external influences.[74]

The analysis also showed that it is important not to overestimate the influence of bilateral party relations upon their programmatic development with regard to policy transfer. While geographical and cultural proximity, networking and the intensity of contacts increase the likelihood of transfer taking place, the close co-operation with the SPD did not visibly translate into a programmatic convergence between German and Polish social democracy. Although the concept of 'social state' in SLD programmes clearly drew upon the SPD documents, in more detailed issues the SLD did not necessarily follow its German sister party. Schröder's concept of the *Neue Mitte* was not even echoed in the party's internal programme debates, and the Schröder–Blair paper was met with a good deal of scepticism by party leaders and intellectuals. What is much more noticeable is that certain ideas have been 'cherry picked' by the party, and this voluntary 'lesson drawing' is the most prominent form of concrete policy transfer. The blueprint for the reform of the labour law was taken from New Labour, while the interpretation of the concept of the 'Third Way' followed that of the French Socialists. The case of the SdRP/SLD also shows that those politicians who specifically engage in international party contacts have mostly had very little influence upon the programmatic issues.

If the party looked for external inspiration it was rather to the documents of the SI and PES than programmatic concepts of individual West European social democracies that it turned. Celiński, chairman of the SLD Programme Committee, admitted that the SI documents provided an intellectual framework for his work. The actual priority given to inspiration from the international organizations of the left fits well with the rather superficial interest invested by the SLD in programmatic work and the domestic constraints for a successful transfer of concrete policy concepts. Both the SI and PES form a platform for co-operation between social-democratic (or socialist) parties based on the highest common factor. They could help construct a social-democratic identity in terms of values and abstract ideas but are much less useful for policy programmes. As the above analysis has shown, it was the former rather than the latter that primarily interested the SLD.

Admittedly, even this kind of transfer would have been inconceivable without the SLD being part of the social-democratic community. Contrary to the SLD politicians' claim of following a 'Polish way' of social democracy (and thus not being particularly inclined to emulate external policy concepts), there is no distinctive Polish model. It is a very day-to-day policy-oriented approach to solving political and economic problems rather than a vision of state and social relations that characterizes the Polish social-democratic party.

NOTES

1. D. Hough, 'Learning from the West: Policy Transfer and Programmatic Change in the Communist Successor Parties of East-Central-Europe', in this collection, pp.5–19.
2. A. Szczerbiak, 'Party Structure and Organization in Post-Communist Poland', paper presented at the Political Studies Association–UK 50th annual conference, London, 10–13 April 2000, p.13. At the first party congress in 1990, the election of the party leadership was almost a formality: Aleksander Kwaśniewski won 90 per cent of the votes and was given the right to name 60 out of 150 members of the Head Council.
3. See E. Nalewajko, *Protopartie i protosystem? Szkic do obrazu polskiej wielopartyjności* (Warsaw: Instytut Studiów Politycznych PAN, 1997).

4. Szczerbiak, 'Party Structure and Organization in Post-Communist Poland', p.13.
5. For the 2001 election, see the analysis by the Pracownia Badań Społecznych, quoted in 'Kto ich wybrał', *Gazeta Wyborcza*, 25 Sept. 2001; for a deeper analysis, see M. Grabowska and T. Szawiel, *Budowanie demokracji: Podziały społeczne, partie polityczne i społeczeństwo obywatelskie w postkomunistycznej Polsce* (Warsaw: Wydawnictwo Naukowe PWN, 2001).
6. See N. Kraśko, 'Sojusz Lewicy Demokratycznej – legitymizacja przeszłości', in E. Tarkowska (ed.), *O czasie, politykach i czasie polityków* (Warsaw: Instytut Filozofii i Socjologii PAN, 1996), pp.115–29.
7. A. Grzymała-Busse, *Redeeming the Communist Past: The Regeneration of Communist Parties in East Central Europe* (Cambridge: Cambridge University Press, 2002), p.137.
8. 'Sojusz idzie na wojnę', *Rzeczpospolita*, 20 Oct. 2003.
9. Grzymała-Busse, *Redeeming the Communist Past*, p.161.
10. 'The Polish party especially could evolve its views towards a strong support for economic reform, as a result of its centralized, flexible program-writing mechanisms ... The more centralized the party, the more easily it could pursue a broad, pro-reform, strategy', ibid., p.135.
11. A. Celiński, interview by the author, Jan. 2003.
12. R. Kalukin, 'SLD szuka wartości', *Gazeta Wyborcza*, 4 March 2004.
13. See J. Rolicki, 'Zachłyśnięcie się władzą', *Rzeczpospolita*, 6 Aug. 2003; J. Rolicki, 'Zagubiona tożsamość SLD', *Rzeczpospolita*, 21 Oct. 2003; M.F. Rakowski, 'Zaraza niewiary na lewicy', *Rzeczpospolita*, 7 Nov. 2003.
14. S. Golinowska, 'Polityka społeczna okresu transformacji: Koncepcje, środki, instytucje', in S. Golinowska (ed.), *Dekada polskiej polityki społecznej: Od przełomu do końca wieku* (Warsaw: Instytut Pracy i Spraw Socjalnych, 2000), pp.87–208.
15. G. Esping-Andersen, *The Three Worlds of Welfare Capitalism* (Cambridge: Polity Press, 1997).
16. S. Golinowska, *State Social Policy and Social Expenditure in Central and Eastern Europe* (Warsaw: Centre for Social and Economic Research, May 1996), p.7.
17. Interview by the author, Jan. 2003.
18. On the reformist circles in the PZPR, see J.J. Wiatr, 'Drogi i bezdroża reformatorów w PZPR', *Dziś*, No.1 (1991).
19. See Z. Siemiątkowski, 'Czym był Ruch 8 Lipca', *Przegląd*, 11 June 2003.
20. Interview by the author, Jan. 2003.
21. 'Deklaracja Socjaldemokracji Rzeczypospolitej Polskiej', in *Podstawowe dokumenty Kongresu Założycielskiego Socjaldemokracji Rzeczypospolitej Polskiej* (Warsaw: SdRP, 1990), p.4.
22. In a resolution addressed at the Socialist International issued in March 1993, the Second Congress of the SdRP complained about the SI 'underestimating the processes going on in East-Central Europe', among them the 'phenomenon of the social-democratic left in this region whose role is obviously increasing'. It should be noted that the document also stressed the party's adherence to the official SI programmatic stances adopted at the Berlin Congress. The programmatic conformity was clearly used as an argument in favour of accession.
23. See T. Iwiński, 'SdRP w Europie i świecie', in *Dekada SdRP 1990–1999: Materiały IV Kongresu Socjaldemokracji Rzeczypospolitej Polskiej, Warszawa 16.06.1999 r.* (Warsaw: SdRP, 1999), pp.64–80.
24. 'O programowych zadaniach polskiej lewicy', *Myśl Socjaldemokratyczna*, No.1 (1999), p.19.
25. These efforts resulted in, for instance, the publication of a selection of articles presenting various opinions on the European debate; however, as the representative of FES in Warsaw admitted, the interest of the party leadership in discussing the programmatic issues was very limited: see T. Kowalik (ed.), *Spory wokół Nowej Trzeciej Drogi* (Warsaw: Scholar, 2001).
26. A. Szejna (Head of the Bureau for Foreign Affairs of the SLD), interview by the author, Jan. 2003.
27. See for example *Program SdRP* (Warsaw: SdRP, 1997).
28. 'Socjaldemokracja Rzeczypospolitej Polskiej: Program społeczno-gospodarczy' [1990], in I. Słodkowska (ed.), *Programy partii i ugrupowań parlamentarnych 1989–1991: Cz. 1*

(Warsaw: Instytut Studiów Politycznych PAN, 1995); 'Program społeczno-gospodarczy Socjaldemokracji Rzeczypospolitej Polskiej: Polska postępu, prawa i demokracji' (Warsaw: 1991).
29. The 1999 party programme states: 'We consider it to be our basic obligation to argue for the rights of the poor and the weak'. In this document the already mentioned warning of 'becoming a society of inherited poverty ... with an increasing number of people excluded from the benefits of the growth and social development of Poland' refers for the first time explicitly to the concept of 'social exclusion': see *Manifest programowy Sojuszu Lewicy Demokratycznej: Nowy wiek – nowy Sojusz Lewicy Demokratycznej. Socjaldemokratyczny program dla Polski*, at <http://www.sld.org.pl>.
30. A. Wiktorow, 'System emerytalno-rentowy', in *Dziesięciolecie Polski niepodległej*, pp.970–73.
31. J. Lityński, 'Mit politycznej poprawności', *Rzeczpospolita*, 5 Sept. 2003.
32. T. Szawiel, 'Bez dopingu', *Rzeczpospolita*, 28–29 June 2003.
33. 'Program społeczno-gospodarczy' (1990).
34. 'Program społeczno-polityczny SdRP. Demokracja i sprawiedliwość', *Trybuna*, No.134 (1991).
35. See 'Program społeczno-gospodarczy Socjaldemokracji Rzeczypospolitej Polskiej'.
36. 'Program społeczno-gospodarczy' (1990).
37. J. Staczkowski, *G.W. Kołodko: Strategia dla Polski* (Warsaw: 1994), p.61.
38. 'Zmniejszanie bezrobocia i tworzenie nowzch miejsc: 18 kwietnia 1999', in *Propozycje programowe Sojuszu Lewicy Demokratycznej dotyczące najważniesjych dziedzin życia gospodarczego i społecznego prezentowane na konferencjach prasowych w drugim kwartale 1999 roku* (Warsaw: SLD, 1999).
39. 'Dokąd prowadzi "Nowa Trzecia Droga": Spotkanie z Tadeuszem Kowalikiem, Andrzejem Szejną i Adrianem Zandbergiem, 26 czerwca 2002, Warszawa', *Zeszyty Klubu Dyskusyjnego Starówka 5* (Warsaw: 2002), p.17.
40. *Przedsiębiorczość–Rozwój–Praca. Strategia gospodarcza rządu SLD–UP–PSL* (Warsaw: 2002).
41. Ibid., p.27.
42. According to Robert Ladrech the process of Europeanization (reorienting the direction and shape of politics to the degree that EC political and economic dynamics become part of the organizational logic of national politics and policy making) in the party programmes can be measured quantitatively (increased mention of the EU – also with regard to the issues traditionally considered domestic) or qualitatively (references to the EU as an additional factor in the pursuit of policies traditionally considered domestic). R. Ladrech, 'Europeanization and Political Parties: Towards a Framework of Analysis', *Queen's Papers on Europeanization 2* (Belfast: The Queen's University, 2001).
43. 'Program SLD: Tak dalej być nie może' (Warsaw: SLD 1993).
44. 'Polska postępu, prawa i demokracji' (1991).
45. 'Program SdRP' (1997).
46. Ibid.
47. 'Polska Socjaldemokracja a Europa: Uchwała III Kongresu SdRP', Warsaw, 19 Dec. 1997.
48. 'Manifest programowy SLD: Nowy wiek – nowy Sojusz Lewicy Demokratycznej. Socjaldemokratyczny program dla Polski' (Warsaw: SLD, 1999).
49. J. Jaskiernia, intervention in the parliamentary debate on information about the work of the European Convention, 24 July 2002, at <http://www.sejm.gov.pl>.
50. 'MSZ będzie w tle', interview with Leszek Miller, *Unia i Polska*, 19 March 2001.
51. T. Blair and L. Miller, 'Bringing Europe Closer to its Citizens: Polish–British Contribution', 2 Nov. 2001.
52. W. Cimoszewicz, 'Polska wizja Europy', *Rzeczpospolita*, 19 Feb. 2002.
53. R. Trzaskowski, *From Candidate to Member State: Poland and the Future of the EU*, ISS Occasional Papers No.37 (Paris: European Union Institute for Security Studies, 2002), p.38.
54. 'Program SLD: Tak dalej być nie może'.
55. 'Program społeczno-polityczny SdRP. Demokracja i sprawiedliwość' (1991).

56. T. Iwiński, intervention in the parliamentary debate on the information of the ministry of foreign affairs about the main foreign policy directions, 8 May 1992, at <http://www.sejm.gov.pl>.
57. Ibid.
58. 'Socjaldemokratyczna alternatywa: Polska demokratyczna, sprawiedliwa, bezpieczna' (Warsaw: SdRP, 1993).
59. WEU stands for the West European Union and CSCE stands for the Conference on Security and Co-operation in Europe (subsequently renamed Organization for Security and Co-operation in Europe, or OSCE).
60. 'Program SLD: Tak dalej być nie może'.
61. Kwaśniewski, intervention in the parliamentary debate on the information of the ministry of foreign affairs about the current situation in the international relations and possible threats for Poland, 21 Jan.1994, at <http://www.sejm.gov.pl>.
62. Ibid.
63. 'Program SLD: Tak dalej być nie może'.
64. Nowakowska, 'Partia protestu, partia sukcesu, partia władzy', *Gazeta Wyborcza*, 26–27 July 1997.
65. L. Miller, intervention in the parliamentary debate on the information of the ministry of foreign affairs about the main foreign policy directions, 8 April 1999, at <http://www.sejm.gov.pl>.
66. 'Nie ma trzeciej drogi w gospodarce', interview with A. Celiński, *Rzeczpospolita*, 15 Oct. 1999.
67. 'O programowych zadaniach polskiej lewicy', *Myśl Socjaldemokratyczna*, p.18.
68. 'Nie wykłócajmy się z historią', interview with A. Celiński, *Trybuna*, 20–21 Nov. 1999.
69. 'Nie ma trzeciej drogi w gospodarce', interview with A. Celiński, *Rzeczpospolita*, 15 Oct. 1999.
70. 'Nie wykłócajmy się z historią'.
71. 'XXI wiek: wyzwania dla socjaldemokracji. Problemy "trzeciej drogi": wokół Manifestu socjaldemokratycznego Tony Blaira i Gerharda Schrödera', *Myśl Socjaldemokratyczna*, No.2 (2000), p.34.
72. W. Cimoszewicz and B. Góralczyk, 'Lewica idzie', *Gazeta Wyborcza*, 21 June 2001.
73. 'Nie wykłócajmy się z historią'.
74. See R. Misik, *Die Suche nach dem Blair-Effekt: Schröder, Klima und Genossen zwischen Tradition und Pragmatismus* (Berlin: Aufbau Verlag, 1998).

Between Emulation and Adjustment: External Influences on Programmatic Change in the Slovak SDL

VLADIMÍR HANDL AND VLADIMÍR LEŠKA

Introduction

In its short life, the SDL (*Strany Demokratickej L'avice* – Party of the Democratic Left), the successor to the Communist Party of Slovakia (KSS), underwent the most dramatic changes in political and electoral fortunes of all the East and Central European communist successor parties (CSPs).[1] During the period 1990–93, energetic leaders pushed the party on a fast track to social-democratic transformation.[2] By the mid-1990s, the party was participating in a broad coalition of democratic parties and had become an internationally recognized player. At the same time, a process of internal polarization was taking place, ending with the disintegration of the party and its political marginalization by 2003. At the 2002 election there were five non-communist left-wing parties in Slovakia, yet none of them

---

Vladimír Handl is with the Institute of International Relations, Prague, and a former research fellow at the Institute of German Studies, University of Birmingham.
Vladimír Leška is Chief Researcher for Czech–Slovak relations at the Centre of Regional Analysis, Institute of International Relations, Prague.

managed to pass the five per cent threshold needed to enter parliament. Instead, the centre-left *Smer* and the communist KSS *de facto* 'replaced' the SDL in parliament.

This essay investigates the nature of policy development and policy transfer between the SDL and foreign parties and international actors. It analyses when and to what extent bilateral (as well as multilateral) transfer networks, and emulative and coercive transfer between the SDL and the non-communist West European Left, actually took place.[3] The analysis reveals that the SDL engaged in an acknowledged and deliberate emulation of programmatic and political ideas from Western social-democratic parties, the Socialist International (SI) and the Party of European Socialists (PES).

Policy transfer facilitated the rapid transformation of the KSS into the SDL during the first half of the 1990s. At the same time, radical modernization of the party's programme was not being absorbed by the party's grassroots or organizational apparatus, which stuck broadly to conservative socialist appeals. The emulation of programmes across space was elite-driven and remained largely elite-confined, detached from wider discourse within the party. Beyond a narrow stream of modernizers, 'Third Way'[4] approaches tended to meet with outright rejection. Consequently, policy transfer became one of the key motors behind the party's internal polarization, division and eventual implosion.

Post-Communist Transformation and Political Opportunities

Even though they enjoyed significant historical similarities, the paths of transformation of the communist successor parties in the Czech Republic and Slovakia could hardly have been more different. In Slovakia, conditions for a social-democratic, non-communist transformation of the KSS were initially not favourable. The radical transition that took place in Slovakia in the early 1990s was preceded in the years beforehand by slower and more disjointed processes of cultural modernization, numerous regime changes as well as continual ruptures in the social structure.[5] Paternalist expectations of the state remained strong. The rejection of communism after 1990 was subsequently less radical in Slovakia than elsewhere in Eastern and Central Europe. Yet Slovaks experienced an unprecedented modernization of their society under communist rule and the oppression witnessed in Czech territories following the Prague Spring was not as evident in Slovakia.[6] The latter explains why Soviet *perestroika* led to more discussion and activity within the Slovak KSS than it did in the Czech part of the communist party.

On the other hand, after 1989 the rapid decline and deterioration of economic and social conditions were much more intense in Slovakia than they were in the Czech Republic.[7] Modernizers, headed by Peter Weiss, took over the leadership of the party in December 1989, and they sought a fast-track transformation of the KSS into a non-communist party. In the elections of June 1990 the party polled 13.3 per cent of the vote and became the fourth strongest in parliament. In order to exercise control from the centre, the modernizers centralized the party's organizational structures and gave it a new name (SDL). A re-registration of the membership cut the party off from the most orthodox communists and the membership base shrank from 440,000 to approximately 47,000.[8] The SDL split from the Czech Communist Party in order to prevent it discrediting its own radical transformation.[9] Slovak orthodox communists founded *Zväz kommunistov* (Union of Communists) and the Communist Party of Slovakia '91 (KSS '91) although they rapidly (in 1992) merged to form the new Communist Party of Slovakia (KSS).

Following the fall of Vladimír Mečiar's government in March 1994, the SDL joined a broad democratic anti-Mečiar government with conservative parties, having accepted, most notably, the difficult finance portfolio. However, the leadership, having overestimated the party's supporter base, pushed for extraordinary elections in 1994 – at which the party registered a disappointing 10.4 per cent. These mistakes had a considerable impact on the party's confidence and were something of a 'debilitating cocktail', as infighting began to break out.[10] Programmes remained important to the SDL, and modernizers and conservative socialists continued to have disagreements about what note the SDL's programme should strike. The modernizers sought to develop a substantial soft-left programme and to attract centrist voters. The conservative socialists sought to consolidate their power through the cultivation of ties with the grassroots and with district organizations. Slowly, the conservative socialists gained in influence, and the party began to acquire the features of a clientelistic party rather than that of a more traditional 'programmatic party'.[11]

While the top-down radical reorganization of the party was broadly successful, this did not bring with it any sort of programmatic cohesion. The party's programmatic reform put the SDL at the left-liberal end of the spectrum among the other post-communist parties, but a large part of the membership stuck to a traditional socialist agenda and it struggled to appeal convincingly to a broad spectrum of voters.[12] Through the 1990s the political space on the centre-left was dominated by the national populist Movement for a Democratic Slovakia (HZDS), headed by Vladimír Mečiar.[13] The SDL found this challenge difficult to come to terms with in both an ideological and a pragmatic sense, and subsequently split over its attitude towards the HZDS. At the fourth congress of the SDL in 1996 Josef Migaš replaced Peter Weiss as party chairman, and the conservative socialists became dominant within the party.[14] The political programme adopted was still, however, drafted under the leadership of Weiss, and called for the creation of an SDL policy platform that was fully compatible with that of the Socialist International. The action programme, adopted in parallel, nevertheless marked a dividing line between the modernizers and the conservative socialists within the SDL. The declared goal of the chairman, Migaš, was to 'return to left values'.[15] In the second anti-Mečiar coalition (1998–2002) relations between the SDL party fractions worsened to such an extent that the conservative socialists often attacked their own government in parliament, prompting the party leadership to seek effective control over both the SDL deputies in parliament and the party in government.[16]

Competing with Mečiar on his own terms, the new leadership could never go as far as the HZDS or the KSS in playing the populist card. The failure of Migaš to accommodate the ambitions of the most popular SDL politician, vice-chairman Robert Fico, proved to have a highly detrimental effect. Fico left the SDL and founded his own party – Smer – confirming the failure of the SDL's strategy of integrating and uniting the left of the political spectrum.[17] Socio-economic difficulties, particularly spiralling unemployment, placed a heavy burden on the SDL, and the party's core constituency became extremely dissatisfied with the party and democracy as a whole.[18] The tension between the conservative socialist party leadership and the modernizers culminated in the resignation of left-liberal economist Brigita Schmögnerová from her post as finance minister and a split became unavoidable. Peter Weiss subsequently founded a new left-wing political movement in April 2002 – the Social-Democratic Alternative (SDA) – with Milan Ftáčnik becoming its chairman. The break-up of the party and the subsequent failure in the September 2002 election reflected the depth of the crisis for the non-communist left in Slovakia, with the SDL and SDA both failing to reach the five per cent threshold. The party's decline was caused by both external and internal factors. Political competition in Slovakia was not structured along a single, straightforward left–right axis, but was dominated by the struggle between 'Mečiarism' and 'anti-Mečiarism'.[19] As Tim Haughton has shown such a 'dichotomization' of the Slovak political scene was detrimental to the SDL as it offered it little room for the implementation of left-wing policies.[20]

International Co-operation

The programmatic transformation of the SDL was driven primarily by indigenous factors. None the less, external influences were also at work. International influences have been highly visible in regime change across Eastern and Central Europe in general, and the region has historically been very exposed to international pressures.[21] The KSS/SDL has been influenced by foreign influences in a number of ways and in a number of phases.

- During the formative period, between 1990 and 1993, the party gradually detached itself from the Czech Communist Party, establishing contacts with post-communist parties across the region – most importantly in Italy – while avoiding contacts with neo-communist parties such as the German PDS. Instead, it sought relations with the West European social-democratic left, although the West European parties tended to see their main partner as the Slovak Social Democratic Party (SDSS).[22]
- The SDL participated in a broad anti-Mečiar coalition in 1994 and this assisted the SDL in obtaining international recognition. Governmental participation led to a period (lasting until 2000) of a promising, but ultimately unfulfilled, Europeanization of the party in terms of its external ties and identity. The SDL achieved a respected position in the region while still being treated with caution because of its internal divisions. Moreover, external relations tended to be conducted by a narrow reform-oriented elite and their Europeanization had only a limited spillover effect on the rest of the party.
- The period 2000–02 saw the SDL slip into an ever-deepening crisis, and the party's external relations increasingly lacked any sort of substance. From 2002 until its implosion in 2003, the party sought to rejuvenate itself completely following heavy election defeats and the defection of many significant figures.

Bilateral Partners

The first and most intensive contacts were developed with the Italian PCI in 1990, while regular contacts with the Austrian Social Democrats (SPÖ) and, less prominently, the German SPD were established a little later in 1992–93. The reason for the orientation towards the SPÖ was not only geographical proximity, but also the considerable number of Slovak German-speakers who were active within the SDL. Before 1989, the most widely spoken foreign languages in Slovakia were German and Russian, and people in western Slovakia – and Bratislava, in particular – used to watch ÖRF, the Austrian public television and radio service.[23] Contacts with the Czech social democrats (ČSSD) developed after only Miloš Zeman became the chairman of the party in 1994, and they intensified following the elections in 1998 when both parties entered government.[24] Traditionally, the SDL therefore maintained very good relations primarily with the Czech, Hungarian and Austrian social democrats.[25]

In 1992–93 the Ladislav Novomeský Foundation of the SDL developed more or less regular contacts with the Friedrich Ebert Foundation (FES – associated with the German SPD) and with the Karl Renner Institute (of the Austrian SPÖ).[26] The contacts between the Friedrich Ebert Foundation and the SDL cannot, however, be described as particularly intensive. Under

Migaš and Koncoš, co-operation became even more irregular. The Friedrich Ebert Foundation therefore shifted its focus towards non-governmental organizations.[27] Michael Petráš, head of the FES in Bratislava, has argued that the SPÖ had perhaps the most extensive influence on the programmatic work of the SDL, and Weiss and Petráš have agreed that the German SPD was viewed mainly as a source of practical know-how regarding party organization and general political activities.[28] Ján Richter highlighted the intensive, regular and institutionalized relations developed with Swedish social democrats in particular in the second half of 1990s, and more recently with the British Labour Party and the Dutch social democrats. This co-operation, based on bilateral annual programmes, focused on sharing know-how on how modern political parties should function, organize and prepare for election campaigns, rather than on programmatic issues. A number of party officials also received special training in the institutions and headquarters of the partner parties.[29]

Individual personalities played a more important role than official party bodies. This was mainly on account of the underdeveloped institutional and procedural basis of international relations in the party throughout most of the 1990s. Ideological compatibility, a credible political record, education and foreign language competence became the main preconditions for the development of intensive international contacts. It was mainly the 'modernizers' of the party (Peter Weiss, Pavol Kanis, Milan Ftáčnik, Brigita Schmögnerová and a small group of others), and – later – also several 'pragmatists' (Ľubomír Fogaš) who shaped the party's international activities as well as its image. Migaš and Koncoš, on the other hand, were neither qualified to cultivate the party's international contacts, nor indeed cared very much about this.[30]

Among foreign representatives, the Italian Piero Fassino (Italian Communist Party – PCI and later PDS), the Austrian Heinz Fischer (SPÖ), the Germans Wolfgang Roth, Markus Meckel and Günter Verheugen (SPD), and later also Jan Wiersma of the Party of European Socialists, developed close contacts and intimate knowledge of the Slovak political scene.[31] Mutual contacts were facilitated by two factors. First, leading SDL representatives were involved in conducting Slovak EU policy in 1994 and 1998–2002. In fact, the SDL often developed a more proactive attitude towards the EU than did their coalition partners. Second, most of the EU member states were run by social-democratic governments in the second half of the 1990s, boosting more general contacts across the European left.

The multilateral institutions of the European social-democratic left played a crucial role as ultimate 'gatekeepers' for the international acceptance of the SDL. Having accepted the SDL as an equal partner, they also enhanced the domestic coalition potential of the party. Less certain was the impact on the party's domestic legitimacy. Throughout the post-1989 period a considerable part of the Slovak population maintained a cautious attitude to anything foreign.[32] In the early 1990s, though, the parties of the Socialist International chose the SDSS, headed briefly by Alexander Dubček (1992), as their partner and they made Dubček agree to withdraw from a co-operation agreement with the SDL prior to the elections in June 1992. The Socialist International in effect prevented a merger of the Slovak non-communist left which might have altered the balance of political power in the country and perhaps even hindered the division of Czechoslovakia.[33]

In sum, since the mid-1990s the reform-oriented leaders participated in what Stone has termed 'networking and interaction via trans-national policy communities'.[34] Most importantly, the SDL's transformation efforts were rewarded by admission to the Socialist International in 1996. SDL representatives also began taking part in meetings of the PES. The modernizers sought to integrate themselves into the 'epistemic community' of the Western left, and participate in the discourse of the international left. The conservative socialist leaders of the SDL, on the other hand, hardly took part in this 'elite networking' at all.

Foreign partners played a constructive role, particularly amid the background of growing internal unrest in the SDL in the late 1990s. They tried to smooth personal relations between leading representatives.[35] The Swedish Olof Palme Institute even provided the SDL with an analysis that warned against the disintegration of the Slovak left.[36] In fact, Ján Richter, secretary general of the SDL, regretted that the PES had not exercised more influence on the party and its fractions before the split became inevitable.[37]

Programmatic Inspiration

External models did play a significant role in the programmatic development of the party, both before and after 1989. The 'Young Turks' from the Institute for Marxism-Leninism,[38] a small group around Peter Weiss (labelled an 'enlightened communist' by prominent dissident Fedor Gál)[39] and Pavol Kanis, were inspired by Gorbachev's *perestroika* and *glasnost'* and by the discourse of the West European democratic left during the late 1980s.[40] In the immediate post-1989 period they continued to co-operate on programmatic issues with the Czech KSČM, and their economic experts worked together reasonably intensively. From the very beginning the orientation towards 'modern patterns of policy making and models' was none the less more prevalent in Slovakia.[41]

During this formative period and up until the introduction of the 1996 programme, the SDL leaders actively searched for policies and a programmatic template that they could use in the specific Slovak context. Peter Weiss developed intensive personal contacts with the PCI and he has since argued that the know-how of the Italian post-communists was the most significant source of inspiration in 1990–91. The most visible example of the Italian influence was the change of name from KSS to SDL, along with the form of internal reorganization that took place.[42] Throughout the 1990s, the Socialist International and the Party of European Socialists (and especially the latter's European Forum of Democracy and Solidarity) were instrumental in shaping the political and programmatic framework of the SDL.[43] Their programmatic influence was acknowledged and relatively uncontroversial because the concept of 'democratic socialism' was broadly accepted and the framework remained general in its content. There was not one particular party model or example of political know-how which the SDL could or would have imported after 1989. The party tended to be inspired by specific elements of know-how from a variety of partners: an example of this would be the way that a number of SDL activists looked to the experiences of the Polish social democrats in coming to terms and coexisting with an active and influential Catholic movement.[44] While the SPÖ has been a particularly important source of programmatic inspiration, it remains clear that the uniqueness of the Slovak political system has rendered the systematic import of policy largely inapplicable.[45]

The party professed allegiance to the 'model of European society implemented in the West' and support for 'political orientations manifested in the Socialist International'.[46] The latter offered a 'model consisting of democracy, a mixed economy, a socially responsible state and international co-operation based on equality'.[47] The political programme of 1996 was particularly important as it established the programmatic compatibility of the SDL with Western social democracy. The programme acknowledged its debt to the 'Declaration of Principles' of the Socialist International, using democratic socialism as its ideological core.[48]

The situation changed only marginally during the Europeanization period, 1994–2000, and after 2000. Even under Koncoš, the SDL declared its goal to be an implementation of the values of solidarity, social justice and a pluralist society together with the other parties of the Socialist International. Slovakia must not stay outside a 'unified Europe of social justice and solidarity'.[49] In fact, the tension between the modernizers and conservative socialists had a significant conceptual and programmatic dimension. Most visibly, the two streams differed in their approaches and understandings of 'Third Way' ideas. The programme commission established in 2000 studied the manifesto of the Party of European Socialists and programmes of individual Western social-democratic parties. The chairman of the commission, Eduard Chmelár, a young unorthodox leftist intellectual, found the Swedish social-democratic party, French eco-socialists (and especially left-wing activists and the discourse around *Le Monde Diplomatique*) and the European Social Forum particularly interesting. He also followed the theoretical contributions of the neo-communist leaders Miloslav Ransdorf (Czech KSČM) and Pavol Ondryáš (KSS), while possessing a critical attitude towards the stream of modernizers represented in the commission. He claims that they borrowed ideas from the intellectual and academic discourse of the West European left in the 1970s and 1980s, and were out of touch with the trends and debates of the 1990s, and particularly with those of the Swedish social democrats and French socialists.[50] Others argue that programmatic discourse was also influenced by the programmatic work of the British Labour Party and the German SPD including, even if only marginally, 'Third Way' ideas.[51] While rejecting the economic element of the 'Third Way', Chmelár acknowledges that he was inspired by the emphasis on the development of civil society, political liberalism and environment protection.[52] Such a position clearly conflicted with the preferences of the conservative socialists: the latter apparently hoped that modernizers would be defeated on the 'Third Way' issue in the commission. In reality, though, the commission failed to arrive at any common position and young leftist intellectuals such as Chmelár turned against both the modernizers and the conservative socialists.[53]

The declining interest in programmatic work and the dispute around the 'Third Way' ideas prompted the leadership of Migaš and Koncoš to take a dimmer view of the Socialist International. The SI nevertheless assumed a corrective role: the rhetoric of the SDL leaders did not change substantially even if their policy preferences did.[54] Membership of the SI was too important an asset even for the conservative socialists to put in jeopardy. With the election defeat of 2002, the attachment to the SI and the Party of European Socialists again increased. The SDL leaders perceived the parties in the PES as their closest allies, while still emphasizing that they followed no particular foreign model.[55] The search for programmatic know-how remained specific and focused. The 2002 election programme of the Czech ČSSD, for example, substantially influenced a similar programme produced by the SDL.[56]

Socio-Economic Issues

The development of the SDL's economic policy proved to be of crucial importance in dictating the success or failure of the party's transformation. Party experts contributed to the elaboration of the economic section of the programme of the then Czechoslovak Communist Party in 1990–91, even though Slovak experts perceived themselves as more liberal than their Czech counterparts. Their receptivity towards more centre-left approaches was prompted by considerable differences in the economic conditions of the two federal republics.

The SDL looked to the experiences of German unification, including the model of the *Treuhandanstalt* (state holding company) as a worthy model for possible emulation.[57] Between 1993 and 1995 the party's experts engaged in an exchange of ideas with the German SPD over economic issues, although the decreasing programmatic and theoretical activity of the party froze out any positive outputs from such exchanges.[58] By 1996, the party was more sceptical. It criticized the growing gaps in property relations, income differentiation and the social exclusion of large groups of citizens, who had been pushed to the margins of society.[59] The programme of 1993, and certainly the political programme of 1996, introduced the key tenets of West European social democracy. The SDL distanced itself from the concept of equality as this was elaborated by communists, and began to stress the importance of equality of opportunity, deepening democratization and social justice.[60]

The pressure of pragmatic policy making was not, however, conducive to the development of any substantial programmatic discourse. In fact, by the late 1990s the idea of the 'Third Way' became a subject of political and ideational differentiation. Brigita Schmögnerová, the party's finance minister in 1994 and 1998–2002, was criticized by radical socialists for having advocated 'Third Way' ideas, although her supporters argue that she was in fact behaving pragmatically, not ideologically.[61] She sought an interpretation of the 'Third Way' that would fit the unique conditions of Slovakian discourse.[62] Her critics among the young unorthodox left maintained that she had originally been influenced by Oskar Lafontaine, and only later sought her political anchor in the 'Third Way'.[63] The outright rejection of the 'Third Way' in the draft of the new programme (2000) was criticized by the modernizers as a manifestation of political dilettantism: the SDL, it was argued, had withdrawn from the ground necessary for an exchange of programmatic ideas with the SI and PES.[64] In fact, as Weiss put it, the SDL 'rose up' against Schmögnerová in 1994 and again in 1998.[65] Her emphasis on macroeconomic stabilization was indeed perceived as being close to the views of the IMF and Milton Friedman.[66] She was seen in the same light as the Hungarian reformer Bokros or the Pole, Balcerowicz.[67] In fact, the critics of Schmögnerová stuck rigidly to discussion of ideology and rarely allowed themselves to participate in debates on strategy and everyday politics (attempts to outflank her ideologically failed spectacularly to spawn a coherent counter-strategy).[68] In the end, the SDL became ideationally redundant and lacked the credible programmatic and political competence that might win over a substantial number of voters.

In terms of labour market policy, the SDL incorporated the EU's stated goal of full employment into its programme. The party none the less tended to focus upon the goal of achieving a high and sustainable level of employment rather than full employment in the literal sense. The 1991 programme argued that state investment in job creation should provide large employers – some of Slovakia's key enterprises – with a clear plan for the future.[69] The 1993 social programme developed this to include goals of high and sustainable employment and a high level of worker protection, while the programme of 1996 described the SDL as a 'labour party', directly importing the EU goal of full employment, the principle of labour market flexibility, closeness to the trade unions, social partnership and solidarity.[70] The emphasis on the role of the state increased in the late 1990s. The conservative socialists advocated extensive state support for failing enterprises. With respect to bad management under the SDL minister for social affairs, Peter Magvaši (1998–2002), who failed to use the instruments and financial resources of his office effectively, employment policy has been viewed as the single biggest failure of the party.[71]

The European Union

The Slovak political class has overwhelmingly recognized that the countries of ECE 'never had a choice but to seek reintegration in Europe'.[72] Modernizers in the SDL not only accepted the popular slogan of a 'return to Europe', they placed integration high on their political agenda. Narrowing the slogan down to concentrate on EU accession, however, has been more problematic. The modernizers turned towards the EC/EU as a beacon of European political and economic development and sought Slovak accession to the EU from the early 1990s. The extent to which party members adopted the idea and – even more importantly – understood its implications, is less clear. The SDL's perception of the EU was shaped not only by the European Union itself but also by other social-democratic parties, their programmes and policies. No less important was the personal engagement of politicians such as Günter Verheugen and, more recently, Jan Wiersma, and the gradual involvement of the SDL in EC/EU policy making in the SI and PES.[73] The resulting socialization effect has been of fundamental importance in shaping the party's position on EU integration. The SDL supported PES ideas on EU reform and claimed to share their 'social-democratic vision' of the EU, combining economic management with international co-operation and social justice. The party sought 'membership on the basis of equality' and welcomed 'exchanges of know-how' through training and education programmes.[74] According to Peter Weiss, the attitude of Germany, in particular, and its voluntary submission to the European integration process, became a major source of inspiration for the SDL.

The generally positive attitude to the EU did not change even after the conservative socialists took control of the party. The election manifesto of 2002 underlined the fundamental interest of Slovakia in accession to the EU. The EU was perceived as a community of values, encompassing a commitment to freedom, human rights and social justice.[75] Yet political and programmatic influence has never been exclusively one-sided. By arguing for an accelerated EU enlargement, the SDL acted to speed up the process itself. Together with the social-democratic left in other former communist countries, the SDL exercised indirect but real pressure on its Western partners.

NATO

Much more controversial was the area of security policy. SDL programmatic positions in this area were driven mainly by internal pressures. A group of SDL security and military experts (composed mostly of high-ranking officers in the army) was able to continue its work on theoretical questions of international security begun under the communist regime in the late 1980s. Materials from the Czech ČSSD and other non-communist left parties in Europe were also studied in considerable detail.[76] Party experts developed close ties with Polish, Austrian and Czech colleagues in some of the newly expanded institutions and political foundations. The FES in Bratislava and the security policy section of the SDL, for example, held seminars on defence and military reform.[77] The party held the post of minister of defence in 1994 and 1998–2002 and shaped Slovak security, defence and military policy during these periods. Most importantly, the SDL was the first party in Slovakia to adopt the goal of NATO accession in 1993, and the initiative was driven primarily by the political activism of Pavol Kanis.[78] He emphasized the need for a pan-European system of co-operative security and supported 'bringing the Slovak Republic closer to NATO' as early as the SDL's congress in Žilina in 1993.[79] Integration into 'international security organizations such as NATO and the WEU' was viewed as the way to lead Slovakia into 'European security and co-operation structures' and the party remained ahead of the SI in its attitudes to NATO enlargement.[80] As with EU enlargement, the SDL assumed the role of a 'policy exporter' in these issues *vis-à-vis* social-democratic partners in Western Europe. However, non-left-wing partners and institutions from Western Europe had a significant impact on SDL policy in that party modernizers saw support for NATO accession as proof that it had become a responsible and reliable political partner.[81]

However, defence issues and reform of the army also became areas of dispute within the party. Significantly, the Action Programme of 1996 did not mention NATO accession as a goal of the SDL.[82] By the end of the 1990s, the conservative socialist leadership of the party, represented by Migaš and Koncoš, took a 'shy-neutral position' and only rarely presented in public their preferences for a pan-European or non-bloc security arrangement. The party's external image, however, was still shaped by the 'modernizers' who continued to support NATO enlargement.[83]

Conclusion: SDL Transformation and Policy Transfer

External influences have been a significant factor in the development of the SDL. This essay argues that ideological disposition, language, tradition, regional ties and geographic proximity have all influenced policy transfer in, from and to the SDL.[84] In addition, the experience of the SDL emphasizes the importance of the societal and socio-economic context of transfer. At different periods in time SDL elites have placed different emphases on whom and what they looked to for programmatic inspiration, illustrating how national context shapes the acceptable paths open to party elites.

The nature of external programmatic influence developed in phases. A group of SDL modernizers were already looking for policy inspiration from the West European 'soft left' before 1989, and they subsequently worked with the templates set out by the Socialist International during the first half of the 1990s. The most important result of this was the SDL programme of 1996, fully compatible as it was with the programmatic orientation of the SI and the PES. The next phase, however, turned out to be much more controversial within the SDL. With the social situation deteriorating, the modernizers were gradually ousted from their positions and replaced by conservative socialists: this led to ideological incoherence and eventually prompted the party to split.

In terms of individual parties, it is difficult to single out the most important source of inspiration as the SDL looked for assistance in all directions. Bilateral co-operation with Western former communists and social-democratic parties mostly had a practical focus. Often, individual personalities rather than parties played the decisive role on both sides. In 1990, the Italian former communists exercised the greatest influence on the SDL in terms of its fast-track transition from communist to non-communist left, including the way that the KSS was renamed. Project-oriented co-operation with the German FES and the SPD started in 1992–93. In general, the role of the SPD has been less than could perhaps have been expected and even the extensive activities of the FES did not result in direct programmatic influence. It was the Austrian SPÖ that developed the closest ties with SDL in the mid-1990s. A combination of different factors explains this: geographical proximity, the knowledge of Germany and (indirectly) of Austria, personal engagement on the Austrian side (primarily on the part of Heinz Fischer) and institutional resources (the Karl Renner Institute of the SPÖ). Since the late 1990s, the Swedish and Dutch social democrats and the British Labour Party have most pro-actively and regularly promoted their political and organizational know-how in the SDL, assisting the party in establishing efficient internal organization and preparing for political competition with other parties. Programmatic issues have not been at the core of the annual plans for bilateral co-operation.

The SDL (and other social-democratic parties in Eastern and Central Europe) also influenced its Western partners. The temporal link between the 'convergence and incorporation', between member parties (and prospective member parties) of the SI, prompted interaction and convergence on both sides.[85] The Western partners conversely had to move towards the Eastern applicants, and the recalibration of their attitudes towards NATO and EU enlargement was perhaps the most notable example of this.

The West European non-communist left (and principally the SI and PES) helped the party to transform, modernize and establish itself as a social-democratic party on the international scene. The programmatic template was readily imported and, by the mid-1990s, openly acknowledged. At the same time, the Western partners – with the exception of the Italian former communists – rarely sought intensive contacts with Slovak post-communists until 1993–94. In fact, the Western left used its influence in order to prevent co-operation between the SDL and the Slovak social-democratic SDSS in 1992. A rapprochement of the Slovak left might have fundamentally changed the constellation on the left part of the political spectrum and held back the rise of Mečiar's HZDS. After the more conservative socialists took over in the party, the goal of EU accession remained at the top of the agenda and membership of the SI (and of the PES) was of great value. The SDL leadership therefore may have changed its policy, but was careful not to cast doubt upon the party's compliance with the rules of SI and PES membership. The trans-national party organizations thus played the role of an important promoter of policy transfer as well as a 'corrective' force in the political development of the party.

Programmatic change, however, strained internal cohesion within the party. On the one hand, a 'mechanical application of the principles of the SI has been seen as one of its critical failures'.[86] On the other hand, the dichotomy between the party's modernizers and conservative socialists gradually deepened. The main body of the party was able to live with the 'democratic socialism' of the Western social-democratic and socialist left of the late 1980s and early 1990s. It became alienated, however, by the shifts in the socio-economic programme and the policies of those advocating a 'third way', as well as by security issues, such as NATO enlargement, which the party's modernizers endorsed. In fact, the two major streams exercised very different kinds of policy import. The modernizers were well informed of the intellectual discourse in the western left and sought inspiration from it. They also worked for the translation of their own programme into policy. The mostly conservative socialist majority of the party, however, had no experience with or knowledge of this pre-1989 discourse. They merely adjusted themselves to the programmatic orientation imposed upon the party by the sweeping changes and by the activism of the modernizers. In fact, the conservative socialists had little contact with the general non-communist discourse of the West

European left. They internalized programmatic change only halfway and their policy preferences tended to depart from the programmatic postulates they had formally accepted. Indeed, the conservative socialists exercised a rather superficial understanding of the programmes the party had adopted. As a result, while the official social-democratic programmatic orientation and international links were accepted and remained largely unchanged, two increasingly distinct and incompatible discourses developed within the SDL. The different approaches towards external programmatic models manifested themselves in the growing programmatic incongruity of the party, becoming one of the most tangible reasons for the party's implosion and unsuccessful election campaign in 2002. In January 2005, the SDL along with the SDA and the SDSS merged with the centre-left party of SMER.

NOTES

The authors extend thanks to numerous past and present SDL representatives and especially to Peter Weiss, the former chairman of the party. We are greatly appreciative of the friendly and efficient assistance of Ms Fogelová of the SDL staff. The authors extend their gratitude also to William E. Paterson, James Sloam and Dan Hough for their useful comments, and to Dan Hough for his careful editing of the text.

1. M. Rybář, *Slovak Political Parties Before Parliamentary Elections 2002* (Bratislava: Friedrich Ebert Stiftung, 2002), available at <http://www.fes.sk/arch_en/2002_elections.pdf>, p.9; accessed 1 June 2004.
2. A. Grzymala-Busse, *Redeeming the Communist Past: The Regeneration of Communist Parties in East Central Europe* (Cambridge: Cambridge University Press, 2002); L. Kopeček, 'Strana demokratické levice 1989–2002: úspěch či neúspěch slovenských postkomunistů?', in V. Hloušek and L. Kopeček (eds.), *Rudí a růžoví, Transformace komunistických stran* (Brno: MPÚ, 2002), pp.100–37; T. Haughton, 'Explaining the Limited Success of the Communist Successor Left in Slovakia: The Case of the Party of the Democratic Left (SDL)', *Party Politics*, Vol.10, No.2 (2004), pp.177–91; P. Weiss, 'K príčinám krízy slovenskej nekomunistickej l'avice', *Poliotologická revue*, Vol.9, No.1 (2003), pp.154–64; B. Schmögnerová, *Moderná l'avica: Úvaha o slevenskom socialistickom a sociálnodemokratickom myslení* (Bratislava: SDL', 2001). For broader analyses of the SDL in the context of Slovak social and political transformation, see V. Leška, *Slovensko rok před pravidelnými parlamentními volbami: vnitropolitická situace ve druhém roce předvstupních jednání s Evropskou unií* (Prague: Studijní sešity ÚMV, 2001); G. Mesežnikov, 'Domestic Policies and the Party System', in G. Mesežnikov, M. Kollár and T. Nicholson (eds.), *Slovakia 2002: A Global Report on the State of Society* (Bratislava: Institute for Public Affairs, 2002), pp.23–86; S. Szomolányi, 'Slovakia between Eastern and Central European Ways of Transition', in V. Dvořáková (ed.), *Success or Failure? Ten Years After* (Prague: Friedrich Ebert Stiftung, 1999), pp.24–38; G. Evans and S. Whitefield, 'The Structuring of Political Cleavages in Post-Communist Societies: The Case of the Czech Republic and Slovakia', *Political Studies*, Vol.XLVI (1998), pp.115–39; J.T. Ishiyama and A. Bozóki, 'Adaptation and Change: Characterizing the Survival Strategies of the Communist Successor Parties', *Journal of Communist Studies and Transition Politics*, Vol.17, No.3 (2001), pp.33–50; J.T. Ishiyama, 'The Communist Successor Parties and Party Organizational Development in Post-Communist Politics', *Political Research Quarterly*, Vol.52, No.1 (1999), pp.87–112; J.T. Ishiyama, 'The Sickle or The Rose? Previous Regime Types and the Evolution of the Ex-Communist Parties in Post-Communist Politics', *Comparative Political Studies*, Vol.30, No.3 (1999), pp.299–330.

3. We build primarily on the following literature: D. Dolowitz and D. Marsh, 'Who Learns What from Whom: A Review of the Policy Transfer Literature', *Political Studies*, Vol.XLVI (1996), pp.343–57; D. Dolowitz and D. Marsh, 'Learning from Abroad: The Role of Policy Transfer in Contemporary Policy-Making', *Governance*, Vol.13, No.1 (2000), pp.5–24; C. Radaelli, 'Policy Transfer in the European Union: Institutional Isomorphism as a Source of Legitimacy', *Governance*, Vol.13, No.1 (2000), pp.25–43; D. Stone, 'Learning Lessons and Transferring Policy across Time, Space and Disciplines', *Politics*, Vol.19, No.1 (1999), pp.51–9; D. Stone, 'Non-Governmental Policy Transfer: The Strategies of Independent Policy Institutes', *Governance*, Vol.13, No.1 (2000), pp.45–62.
4. We proceed here from an understanding of the 'Third Way' as a general political goal and policy programme that seeks to modernize social democracy and the left in broader terms. This approach is discussed in more detail in A. Giddens, 'Introduction', in A. Giddens (ed.), *The Global Third Way Debate* (Cambridge: Polity Press, 2001), pp.1–21.
5. V. Krivý, V. Feglová and D. Balko, *Slovensko a jeho regiony: sociokultúrne súvislosti volebného správania* (Bratislava: Nadácia Médiá, 1996), p.9; V. Krivý, 'Results of the 2002 Parliamentary Elections', in Mesežnikov *et al.* (eds.), *Slovakia 2002*, pp.87–111.
6. See K. Henderson, *Slovakia: The Escape from Invisibility* (London and New York: Routledge, 2002), pp.20–26; K. Henderson, 'The Path to Democratic Consolidation in the Czech Republic and Slovakia: Divergence or Convergence?', in G. Pridham (ed.), *Prospects for Democratic Consolidation in East–Central Europe* (Manchester: Manchester University Press, 2002), pp.206–38, at pp.210–11; see also J. Krejčí and P. Machonin, *Czechoslovakia, 1918–92: A Laboratory for Social Change* (Basingstoke: Macmillan, 1996).
7. Krejčí and Machonin, *Czechoslovakia, 1918–92*, p.239.
8. Grzymala-Busse, *Redeeming the Communist Past*, pp.93–4; Kopeček, 'Strana demokratické levice 1989–2002', p.122.
9. Authors' interview with Peter Weiss, chairman of the party 1990–95, Bratislava, 20 Jan. 2003.
10. T. Haughton, 'Explaining the Limited Success of the Communist Successor Left in Slovakia', p.6.
11. We prefer the term 'conservative socialists' to others (such as 'traditional socialists' used by Kopeček, 'hard-liners' used by Haughton, or the 'traditional left' as used by Schmögnerová) that are used elsewhere. The ideological preferences of this stream orientated the group towards the concept of 'democratic socialism', although their ideology also included elements of familiar communist beliefs.
12. M. Dauderstädt, A. Gerrits and G. Márkus, *Troubled Transition* (Bonn and Amsterdam: Friedrich Ebert Stiftung, 1999), p.86.
13. Kopeček, 'Strana demokratické levice 1989–2002', pp.127–8.
14. Authors' interview with Jozef Košnár, head of the SDL commission for national economic matters, Bratislava, 20 Jan. 2003.
15. J. Migaš, 'Zahajovací prejav na 5. sjezdu SDL, 23–24 October 1998', Zvolen, in *Lavicové noviny*, Nov. 1998, p.1.
16. V. Leška, *Vnitropolitická situace Slovenské republiky v roce 2000* (Prague: Studijní sešity ÚMV, 2000), pp.20–21; G. Pridham, 'The European Union's Democratic Conditionality and Domestic Politics in Slovakia: The Mečiar and Dzurinda Governments Compared', *Europe–Asia Studies*, Vol.51, No.2 (2002), p.218.
17. Mesežnikov, 'Domestic Policies and the Party System', p.80.
18. Ishiyama and Bozóki, 'Adaptation and Change', pp.44–5.
19. Schmögnerová, *Moderná l'avica*, p.20.
20. Haughton, 'Explaining the Limited Success'; similarly Mesežnikov, 'Domestic Policies and the Party System', p.80.
21. G. Pridham, 'Rethinking Regime-Change Theory and the International Dimension of Democratization: Ten Years After in East–Central Europe', in G. Pridham and A. Ágh (eds.), *Prospects for Democratic Consolidation in East–Central Europe* (Manchester: Manchester University Press, 2001), pp.54–95; J. Batt, 'The International Dimension of Democratization in Hungary, Slovakia and the Czech Republic', in G. Pridham, E. Herring and G. Sanford

(eds.), *Building Democracy? The International Dimension of Democratization in Eastern Europe* (London: Leicester University Press, 1997), p.168.
22. G. Pridham, 'Complying with the European Union's Democratic Conditionality: Transnational Party Linkages and Regime Change in Slovakia, 1993–1998', *Europe–Asia Studies*, Vol.51, No. 7 (1999), pp.1231–2; also authors' interview with Peter Weiss, 20 Jan. 2003.
23. Authors' interview with Michael Petráš, head, Friedrich Ebert Foundation, Bratislava, 20 Jan. 2003.
24. Authors' interview with Ján Richter, Secretary General of the SDL, Bratislava, 22 Jan. 2003.
25. Authors' interview with L'ubomír Petrák, chairman of the SDL, Bratislava, 22 Jan. 2003.
26. Authors' interview with Michael Petráš, 20 Jan. 2003.
27. Ibid.
28. Authors' interview with Peter Weiss, 20 Jan. 2003, and with Michael Petráš, 20 Jan. 2003.
29. Authors' interview with Ján Richter, 22 Jan. 2003. Mr Richter received training in the organization and administration of political parties by the British Labour Party.
30. Ibid.
31. Authors' interview with Peter Weiss, 20 Jan. 2003.
32. Interview with Vladimír Krivý, Institute for Sociology, Bratislava, 21 Jan. 2003.
33. P. Weiss, 'K príčinám krízy slovenskej nekomunistickej l'avice', p.157.
34. D. Stone, 'Non-Governmental Policy Transfer', p.50.
35. Authors' interview with Ján Richter, 22 Jan. 2003.
36. Authors' Interview with Peter Weiss, 20 Jan. 2003.
37. Authors' Interview with Ján Richter, 22 Jan. 2003.
38. T. Haughton, 'Explaining the Limited Success of the Communist Successor Left in Slovakia'; authors' interview with Jozef Košnár, 20 Jan. 2003, and with Peter Weiss, 20 Jan. 2003.
39. M. Žiak, *Pád komunismu na Slovensku* (Bratislava: Archa, 1994), p.24.
40. According to Pavol Kanis, the IML translated a number of Western publications and was therefore able to reach a broader readership: authors' interview with Pavol Kanis, former deputy chairman of the SDL and minister of defence 1994 and 1998–99, Bratislava, 24 Jan. 2003.
41. Authors' interview with Jozef Košnár, 20 Jan. 2003.
42. Authors' interview with Peter Weiss, 20 Jan. 2003.
43. Authors' interview with Milan Ftáčnik, former deputy chairman of the SDL, minister of education 1998–2002, currently chairman of the SDA, Bratislava, 24 Jan. 2003.
44. Authors' interview with Ján Richter, 22 Jan. 2003.
45. Ibid.
46. 'Zahranično-politický program', in *Dokumenty druhého zjazdu Strany demokratickej l'avice, 22.-23.mája 1993, Žilina* (Bratislava: VV SDL, 1993), p.79.
47. Ibid., p.84.
48. 'Politický program SDL', *4. zjazd Strany demokratickej l'avice v Nitre 27–28. Apríla 1996* (Bratislava: VV SDL, 1996), p.54.
49. 'Nová nádej', *Volebný program SDL* (Bratislava: SDL, 2002), pp.1, 8.
50. Authors' interview with Eduard Chmelár, chairman of the programme commission of the SDL 1999–2003, Bratislava, 23 Jan. 2003.
51. Authors' interview with Ján Richter, 22 Jan. 2003.
52. Authors' interview with Eduard Chmelár, 23 Jan. 2003.
53. See the critical speech of Eduard Chmelár during the seventh congress of SDL, in *Sedmý sjezd SDL* (Bratislava: VV SDL', 2001), p.80.
54. Authors' interview with Michael Petráš, 20 Jan. 2003.
55. Authors' interview with Lubomír Petrák, 22 Jan. 2003.
56. Authors' interview with Ján Richter, 22 Jan. 2003.
57. Authors' interview with Jozef Košnár, 20 Jan. 2003.
58. Ibid.
59. 'Politický program SDL', p.53.
60. Ibid., pp.55–6.
61. Authors' interview with Peter Weiss, 20 Jan. 2003.

62. B. Schmögnerová, *Moderná ľavica*; authors' interview with Peter Weiss, 20 Jan. 2003.
63. Authors' interview with Eduard Chmelár, 23 Jan. 2003.
64. Authors' interview with Jozef Košnár, 20 Jan. 2003.
65. Authors' interview with Peter Weiss, 20 Jan. 2003. This had the same effect on the attitudes of politicians such as Milan Ftáčnik, who promoted liberal approaches and advocated the introduction of fees in Slovak universities: authors' interview with Daniel Šmihula, Institute for Political Sciences, Bratislava, 21 Dec. 2003, and with Ján Richter, 22 Jan. 2003.
66. Authors' interview with Milan Ftáčnik, 24 Jan. 2003.
67. Authors' interview with František Škvrnda, independent political analyst, Bratislava, 23 Jan. 2003.
68. Authors' interview with Milan Ftáčnik, 24 Jan. 2003.
69. 'O čo sa usiluje SDL', in *Dokumenty prvého zjazdu SDL', 14.–15. Decembra 1991, Trenčín* (Bratislava: VV SDL', 1991).
70. 'Sociálny program', in *Dokumenty druhého zjazdu Strany demokratickej ľavice, 22.–23. Mája, Žilina 1993* (Bratislava: VV SDL', 1993), p.61; 'Politický program SDL', pp.70–72.
71. P. Weiss, 'K príčinám krízy slovenskej nekomunistickej ľavice', p.160.
72. Batt, 'The International Dimension', p.168.
73. Authors' interview with Peter Weiss, 20 Jan. 2003, and with Milan Ftáčnik, 24 Jan. 2003.
74. 'O čo sa usiluje SDL', p.28.
75. 'Nová nádej', p.8.
76. The research project IX/55, an indirect continuation of strategic military thinking that began during the Prague Spring of 1968, was completed in spring 1989 and successfully defended at the Institute for Marxism and Leninism (the theoretical body of the Central Committee of the KSČ) in Prague. The Military Academy, Military–Political Academy and other research institutions of the Army actually conducted the research: authors' interview with Peter Barták, head of the defence policy section of SDL, Bratislava, 19 March 2003.
77. Authors' interview with Peter Barták, 19 March 2003.
78. Authors' interview with Ján Richter, 22 Jan. 2003, and with Pavol Kanis, 24 Jan. 2003.
79. 'O čo sa usiluje SDL'', p.32.
80. 'Zahranično-politický program', p.76.
81. Authors' interview with Peter Weiss, 20 Jan. 2003.
82. 'Akčný program Strany demokratickej ľavice', in *4. zjazd Strany demokratickej ľavice v Nitre 27–28 Apríla, 1996* (Bratislava: VV SDL', 1996), pp.85–110.
83. Authors' interview with Peter Barták, 19 March 2003.
84. On general conditions of policy transfer, see the essay by W.E. Paterson and J. Sloam, 'Learning from the West: Policy Transfer and Political Parties', in this collection, pp.37–51.
85. G. Pridham, 'The European Union's Democratic Conditionality', p.205.
86. Authors' interview with Dušan Leška, faculty of physical education and sports, Comenius University, Bratislava, 23 Jan. 2003.

Choosing Between China and Europe? Virtual Inspiration and Policy Transfer in the Programmatic Development of the Czech Communist Party

VLADIMÍR HANDL

Introduction

The Communist Party of Bohemia and Moravia (KSČM) is an interesting – if perhaps somewhat surprising – case study of how the need to reform programmatically can be facilitated by transferring in ideas and policies from other political settings. Since 1993 the KSČM has perceived itself as the only genuinely left-wing party in the Czech Republic, representing what it terms a revolutionary alternative and perceiving itself as a vanguard party in the fight against capitalism. Its long-term objective is, indeed, the imposition of systemic change across the Czech Republic, with a rather ill-defined form of socialism eventually replacing capitalism altogether.[1] Expansive claims such as these have not prevented the KSČM from developing elaborate and detailed programmatic documents and the KSČM is certainly not afraid of

---

Vladimír Handl is with the Institute of International Relations, Prague, and a former research fellow at the Institute of German Studies, University of Birmingham.

announcing what it would do differently should it be given the chance – even if the alternatives it articulates remain, for the most part, vague and ill-defined.[2]

As a rule, Czechs regard the programmatic positions that parties take up – in stark contrast to their Polish counterparts – as being of genuine significance.[3] Indeed, opinion polls reveal that programmes play an important role in shaping individual electoral preferences and moulding a party's internal and external identity.[4] The KSČM has subsequently managed to pull off the trick of simultaneously remaining a party wedded to a seemingly clear ideology, while being pragmatic enough to participate – where the opportunities arise – in sharing power at sub-national levels. Ideology has played a particularly prominent role in prompting internal programmatic consolidation within the party. In recent times electoral success and the ageing of the party faithful have none the less led to an intensification of debate on how, and whether, the party should be modernized, further emboldening party elites to act in more pragmatic ways than they have done in the past.

This article analyses how and when party elites have sought ideological and political inspiration from external sources when constructing their own programmatic identity. It builds on the growing body of literature on emulative and coercive policy transfer.[5] The explicit transfer of policies from abroad has not attracted much attention within the KSČM itself, and it has subsequently found little resonance in the academic literature published so far on the party.[6] In the early 1990s the KSČM's strategy was simply one of survival; and, although approaches differed concerning what such a strategy should look like, there was little talk (anywhere within the party) of mimicking programmes adopted elsewhere. All of the analysis of the KSČM to date has therefore indicated that programmatic development is primarily indigenous.

Here it is argued that before 1993 there was a genuine – if short-term – interest in extensively importing elements of the social-democratic agenda. Second, and no less importantly, the programmatic development of the party has always been open to a certain level of external inspiration and, in the late 1990s, the party continued to grow into the role of an active policy exporter and the facilitator of two-way exchanges of policy. More recently, the orientation of the Czech Republic towards the normative, political and institutional framework of the EU naturally tied in with the import or emulation and diffusion of particular policy models.[7]

Given the internal ideational divisions within the party, however, the conservative and neo-communist streams often appear to look in different directions when doing this. Most articulate representatives of the former, conservative, group tend to present Chinese communism as a model that the KSČM should look to emulate, unwilling as they are to accept the project of EU integration as being anything other than a neo-liberal plot. The latter, neo-communist, group looks to learn from the political experiences that they and other left movements (both radical and 'soft') have accumulated in the EU.

The Post-1989 Transformation

The KSČM has been a prominent actor in Czech politics since 1989. It has been variously viewed as a traditional mass party, an anti-system party, one of the so-called 'semi-loyal opposition parties', a 'sub-cultural party', an 'orthodox Marxist-Leninist party', or – as Fausto Sorino from the Italian Party of the Communist Refoundation (PRC) argues – simply a 'Leninist party'.[8] Its support in national elections has increased from 10.3 per cent (1996) to 18.5 per cent (2002), and recently to 20.4 per cent (in the 2004 elections to the European parliament). KSČM leaders have claimed that this recent surge in electoral support illustrates that the party is taking up a dominant position on the Czech left.[9]

As was the case with other communist successor parties (CSPs), the window of opportunity in terms of implementing radical programmatic transformation existed primarily in the very early 1990s. Both leaders of the party in the immediate post-1990 period – Vasil Mohorita (1990) and Jiří Svoboda (1990–93) – sought, more or less consistently, to open the party up to non-communist modernization. Yet, by virtue of the sheer size of the KSČM membership base and the permanent electoral constituency that it represented, the party's survival did not depend exclusively on gaining support from the wider public. The party's organizational structures were decentralized and the executive committee rendered weak and financially and organizationally dependent on the district organizations. This gave the more conservative forces – after 1991 – the ideal opportunity to regain influence through and within the district organizations.[10] The grassroots, comprising the lower strata of the former ruling class and the intelligentsia, increasingly began to influence the party's programmatic transformation, eventually becoming the ultimate arbiter of party decisions.[11] They sought in effect to preserve the party as an ideological, political and emotional sanctuary safe from transformative pressures.[12]

The party programmes adopted at the two congresses at Kladno (1992) and Prostejov (1993) confirmed that the party had opted very much for the communist path. Ishiyama and Bozóki argue that the leadership chose a 'strategy of leftist-retreat' that involved an embracing of an 'orthodox communist' ideology.[13] Hanley refers to a 'neo-communist strategy' with 'innovative and democratic elements'.[14] Yet the KSČM's programmatic transformation is perhaps not as clear-cut as such labels suggest. The KSČM certainly did opt for a strategy of leftist retreat in a broad sense, but it did not adopt an exclusively conservative orthodox model. It also appears difficult to characterize this strategy as purely neo-communist: in reality, the strategies represent the *modus vivendi* among the individual communist streams within the party at that particular time, and they have most certainly been open to adjustment over the years. This process was accelerated by two particular external influences – the increasing electoral successes of the party and the prospect of EU accession. Both of these developments intensified debates in the run-up to the crucial sixth party congress, which took place in May 2004.

One thing the KSČM clearly is not, however, is a 'non-communist' party. In 1993 the non-communist stream was forced out of the party, as were a group of extreme Stalinists, headed by Miroslav Štěpán. The two most articulate elite streams that remained within the KSČM were therefore the neo-communists and the conservatives. Yet the traditionalist majority of the party represents a heterogeneous stream of its own.[15] The latter two streams (conservatives and the traditionalist majority) represent a tacit 'retreat coalition', a bulwark of the strategy of leftist-retreat. They maintain elements of traditional communist ideology and preserve the Marxist-Leninist identity of the party; they use familiar language and pander to particularly significant points of ideological and historical reference – namely by using a particular form of pan-Slavic revolutionary discourse that is reproduced primarily in the party's daily newspaper, *Haló noviny*.

Other characteristics of the communist faith are treated as untouchable and remain objects of self-identification – most crucially the party's name, but also the icons of its Russophile attitude or unreserved support for 'socialist' states such as Cuba and North Korea and sympathy with any other 'leftist' parties, and adversaries of the United States and 'imperialism' as a whole (Milošević's Yugoslavia, partly even Mugabe's Zimbabwe or Saddam Hussain's Iraq). The most pronounced of these developments is the newly discovered (or rediscovered) fascination with communist China. The anti-capitalist orientation of the party's majority has always been essentially 'anti-Western' and 'anti-liberal' by definition, biased mainly against Germany and the US, and interest in the 'success story' of contemporary China links well with these other long-held ideological beliefs.

The party's electoral successes in recent years certainly indicate that the survival strategy has worked well so far.[16] These successes can be explained by the loyal voting habits of communist voters, as well as being a result of the overwhelmingly one-dimensional form of party competition evident in the Czech Republic to date:[17] put another way, it really is a case – as Bill Clinton once famously said – of it being 'the economy, stupid'. The KSČM also attracts protest voters who want to punish the social democrats for their performance in government. Yet, according to some, the KSČM has become a part of the political mainstream. According to Jan Hartl, director of STEM, an influential institute for public opinion research in Prague, all taboos regarding the party have been removed and the KSČM is actively trying to move beyond 'simply attracting frustrated voters'.[18] Yet the KSČM appears to be approaching the limits of its growth and if it is unable to reach out towards the young, well-educated urban population it is likely that its recent electoral successes will prove to be a high before an inevitable fall. Vlastimil Balín argues that the party, like the German PDS, is getting older and older, and that the limited number of new members cannot balance this ageing process out. In 2003, the average age of a party member was 68.1 years, and half of the membership was aged 70 or older.[19] The 'neo-communists' and the policy-oriented 'traditionalists' are conscious of this and argue in favour of a modernization of the party to counteract this trend. Before the sixth congress, the then deputy chairman of the party, the prominent 'neo-communist' Miloslav Ransdorf, argued that the KSČM had to go beyond a narrow class-based bedrock of support and ideas. It should transform itself into a political party mediating between groups, layers and classes in society, developing into what he vaguely describes as an 'information party', leaving its 'cultural ghetto' behind.[20]

Contrary to this, representatives of the 'retreat coalition' reject attempts to make any substantial change to the general direction of the party. The traditional conviction is that the KSČM should be able to make better use of its main asset – 'the largest and most experienced' membership base of any communist successor party in Eastern and Central Europe.[21] The majority of the predominantly conservative and powerful district committees are afraid of weakening their own position and watering down the identity of the party. They oppose even the most basic attempts to turn intermediate co-ordinating bodies (regional councils) into fully-fledged regional organizations that would exist between them and the centre.[22] One result of the deepening internal division has been the increasing degree of pragmatism exhibited by the party elite, plus a focus on maximizing the party's power and influence in everyday politics. Somewhat bizarrely, the KSČM relates increasingly to liberal conservative and Eurosceptic politicians with a populist touch such as the current president, Václav Klaus, and the party has even linked up with the controversial media magnate Vladimír Železný.[23]

In preparation for the sixth congress in 2004, Ransdorf directly challenged the chairman, Grebeníček, for the first time and turned to party members with a personal appeal to change the party in order to enable political co-operation with the social-democrat ČSSD.[24] Given the predominantly self-satisfied atmosphere that existed within the party, and its general aversion to social democrats, he inevitably failed in his quest and gave up his position as deputy chairman. In order to modernize the party, the 'neo-communists' will have to challenge the 'cultural hegemony' of the 'conservatives', manifested and reinforced daily by *Haló noviny*.

International Relations and Programmatic Development

Both the past and present party elites have claimed – and still do – that external influences on the KSČM's programmatic orientation have been minimal. They argue – plausibly – that the KSČM has never developed a one-dimensional orientation towards one particular communist or social-democratic party. Yet, party representatives from all streams claim that the party has observed and analysed the programmatic platforms of a number of foreign parties more carefully than any other political party in the Czech Republic. As both of the party's deputy chairmen, Ransdorf and Exner, observed in 2003, 'anything that can inspire us and can serve as an impetus for internal debate is welcome'.[25] In terms of ideology, the party has been clearly distinct from the parties of the Socialist International (SI), as well as most other postcommunist parties and most of the European hard left in that it has not sought openly to adopt a social-democratic identity. Only Zyuganov's Communist Party of the Russian Federation is seen as having anything like a similar ideological self-understanding.[26] In political terms, the KSČM has been mostly ignored, isolated and pressurized by anti-communist forces both at home and abroad. The KSČM itself has been primarily inward looking and has preferred self-isolation to exposing itself to a dialogue across the left spectrum and beyond. The SI, for its part, has been seen as departing from a vision of the left with which the KSČM can identify, ironically just as the party has been returning to 'socialism' in its programme.[27]

There are also substantial institutional limitations on any attempt to transfer policy inwards. Only a small number of individuals in the leadership of the party have been capable of conducting a search for foreign inspiration and, moreover, such activities have never been part of their day-to-day political agenda.[28] A research-orientated think tank (TAP) has been established by the party's central committee, and a well developed, yet understaffed, structure of so-called 'expert commissions' also exists.[29] The scope of their remits is, however, fairly limited.[30] The KSČM has none the less established relations with more than 200 mostly hard-left parties around the world. But it has made no moves to co-ordinate policy with any of them in a formal sense, and the intensity of relations is shaped by the preferences of the individual representatives and ideational streams. KSČM leaders develop their own foreign contacts, linking directly with partners with similar ideological preferences. The conservative stream remains the most well organized and it holds fairly regular conferences, attended by a narrow circle of politicians from the German PDS, the French Communist Party (PCF), the Italian PRC and the Labour Party of Belgium.

Foreign parties, from either the 'hard' or 'soft' left, were rarely active at home in promoting their co-operation with the KSČM in the early 1990s.

The entire communist movement was in a state of crisis, relations between the different parties were subsequently patchy, and, for most of this period, they lacked direction. Only in the late 1990s was there a gradual intensification of programmatic dialogue across the hard left. Since the late 1990s, the German PDS – and in particular its honorary chairman and former MEP, Hans Modrow – has invested considerable effort and funds into the promotion of the idea of EU accession inside the KSČM. However, the mixture of communism and post-communism that is evident within the German PDS and its 'EU-activist' stance prompted considerable KSČM reservations about cooperation with the PDS, as conservatives remained fundamentally distrustful of the EU project.[31] The KSČM therefore only indirectly participated in the creation of an institutionalized platform for co-operation with the PDS-affiliated Rosa Luxemburg Foundation.[32] These forms of co-operation had an important impact on the EU positions that the KSČM adopted. The 'soft no' during the referendum on EU accession – a compromise between neo-communist supporters and conservative opponents of accession – could not have been achieved without the engagement of the PDS.[33] These forms of co-operation have been shown to possess clear limits: in the context of the 2002 elections in Germany, the PDS has been viewed as lacking a profile that differentiates it from the German SPD[34] – which, given the reform agenda at present being pursued by Gerhard Schröder's social democrats, says more about the KSČM than it does about the PDS. The KSČM has subsequently moved closer to the Marxist-Leninist stream within the PDS. The non-communist-oriented PDS leadership has tried to keep a respectable distance from the KSČM and ideas for a joint election platform for the elections to the European parliament in 2004 were quietly dropped by the reforming elements of the PDS leadership.[35]

Since the late 1990s, the KSČM has been growing into the role of a promoter and facilitator of multilateral co-operation across the hard left. Relations with the hard-line communist parties in neighbouring Germany, Slovakia and Poland at the regional level represent a 'natural arena' for the KSČM to play a role as a policy exporter, as well as a facilitator of contacts and networks. The KSČM has initiated regular meetings between the communist and neo-communist parties of the four countries. At the European level, the KSČM convened an international conference – effectively an anti-NATO summit – on 19 November 2002 and a conference on the future of the hard left in the EU on 6–7 March 2004. While in the early 1990s there were few opportunities for such exchanges of views, Ransdorf argues that there is 'now a regular process in which we can find elements of a new strategy'.[36] The Spanish CP even called on the KSČM to assume the role of a co-ordinator of far-left parties on security issues (in the so-called 'Spanish appeal'). The involvement of the KSČM in the Group of the European

United Left/Nordic Green Left (GUE/NGL) group and its relations with the same parties in the Council of Europe has also been of importance in socializing the party into the international arena. The internal divisions within the KSČM may, however, be transported on to the European stage, and this is a danger of which other hard left parties are aware. Future KSČM representatives, as an insider has argued, will need to avoid giving preference to 'so-called national interests' and developing irrelevant debates about the appropriate 'revolutionary attitude to the EP', as such 'diversions' would undoubtedly alienate the KSČM from most of its hard-left partners.[37]

Most importantly, the KSČM may play a role in the further development of the European Party of the Left (ELP). Czech communists were not initially invited to participate in preparing the launch of the party in late 2003. This – unsurprisingly – prompted a disdainful reaction by the KSČM.[38] Moreover, the party is clearly split over what the ELP should do, how it should be organized and how much sovereignty the KSČM should concede to it. Indeed, the party's conservatives opposed outright the creation of the European Party of the Left, viewing it primarily as a Euro-communist creation, with undemocratic structures and a projected trajectory that might water down the communist identity of the KSČM. They therefore prevented the KSČM from joining the ELP during the founding congress in Rome (May 2004) and insisted on maintaining observer status.[39] The conservatives also sought to prevent any enhancing of the position of the 'neo-communists' – and Miloslav Ransdorf in particular – who could well have been asked to play a significant role within the European 'hard left'. The neo-communists and policy-oriented traditionalists, on the other hand, support the creation of a pan-European hard-left organization. Ransdorf stressed that the KSČM had been recognized at the international level as 'a key partner, as one of the decisive parties of our movement at both the European and the global level', and dangers to national sovereignty and the independence of the individual parties were vastly overestimated.[40]

In direct party-to-party terms, the KSČM assumes the role of a policy exporter mainly in its relations with the Communist Party of Slovakia (KSS). It is mostly the conservative and traditionalist streams that share ideological preferences with the orthodox KSS. The Czech neo-communists, for example, failed to persuade the KSS to adopt a more critical stance to its 'socialist' past. On the other hand, given specific domestic circumstances in Slovakia, the KSS decided – unlike the KSČM – to support accession to the EU during the referendum campaign in Slovakia.[41]

External Inspiration in Practice

Despite the party wings waging war on each other between 1989 and 1992, KSČM leaders none the less did search for external models that would help it accrue greater democratic legitimacy. Initially, social-democratic parties were – perhaps surprisingly – interesting objects for prospective policy transfer. In December 1989, Ladislav Adamec, party chairman at that time, referred in positive terms to the experience gathered by the social-democratic parties in their political struggles.[42] Valenčík argues that Jiří Svoboda went even further: 'if there had been an offer, we would have been able to pull the party towards a form of social-democratic development and associate membership of the SI'.[43] Even the present chairman of the party, Miroslav Grebeníček, in 1991 presented the transformation of the Italian PCI into the then PDS as an inspiration for the KSČM.[44]

After 1993, two types of external policy transfer appear to have existed: one largely programmatic and ideological, the other primarily policy-oriented. The first is characterized figuratively by the 'China–EU dichotomy'; the second is less ideological and reflects the growing pragmatism of the conservatives and traditionalists. All streams deny there is a ready-made programmatic model that is directly suitable for their needs, while still acknowledging that they are indeed still searching for inspiration from all sorts of different directions. For example, while elaborating on the new definition of socialism, the deputy chairman of the KSČM, the neo-communist representative Jiří Dolejš, found 'the most recent ideas of the Greens on a sustainable quality of life ... to be most appropriate'.[45] The KSČM has studied SI documents and those of the group of radical European leftist parties in the European parliament. The programmes, however, were seen as not specific enough to give clear answers to the most burning questions that the KSČM faced in its daily affairs. Dolejš also tracks with interest the example of co-operation between social-reformist and environmentalist parties in Western Europe. He finds the attempts of the German PDS 'to get closer to civic initiatives on peace, the environment and social affairs' to be of genuine significance and perhaps of use to the KSČM. Dolejš and those around him are clearly aware that 'a party of a narrowly defined communist type has a relatively limited electorate', and the KSČM has a pressing need to open itself up to new sections of Czech society.[46]

The ideological inspiration for the conservatives comes primarily from the 'hard left': Miroslav Grebeníček has underlined the KSČM's ideological closeness both to the Communist Refoundation in Italy and also to the Marxist-Leninist Communist Party of Portugal.[47] Above all, unreserved admiration for Beijing prompts both the conservatives and traditionalists to look at the Chinese Communist Party as an ideal model.[48] 'The light is coming from the East again', claimed *Haló noviny* in 2003; 'however, from a further distance this time', reflecting the increasing importance of Chinese communism over and above its Russian counterpart. Chinese economic growth is seen as being impressive, precisely because it is part of a 'functioning socialist system' and because in China there is 'more real democracy than in the so-called democratic world'.[49] China is particularly attractive to the orthodox elements in the KSČM who proposed that the sixth congress should look to China for inspiration.[50] The reasoning behind this is simple: the Chinese party has introduced capitalism, while maintaining a monopoly on political power.

The German PDS is less popular with the conservatives. The German post-communist party includes a strong non-communist stream, which has mostly sought to maintain a considerable distance from the KSČM. The 'retreat coalition' within the KSČM has returned the compliment.[51] None the less, the PDS's definition of socialism was referred to in the fifth party congress documents principally as being much more practicable than other definitions that were considered, and the PDS's influence here remains the only 'acknowledged' foreign source of programmatic innovation.[52] The KSČM warmly greeted the electoral success of the PDS in 2004.

Despite the clear absence of overt contacts with social-democratic parties, a considerable degree of inspiration has none the less taken place. The KSČM has emphasized time and again that there is an overlap of 70–80 per cent of its programme with that of the ČSSD.[53] When compared with the pre-1989 communist programme, it is evident that the KSČM has in fact been inspired by the main pillars of the social-democratic and Euro-communist agenda of the 1970s and 1980s: pluralist political democracy, acceptance of a mixed economy, social solidarity and justice, emphasis on the role of the state and a distinct vision of socialism. Paradoxically, the rapprochement in substance prompted efforts by the party to distinguish itself from the social-democratic movement by emphasizing Marxism and revolutionary symbols, most importantly the party's communist name. Policy transfer from sources other than the 'hard left' has therefore often been unacknowledged, flatly denied or promoted subconsciously. For example, the KSČM programmes in 1990–91 included the concept of 'democratic socialism' and referred directly to the political programme of the Socialist International.[54] Later, however, the KSČM chose to drop ideas of democratic socialism and introduce the concept of 'modern socialism' as a replacement.[55] 'Modern socialism' derives from 'democratic socialism' without referring to it – principally because the party needed to distinguish itself clearly from the SI's programmatic orientations.[56]

The sources of policy-oriented inspiration are much more diverse and difficult to pin down. All streams within the KSČM developed their own preferences, which are by no means all best understood as being part of traditional hard-left discourse. In general terms, the single most feasible source of inspiration is inevitably the EU and its member states (and, once again, not only the 'hard left' parties that are active within some of them). By definition, the retreat coalition forms a 'negativist' bloc in terms of its attitude to the EU, and tends to avoid admitting that it may have been inspired by the EU at all. Contrary to this, the neo-communists and the policy-oriented traditionalists take up an 'activist' position *vis-à-vis* the EU. They discuss EU-relevant policy initiatives openly and they attempt to change the anti-EU discourse within the party and thus to add legitimacy to their support for EU accession as well as to their call for modernization of the KSČM itself.

The KSČM's Attitudes to the European Union

In general, the KSČM agrees that 'the process of European integration is inevitable and natural'.[57] However, conservatives have a 'negativist' view of integration and they see it as the ultimate sanctioning of the capitalist system.[58] They stand close to the Eurosceptic position of liberal conservatives and share Václav Klaus's emphasis on maintaining and preserving national sovereignty. The neo-communist 'activists' reject such a stance, pointing out that the EU offers the potential to mobilize both political and economic resources with the aim of increasing Czech influence in a much more interdependent world.[59] The party's only specific document of a genuinely programmatic nature on European policy none the less remains the so-called 'Manifesto for a Democratic Europe' – which is a document that reflects the uneasy balance between the 'negativist' and 'activist' attitudes within the party.

In more policy-oriented documents, EU policies in areas such as social affairs, environmental protection, regional development, structural policy, agriculture and institutional reform are referred to or acknowledged.[60] Consciously or not, the EU has clearly been accepted as the single most important external reference point. At the same time, the KSČM criticizes advancements made in terms of a European security and defence policy. It is also sceptical of the EU's proposed constitution, reflecting the majority opinion of the 'retreat coalition'.[61] The sixth congress took a more positive view, though, defining the KSČM as a proponent of a confederal or 'moderately federal' EU.[62] The KSČM's attitudes so far – and the difficulty it has experienced in finding a commonly acceptable line – indicate that the party may seek a leftist EU '*à la carte*', supporting further integration in areas where internal accommodations are possible, but rejecting it as and when the retreat coalition is able to dictate programmatic orientations.

Socio-Economic Issues

In practical terms and among the party's economists, Marxist doctrines were not seen as offering much inspiration, even though they continued to be of considerable symbolic importance.[63] In terms of the ownership of the means of production, the KSČM seeks a solution where 75–80 per cent of production is completed by publicly owned organizations. The party does not look to create large state-owned companies; rather it seeks to follow the example of the Mondragon co-operatives in Spain or co-operative structures as they exist in Austria, Germany, France and Israel. The KSČM also focuses on employee share ownership programmes (ESOP), the like of which are most well developed in – of all places – the United States.[64] The KSČM also supports employee participation in running the firms where they work.[65] The 'Third Way', as defined by Tony Blair, Bill Clinton and Gerhard Schröder, remains – unsurprisingly – anathema to the party. Jiří Dolejš in particular – a man who positioned himself on the party's 'liberal' side – has always been rebuffed by the hardliners in the party leadership and *Haló noviny*.

In more general economic and social policy terms, the KSČM looks to the experiences of countries such as Ireland, Finland and partly also Portugal for possible prompts in their search for programmatic ideas.[66] The KSČM supported in principle the Lisbon economic reform agenda of 2000 while concurrently maintaining a strong preference for the protection of national producers and for constraints on international competition.[67] The party has elaborated in some detail its views on the standard tools of an active employment policy. Special emphasis is placed on the role of the state and on the importance of active self-government at the lower levels of political activity. The experience of successful EU countries is acknowledged and the EU is referred to when it comes to 'post-material needs' and the necessity to rethink the whole concept of labour.[68] The KSČM has directly 'imported' some ideas, such as the 35-hour week from the PCF, and has not had difficulty in subscribing to the GUE/NGL's employment policy guidelines.[69] Like its Western partners, the KSČM focuses on economic growth based on demand management. Unlike the Blair–Schröder 'Third Way' model, the KSČM emphasizes the importance of increasing labour protection, including particular regulations for fixed-term employment rather than enhancing the flexibility of the labour market.[70]

The KSČM programme integrated the key principles of an expansive welfare state while avoiding using the term directly. As was the case with 'democratic socialism', the party sought a distance from what was seen as a specifically social-democratic agenda.[71] Instead of invoking the term 'social market economy', the KSČM has introduced the concept of a 'socialist market economy'.[72] On the other hand, the 'neo-communist' leaders valued the social policy of West European states. They even took the unusual step of condemning elements of the Swedish model as inapplicable in the Czech Republic, and chose to advocate a more liberal approach.[73] More recently, the welfare state has also become a reference point – as an interim arrangement – for the representatives of the 'retreat coalition'.[74] After all, the adoption of the European Social Charter represents one of the few examples of a direct and acknowledged policy import (emulation) from the EU.

Security Issues

The party's reference to the 'French model' (withdrawal from the military organization of NATO) represents one of the rare examples of acknowledged policy transfer in the security area. The party's military experts also refer to the experience of reform of military forces in a number of other Western countries – Portugal, Greece, Belgium, the Netherlands, Sweden or Denmark – when discussing the proposed transformation of the Czech army.[75] Unlike conservatives, who have a strictly anti-NATO stance, the 'neo-communist' leaders argue that NATO should be transformed into an instrument of all-European security and they voted for ratification of NATO enlargement. They are broadly supportive of the common foreign and security policy (CFSP) and the European security and defence policy (ESDP) and argue in favour of a merger, or at least the increasing synergy, of the multitude of security organizations in Europe.[76] They openly supported a plan to lease JAS-39 Grippen fighter jets instead of US F-16s – thereby stressing the importance of finding 'European' solutions in security affairs. Evidently, the Iraq War prompted a sense of urgency in attempting to create 'European', or at least 'non-American', security arrangements. In its 2004 programme for elections to the European parliament, the KSČM declared support for such an EU foreign and defence policy, while rejecting war as an instrument of conflict resolution.[77] On the other hand, some prominent KSČM experts remain sceptical of the EU's ability to achieve any substantial autonomy as the very existence of NATO guarantees the supremacy of the United States.[78]

During the 'anti-NATO summit' representatives of the individual streams presented their views in an attempt to define and shape party discourse on these matters. The compatibility of the positions of the Czech and international hard left has been very limited, however. The 'neo-communists' viewed the PCF as being closer to them on security issues than the German PDS, because the PDS's identity is indeed closely linked with pacifist ideas. Even then, the PCF is still viewed as having no clearly defined position on the present development of NATO.[79] All in all, the 'neo-communists' tend to adopt a primarily Eurocentric position, whereas the conservative stream has been both anti-American and Eurosceptic. Their main hope is a new multi-polar world in which Russia and China will be able to restrain and counterbalance the US.

Conclusion

It appears that the KSČM engages in policy transfer to a greater extent than has traditionally been assumed. This is both in terms of academic analyses of the party and in terms of what party activists are likely to admit. There has not, however, been any particular pattern of policy transfer. The party has suffered – although it is not clear that all party members see it as such – from existing in a policy vacuum, with sections of the party standing against each other on a number of occasions and over a number of issues. Some representatives of the KSČM, in common with parties of the West European hard left, remain wary of the KSČM's orthodox communist rhetoric, and the social-democratic soft left – both in the Czech Republic and abroad – has largely ignored the party. None the less, individual streams within the party have engaged actively in the search for, and export of, policies that suit their ideological and practical needs. The conservatives and traditionalists, hegemons of the 'strategy of leftist retreat', derive their legitimacy from resisting radical changes within the party, maintaining communist orthodoxy wherever possible, and focusing on the defence of what they see as Czech national interests. They have adopted an essentially defensive or even 'negativist' attitude to the EU. Instead, most conservative elements tend to look to China as an ideational model. However, this particular fascination with China represents a virtual programmatic inspiration rather than a source of genuine policy transfer, as implementing such ideas in practice is hardly feasible. Even China's most active adherents have never translated the admired Chinese model into programmatic or policy propositions. Its rhetorical attractiveness none the less remains. Now that the Czech Republic has joined the EU, the KSČM's unreserved political support for the regimes in China, Cuba and North Korea is bound to spawn conflict not just with other EU states, but also with other hard-left parties that have left orthodox communism behind.

Apart from the virtual inspiration from China, even conservatives and the traditionalist majority within the party tend to emulate programmatic and policy-relevant traditions of the European 'hard' and 'soft' left in various policy sectors. For political reasons, however, such policy import remains largely unconscious, unacknowledged or even denied by the 'retreat coalition'. It is therefore not a straightforward task to substantiate imitation or policy transfer using the criteria defined by Wade Jacoby or Colin Bennett, which take full and even demonstrative acknowledgement of the transfer for granted.[80]

The KSČM's modernizers – the neo-communists supported by a number of pragmatic and policy-oriented 'traditionalists' – do not permit predefined ideological assumptions or ideological or political competition with the 'soft left' to define to whom they look for inspiration. They actively seek to transform the KSČM into a 'new left party' with a broader base of support – and to do this they realize that ideological and programmatic dogmatism would be highly counterproductive. At the same time, they cannot afford and do not intend to break with their mass party ideals and the solid basis that this offers them. Individual 'neo-communist' representatives therefore seek to legitimize their pursuit of change with reference to contacts with other 'hard left' parties – most often the German post-communist PDS. This strand has pursued an 'activist' policy concerning the EU, viewing the EU as a chance for the Czech and European 'hard left' to modernize and broaden its political appeal. The communist 'EU-activists' put considerable emphasis on the potential role of the KSČM in shaping the European 'hard left' in the future, particularly through the newly created European Party of the Left.

Both 'conservatives' and 'neo-communists' seek to enhance the legitimacy of their vision of the KSČM and of how the international 'hard left' movement should develop by focusing on foreign models: either on the 'communist miracle' in China or on Europe. Come what may, the nature of the process of policy transfer and its outcome are heavily obscured by the internal ideological and political dichotomy of the party. This means that the internal ideological conflicts will have a very strong bearing on the party's future development: not just in terms of whom it looks to when shaping its own policies and programmes, but also how other actors see the KSČM. Should the KSČM look to broaden its programmatic appeal, further examples of policy transfer are likely: should it look to 'defend' and protect 'Czech interests' actively against the interests of 'international capitalists', then policy transfer is likely to slip well and truly off the party's political agenda.

NOTES

This study has been written in co-operation with Radomíra Handlová, who contributed mainly by collecting the documents, analysing them and making transcripts of the interviews. I also wish to thank William E. Paterson, James Sloam, Dan Hough and Hana Svobodová for their useful comments, and particularly to Dan Hough for his careful editing of the text.

1. KSČM, 'Zpráva ÚV KSČM o činnosti KSČM v období po IV. sjezdu KSČM', in *Dokumenty V. sjezdu KSČM, 4.–5.12.1999, Ždárnad Sázavou* (Prague: ÚV KSČM, 1999), pp.31, 25, 27.
2. P. Fiala, M. Mareš and P. Pšeja, 'Stranický systém České republiky a jeho vývoj po listopadu 1989', in P. Matějů and J. Večerník (eds.), *Zpráva o stavu české společnosti 1989–1998* (Prague: Academia, 1998), pp.269–291.
3. See P. Buras, 'Polish Social Democracy, Policy Transfer and Programmatic Change', in the present collection, pp.88–108.
4. Eighty-six per cent claim that the ideational orientation of the party they choose to support is important; 85 per cent have the same opinion about the party's programme; 78 per cent also see trust in the leadership as being crucial: D. Kunštát, *Politické strany a jejich příznivci* (Prague: Centrum pro výzkum verejného mínění, Sociologický Ústav Akademie věd České republiky, 2002).
5. D. Dolowitz and D. Marsh, 'Who Learns What from Whom: A Review of the Policy Transfer Literature', *Political Studies*, Vol.44, No.2 (1996), pp.343–57; D. Dolowitz and D. Marsh, 'Learning from Abroad: The Role of Policy Transfer in Contemporary Policy-Making', *Governance*, Vol.13, No.1 (2000), pp.5–24; C. Radaelli, 'Policy Transfer in the European

Union: Institutional Isomorphism as a Source of Legitimacy', *Governance*, Vol.13, No.1 (2000), pp.25–43; D. Stone, 'Learning Lessons and Transferring Policy across Time, Space and Disciplines', *Politics*, Vol.19, No.1 (1999), pp.51–9; D. Stone, 'Non-Governmental Policy Transfer: The Strategies of Independent Policy Institutes', *Governance*, Vol.13, No.1 (2000), pp.45–62.
6. A. Grzymala-Busse, *Redeeming the Communist Past: The Regeneration of Communist Parties in East Central Europe* (Cambridge: Cambridge University Press, 2002); A. Grzymala-Busse, 'Czech and Slovak Communist Successor Party Transformations after 1989: Organizational Resources, Elite Capacities, and Public Commitments', in J.T. Ishiyama (ed.), *Communist Successor Parties in Post-Communist Politics* (Hauppauge, NY: Nova Science, 1999), pp.43–69; S. Hanley, 'Towards Breakthrough or Breakdown? The Consolidation of KSČM as a Neo-Communist Successor Party in the Czech Republic', *Journal of Communist Studies and Transition Politics*, Vol.17, No.3 (2001), pp.96–116; J.T. Ishiyama and A. Bozóki, 'Adaptation and Change: Characterizing the Survival Strategies of the Communist Successor Parties', *Journal of Communist Studies and Transition Politics*, Vol.17, No.3 (2001), pp.33–50; M. Perottino, 'The Position and Role of the Communist Party of Bohemia and Moravia', in L. Cabada (ed.), *Contemporary Questions of Central European Politics* (Pilsen: Aleš Čeněk, 2003), pp.176–97. The most detailed analysis of the party's development is to be found in P. Fiala, J. Holzer, M. Mareš and P. Pšeja, *Komunismus v České republice* (Brno: Masarykova univerzita, 1999); and in M. Mareš, 'Pokusy o reformu komunistické strany a postkomunistické subjekty v České republice', in L. Kopeček and V. Hlošek (eds.), *Rudí a růžoví: Transformace komunistických stran* (Brno: Masarykova univerzita, 2002), pp.83–99.
7. G. Pridham, 'Rethinking Regime-Change Theory and the International Dimension of Democratization: Ten Years After in East–Central Europe', in G. Pridham and A. Ágh (eds.), *Prospects for Democratic Consolidation in East–Central Europe* (Manchester: Manchester University Press, 2001), pp.54–95.
8. See M. Klíma, 'Consolidation and Stabilization of the Party System in the Czech Republic', *Political Studies*, Vol.XLVI (1998), pp.507, 509; Ishiyama and Bozóki, 'Adaptation and Change', p.49; Hanley, 'Towards Breakthrough or Breakdown?', p.97. M. Kubát, *Postkomunismus a demokracie: Politika ve středovýchodní Evropě* (Prague: Dokořán, 2003), p.102; for Sorino, see K. Biggs, 'All Quiet On The Eastern Front? Most Definitely Not!', *Postmark Prague*, No.374, 14 Oct. 2002, at <http://www.solidnet.org>.
9. M. Grebeníček, 'Máme reálnou sílu změnit pořádky nepřátelské vůči obyčejným lidem', *Haló noviny*, 14 April 2003.
10. Author's interview with Radim Valenčík, assistant to Jiří Svoboda, chairman of the KSČM (1991–93), Prague, 29 Dec. 2003.
11. J. Heller, 'Bída analýzy aneb Co překroutili analytici ČSSD', *Alternativy*, No.14 (2003), pp.26–37; Grzymala-Busse, *Redeeming the Communist Past*, p.86.
12. For an impressive analysis of the conflicts between mental barriers and modernization pressures, see H. Fehr, 'Krisen des Übergangs: Überlegungen zur intergrations- und Legitimationsproblematik vor und nach dem revolutionären Umbruch von 1989', in P. Waldeman (ed.), *Diktatur, Demokratisierung und soziale Anomie* (Munich: Verlag Ernest Vögel, 2003), pp.389–407.
13. Ishiyama and Bozóki, 'Adaptation and Change', pp.34, 41.
14. Hanley, 'Towards Breakthrough or Breakdown?', p.97.
15. For a different categorization of the party streams, see the neo-communist analyst Josef Heller, 'Bude KSČM stranou nejprogresívnějších složek dělnické třídy nebo stranou nepoučitelných nostalgiku?', in *Konference o prognóze KSČM*, Oct. 2002, at <http://www.kscm.cz/archiv>, accessed 15 Aug. 2004.
16. The ratio between party members and non-members in the electorate of the KSČM was 1:2.5 in 1990 and 1:7 in 2002: see L. Vacek, 'K příčinám úspěchu KSČM ve volbách', *Alternativy*, No.10 (2002), p.9.
17. S. Oates, W.L. Miller and A. Grødeland, 'Towards a Soviet Past or Socialist Future? Understanding Why Voters Choose Communist Parties in Ukraine, Russia, Bulgaria, Slovakia and

the Czech Republic', in P.L. Lewis (ed.), *Party Development and Democratic Change in Post-Communist Europe: The First Decade* (London: Frank Cass, 2001), pp.16–31; H. Kitschelt, Z. Mansfeldova, R. Markowski and G. Tóka (eds.), *Post-Communist Party Systems: Competition, Representation and Inter-Party Co-operation* (Cambridge: Cambridge University Press, 1999), p.288.
18. J. Hartl, quoted in T. Menschik and V. Dubský, 'Nový cíl komunistů – získat mladé voliče', *Lidové noviny*, 19 Nov. 2003, p.3.
19. In 1992 the Czech Communist Party had 354,549 members in 10,669 grassroots organizations (Zpráva, V. sjezd, 1999, pp.52–4), while in 1999 it had 128,346 members in 5,276 organizations; in 2003, 100,781 members in 4,691 organizations; the average age was 68.1 years, and 95 per cent had been members since before 1990; with 27,783 members younger than 60, the party is still the largest party in the Czech Republic: see 'Zpráva ÚV KSČM o činnosti KSČM v období po V. sjezdu', in *Dokumenty VI. Sjezdu KSČM 15–16.5.2004 České Budějovice*, pp.78–9. Also interview with RSDr. Vlastimil Balín, the then first deputy chairman of the KSČM, Prague, 26 March 2004.
20. M. Ransdorf, 'KSČM 2001: Profil a projekt nové strany', *Alternativy*, No.7 (2001), pp.40–49; M. Ransdorf, 'Komunální politika vyžaduje více pozornosti od nás všech', *Haló noviny*, 28 April 2003; 'Lhostejnost lidí ohrožuje demokracii', *Haló noviny*, 8 May 2003.
21. D. Matulka, 'O co bude boj', *Alternativy*, No.10 (2002), p.16.
22. Author's interview with Vlastimil Balín, 26 March 2004.
23. The KSČM supported its ideological rival, Václav Klaus, the former chairman of the ODS, in his bid for the Czech presidency in March 2003. In November 2003, KSČM senators co-sponsored the establishment of an 'independent group' of senators in the upper chamber of the Czech parliament, the head of which became Senator Železný.
24. M. Ransdorf, 'Je to Tvá věc, o kterou běží', *Haló noviny*, 19 March 2004.
25. Author's interview with Miloslav Ransdorf, the then deputy chairman of the KSČM, Prague, 6 Jan. 2003; and similarly also interview with Václav Exner, deputy chairman of the KSČM, Prague, 7 Jan. 2003.
26. Author's interview with Jiří Dolejš, deputy chairman of the KSČM, Prague, 7 Jan. 2003.
27. Author's interview with Václav Exner, 7 Jan. 2003.
28. Author's interview with Josef Heller, theoretical analytical unit (TAP), professional staff of the Central Committee of the KSČM, Prague, 6 Jan. 2003.
29. The commissions are usually linked with clubs, some of which are agile and intellectually open and do invite non-communist discussants (for example, the club of psychologists and sociologists, headed by Lubomír Vacek, or the club of economists).
30. 'Zpráva o činnosti ÚV KSČM v období po V. sjezdu KSČM', pp.73–5.
31. On the PDS, see D. Hough, 'The Programmatic Development of the Eastern German PDS: Learning What from Whom and Under What Conditions?', in this collection, pp.146–164; and also D. Hough, *The Fall and Rise of the PDS in Eastern Germany, 1989–2000* (Birmingham: University of Birmingham Press, 2002).
32. The platform was designed by one of the neo-communist leaders, the deputy chairman of the KSČM, Jiří Dolejš. Typically enough, though, not the KSČM but its small partner, the Party of Democratic Socialism (SDS), established the Society for European Dialogue in order to enable project co-operation with the Rosa Luxemburg Foundation attached to the German PDS, which has invested up to 100,000 euro into collaborative programmes.
33. The 'soft no' position represented a rejection of EU accession under the current conditions, but not in principle: 'Stanovisko KSČM pro referendum ke vstupu České republiky do Evropské unie', 16 zasedání ÚV KSČM, 22 March 2003.
34. Author's interview with Jaroslav Kohlíček, head of the section for international co-operation of the Central Committee, Prague, 17 Jan. 2003.
35. Author's interview with Jaroslav Kohlíček, Prague, 1 April 2004.
36. Author's interview with Miloslav Ransdorf, 6 Jan. 2003.
37. J. Schwarzová, 'Evropský parlament se formuje už dnes', *Haló noviny*, 22 Sept. 2003.
38. 'Stanovisko k zapojení zástupců KSČM do klubu Evropské sjednocené levice', *Haló noviny*, 6 Oct. 2003.

39. See the position of the head of the international department of the KSČM, H. Charfo, 'Zakládající sjezd Strany evropské levice', *Haló noviny*, 4 June 2004.
40. M. Ransdorf, 'V Berlíně šlo o posílení evropské levice', *Haló noviny*, 15 Jan. 2004.
41. Later, however, the KSS followed the KSČM and voted against the EU accession treaty in the Slovak parliament as it believed the treaty to be disadvantageous to Slovak interests.
42. 'Závěrečné slovo L. Adamce', *Rudé právo*, 22 Dec. 1989.
43. Author's interview with Radim Valenčík, 9 Dec. 2003.
44. M. Grebeníček, *Prameny naděje* (Prague: Futura, 2001), pp.25–6.
45. Author's interview with with Jiří Dolejš, 7 Jan. 2004.
46. Ibid.
47. M. Grebeníček, *Prameny naděje* (Prague: Futura, 2001), p.131.
48. V. Janků, 'KS Číny pro čestnou politiku', *Haló noviny*, 28 Jan. 2003; Oldřich Schwarz, 'Tchen Siao-pching: sto let zrození jedinečného revolucionáře', *Haló noviny*, 23 Aug. 2004.
49. J. Kojzar, 'O Číně, demokracii a všem možném', *Haló noviny*, 14 Aug. 2003.
50. V. Věrtelář, 'Nedělejme si iluze o situaci ve světě i doma', *Haló noviny*, 20 Oct. 2003.
51. On relations between the PDS and the KSČM, see D. Hough and V. Handl, 'The (Post-)Communist Left and the European Union: The Czech KSCM and the German PDS', *Communist and Post-Communist Studies*, Vol.37, No.3 (2004), pp.319–39.
52. KSČM, 'Zpráva ÚV KSČM o činnosti KSČM v období po IV.sjezdu KSČM', p.25.
53. Rozhovor Jiřím Dolejšem', *Český rozhlas 6*, 23 Oct. 2003, at <http://www.rozhlas.cz/cro6/stop/_print/91767>, accessed 25 Aug. 2004.
54. KSČM, 'Program KSČM', in *Dokumenty I. sjezdu KSČM, 13–14 Oct. 1990, Olomouc* (Prague: ÚV KSČM, 1990), p.17.
55. KSČM, 'Zpráva ÚV KSČM o činnosti KSČM v období po IV. sjezdu KSČM', p.25.
56. Author's interview with Professor Zdeněk Hába, expert commission on economics in the Central Committee of the KSČM, Prague, 12 Feb. 2003.
57. KSČM, 'Vystoupení předsedy ÚV KSČM Miroslava Grebeníčka', in *Dokumenty V. sjezdu*, p.12.
58. V. Exner, 'Do Evropské unie nemusíme', *Haló noviny*, 9 Dec. 2002.
59. Head of the expert group of the Central Committee for EU, Member of Parliament, Jiří Maštálka, 'Evropská unie prožívá krizi růstu', *Haló noviny*, 31 May 2003.
60. KSČM, *S lidmi pro lidi, Volební program KSČM* (Prague: ÚV KSČM, 2002); Z. Štefek, 'Vidět rudozeleně neznamená vidět nerudě', *Haló noviny*, 1 Sept. 2004.
61. KSČM, 'Výchozí stanovisko k diskusi o návrhu smlouvy zakládající ústavu pro Evropu', *Haló noviny*, 6 Oct. 2003.
62. KSČM, 'Zpráva o činnosti ÚV KSČM v období po V.sjezdu KSČM', p.30.
63. Author's interview with Zdeněk Hába, 12 Feb. 2003.
64. Z. Hába, 'Spor o vlastnictví', in *Politická ekonomie*, No.38 (1990), pp.1195–7.
65. Z. Hába, 'Zaměstnanecká participace – tichá revoluce?', TAP KSČM, at <http://www.kscm.cz>, accessed 15 Nov. 2003, p.75.
66. Author's interview with Václav Exner, 7 Jan. 2003.
67. KSČM, *S lidmi pro lidi*.
68. V. Exner, 'Zaměstannost – jak a co dál', *Alternativy*, No.10 (2002), pp.32–3.
69. Author's interview with Jiří Dolejš, 7 Jan. 2003.
70. KSČM, *S lidmi pro lidi*, p.10.
71. Author's interview with Zdeněk Hába, 12 Feb. 2003.
72. KSČM, 'Program KSČM', in *Dokumenty III. sjezdu KSČM, 26 June 1993, Prostějov* (Prague: ÚV KSČM, 1993), p.52.
73. J. Dolejš, 'Reforma veřejných financí zatím politickým balancováním', *Haló noviny*, 28 April 2003.
74. M. Grebeníček, 'Vláda neplní své programové prohlášení', *Haló noviny*, 8 April 2004.
75. Author's interview with Karel Hošek, head of the theoretical and analytical unit (TAP), professional staff of the Central Committee, KSČM, Prague, 6 Jan. 2003.
76. Interview with Miloslav Ransdorf for *Mladá Fronta DNES*, 18 June 2004.
77. KSČM, 'S Vámi a pro Vás, doma i v Evropské unii', at <http://www.kscm.cz> accessed 26 April 2004.

78. Interview with Stanislav Suja, expert on foreign policy, professional staff of the Central Committee of the KSČM, Prague, 8 Jan. 2003.
79. Author's interview with Jiří Dolejš, 7 Jan. 2003.
80. W. Jacoby, *Imitation and Politics, Redesigning Modern Germany* (Ithaca, NY and London: Cornell University Press, 2000) p.2; C.J. Bennett, 'Understanding Ripple Effect: The Cross-National Adoption of Policy Instruments for Bureaucratic Accountability', *Governance*, Vol.10, No.3 (1997), p.215, as quoted in Stone, 'Learning Lessons and Transferring Policy', p.56.

The Programmatic Development of the Eastern German PDS: Learning What from Whom and Under What Conditions?

DAN HOUGH

Introduction

The German Party of Democratic Socialism (PDS) is not like other communist successor parties (CSPs). While most, after 1989, were predicted gruesome deaths at the hands of vengeful electorates, none of the CSPs was given less chance of survival than the GDR's Socialist Unity Party (SED) and its successor the PDS.[1] The PDS not only had to introduce democratic structures and shed the worst of its ideological baggage, it had to reinvent itself programmatically and compete with powerful west German political organizations in the open struggle for votes. The PDS was forced to defend the GDR's woeful political, economic and human rights record, and, unsurprisingly, east German electors subsequently chose to punish their former rulers at the first

---

Dan Hough is a Lecturer in Politics at the University of Sussex.

opportunity.[2] The end for the PDS was nigh – or so it was widely hypothesized – and the party was expected to die a quiet death, in disgrace, on the fringes of political life.[3]

The reality has been somewhat different and the PDS has confounded its critics by stabilizing itself as an east German party of social justice, pacifism and political protest.[4] The PDS has stabilized itself in each of the six eastern *Landtage*, it continues to be represented in the European parliament (EP), and it had a significant presence in the German federal parliament between 1990 and 2002.[5] Furthermore, the PDS – like most other communist successor parties – is no longer a party purely of opposition. The PDS has not been involved in governing Germany at the federal level, but, as early as 1994, it tentatively grasped at the reins of power in one of Germany's 16 *Länder* when it 'tolerated' a Social Democratic (SPD)–Green coalition in the eastern state of Saxony Anhalt. By 1998, the social democrats in Mecklenburg–West Pomerania felt secure enough to enter into a fully-fledged coalition with the PDS, continuing this arrangement after the 2002 regional election.[6] Finally, and in the symbolically significant capital city, Berlin, the SPD and PDS joined forces in government again following the 2001 state elections, and it is not beyond the realms of possibility that we may see yet more SPD–PDS alliances in the years to come.[7]

While other communist successor parties have been confronted with similar political dilemmas, the barriers that the PDS faced (strong, well-funded West German political parties; the unique process of German unification and the stigma of representing a state that no longer existed) were greater than those that similar organizations across Eastern and Central Europe (ECE) had to tackle. Developing a new ideological and programmatic agenda was therefore just one of the many challenges that the PDS had to come to terms with as it entered the competitive electoral arena in 1990. The SED had long since been ideologically redundant and the new PDS leadership needed – within a very short period of time – to create policy options that were at once convincing and popular. Furthermore, if the PDS were to be a credible actor, it had to distance itself from the mistakes that its predecessor had made in the GDR, while simultaneously avoiding blanket condemnations of the SED's policies. The PDS needed to perform a delicate balancing act, portraying itself at once as new and progressive, while not alienating those who had worked in the GDR for the just socialism that the SED claimed to be progressing towards.

This essay will look at this programmatic development in more detail, pinpointing why the PDS progressed down the policy tracks that it did and from whom – if, indeed, anyone – it learned in its attempts to rejuvenate itself. This study consciously avoids a pejorative analysis of the PDS: questions concerning the PDS's allegedly anti-democratic and extremist nature have been discussed elsewhere and do not need to be reviewed here.[8] This essay will concentrate, first, on analysing what the PDS perceives itself as standing for and what it aims to achieve; second, it will assess how the PDS has built a programmatic profile out of these beliefs; third, the study moves on to identify which parties and actors have had particular influence on the PDS so far, illustrating that – perhaps surprisingly – the PDS has been both an importer and an exporter of policy ideas; fourth, the impact that the newly constituted Party of the European Left, together with other longer-established cross-national bodies, will have on the PDS's future programmatic development is analysed. The essay concludes by assessing the prospects for the PDS's long-term goal of establishing itself as a reforming party of the socialist left within the German party system.

Pulling Back from the Abyss: From SED to PDS

For a party with intrinsically conservative and anti-reform leanings, the implosion of the GDR and the advent of competitive elections left the SED leadership of late 1989–90 facing a plethora of complex problems. These ranged from choosing a new party name (or perhaps disbanding altogether), to rapidly creating a whole host of new policy proposals, as well as deciding what attitude to take towards the crimes and misdemeanours that were committed in socialism's name in the GDR. A rapid turnover of leadership personnel in late 1989 saw the SED hastily retreat from its most conservative anti-reform stances and it began to accept that internal democratization and an admission that mistakes were made in the GDR were necessary. Yet these unavoidable reforms were not enough to prevent the party from haemorrhaging members, and the SED realized that if it did not fundamentally reinvent itself it would very rapidly slip out of existence. Thankfully for the PDS – and somewhat unwittingly – the party stumbled on perhaps the one man who could save it from implosion: a sharp-thinking, quick-witted East Berlin lawyer named Gregor Gysi. Although a long-time member of the SED, Gysi was no apparatchik and looked to lead the SED away from its dogmatic past, towards a reforming left-wing movement for those critical of capitalism. Gysi helped the party to adopt the name SED–PDS in December 1989, before championing the dropping of the SED title altogether, and in February 1990 the PDS officially came into existence. Despite efforts by the leadership to portray this as a new beginning, with the PDS developing out of reform-minded socialist forces in the SED, the reality was more hard-nosed. As the legal successor to the SED the PDS was entitled to retain considerable amounts of SED funds and property, as well as much of the SED's organizational framework and party cadre.[9] In this sense it remains a genuine communist successor party. The process of internal reform was also both slow and incremental, as successive conferences saw modernizers and conservatives fight for the heart and soul of the party.[10] Gysi and other influential reformers such as Lothar Bisky (the party leader in 2004) usually managed to cajole the party into adopting less dogmatically orthodox positions on ideological questions, but the more traditional socialists and Marxists did enjoy their successes. Indeed, only at the seminal party congress of January 1995 were Stalinists officially excluded from the PDS, and even then no suitably worded declaration could be agreed upon that excluded communists. On the contrary, the party leadership made every effort to reassure communists within the party both that they were welcome and that their opinions and ideas enriched internal party democracy. Indeed, communists still remain active within the high-profile 'Communist Platform'[11] and the 'Marxist Forum', despite persistent calls from all sides for the party to distance itself from such doctrines.

The PDS is, none the less, a considerably different party from the SED, and in many ways it resembles other post-communist parties across Eastern and Central Europe. The PDS has streamlined its organizational structures and made effective electoral capital of increasing disillusionment with the pace and nature of the reform processes that the 'new rulers' have undertaken. The initial reforming zeal of late 1989 saw the party distance itself from one-party government, democratic centralism and the much-feared secret police. It has become obvious that internal party democracy flourishes – as recurrent spats between the membership and the leadership, moderates and conservatives, reformers and traditionalists, testify.[12] Working groups (*Arbeitsgemeinschaften*) and interest groups (*Interessengemeinschaften*) appeal to the interests of different segments of the party membership, tackling different thematic issues and developing programmatic suggestions in particular policy areas. PDS members are therefore involved in impressively pluralist debates on the future of a wide variety of issues, ranging from sport and ecology to the future of the welfare state and gay and lesbian rights. The PDS has, therefore, clearly changed over the course of the 1990s. Ironically, the most unresponsive and incompetent of all the communist parties in ECE has spawned a successor that has been able to adapt to democratic electoral cleavages and convince a significant minority of the electorate of its ability to govern both democratically and competently.[13] The PDS has attempted to develop socialist alternatives to what it describes as the neo-liberal hegemonic discourse, basing its agenda on a commitment to social justice (including a strong commitment to redistributive tax policies), a commitment to the international peace movement (including such ideas as the dissolution of NATO and the banning of German participation in out-of-area activities), and a strong defence of 'eastern German interests'.[14]

The PDS, Internationalism and the Challenges of the Twenty-First Century

Internationalism and the importance of creating socialism across national borders has traditionally been a key tenet of the communist and socialist left's ideological armoury. The PDS – according to its publicly declared self-understanding, at least – abides by this doctrine: it seeks to work together with other like-minded parties and movements to place national politics within an international context and to achieve broadly defined universal goals such as freedom, equality, democracy and social justice. In the twenty-first century, with the seemingly ever-increasing globalization of political, social and particularly economic activity, the PDS argues that internationally co-ordinated programmes and platforms are vital in counteracting the 'asocial' effects of globally integrated markets.[15] Left-wing parties – so the PDS claims – have to accept that only by co-ordinating their activities will they be able to synthesize their programmes and coherently challenge the prevailing pro-market consensus.[16] This philosophy should make parties of the far left particularly open to policy learning and policy networking, stressing the importance of facilitating programmatic co-operation and permitting programmes and policies to emerge from specially created networks.

Nevertheless, internationalist rhetoric aside, the behaviour of the PDS has frequently been shaped by forces very much closer to home, and overt examples of lesson drawing and voluntary policy transfer from abroad are few and far between. Foreign political systems did not offer useful laboratories of policy innovation in any explicit sense because the parameters of political competition in post-unification Germany were so unusual. As the PDS emerged out of the SED it was only very rarely able to coordinate activities with international partners, and its programmatic development was shaped by the peculiarities of the German unification process and the PDS's unique position among far-left parties. The challenge of competing with wealthy, organizationally efficient Western parties on a playing field that the Western parties were instrumental in creating ensured that the PDS began to look for a new role – and a new programmatic orientation – almost as soon as the Berlin Wall fell. It neither had the experiences of far-left groupings in Italy and France, that had long since become used to the existence of capitalist competitor parties, nor could it benefit from the widespread new start that all parties across Eastern and Central Europe were experiencing. The PDS's competitors were experienced, wealthy, organizationally proficient and anti-communist. Templates and patterns for programmatic reform of the PDS were largely absent: the key aim was simply to jettison the worst of the ideological baggage of the GDR era, hold the creaking party together and fight desperately for survival. The PDS therefore needed from the very beginning to develop a programmatic profile that would come to terms with unique German circumstances.

As with other post-communist parties in ECE, through the 1990s the PDS slowly found itself able to benefit from increasing levels of frustration and dissatisfaction with post-communism. In Germany this dissatisfaction took on a slightly different guise from that in other ECE states: Easterners, in the widely held perception, were to become like Westerners and to learn the rules anew.[17] With the benefit of hindsight, it should not be surprising that this prompted considerable tensions between *Ossies* and *Wessies*.[18] The PDS was the first party to incorporate such sentiments into its political appeal. Once the PDS had weathered the tumultuous early period of stabilization, it sought to rebuild itself both organizationally and programmatically by incorporating what it saw as uniquely east German values, beliefs and interests into its programme alongside its socialist and anti-capitalist rhetoric. The two, despite many expectations to the contrary, were mutually reinforcing, as the pro-state, anti-capitalist, resentful attitudes of many easterners fitted well with many of the classic tenets of socialist ideology.[19] For the PDS, the end-product of this reorientation process was the party programme of 1993.[20]

Unlike a number of other CSPs, therefore, the PDS neither wished nor sought to become a genuinely social-democratic entity. The existence of the SPD ensured that any social-democratization of the PDS simply would not have been feasible. Instead, the PDS attempted to broaden its ideological platform to offer a home to those possessing *linkes Gedankengut* (left-wing orientations) who did not, however, define themselves as social democrats.[21] This ideological broadening was seen as imperative if the PDS were to achieve any sort of public acceptance over and above the many party members who remained (and still remain) true to the ideals that they espoused in the GDR. Even those party members who were willing to criticize the GDR and what it stood for did so in very guarded terms and were careful not to de-legitimize the aim of creating the first socialist state on German soil.[22] Once the PDS chose not to disband itself, the intrinsic conservatism of its membership and, more importantly, the radical process of internal democratization and decentralization that had taken place restrained the ability of the elite to dictate ideological and programmatic change – much as was the case in the Czech Communist Party.[23]

The PDS sought to become a *Stück europäischer Normalität* (piece of European normality), positioning itself at the head of the communist–socialist movement and to the left of the SPD. André Brie, former manager of the PDS's election campaigns and current MEP, claimed that the party sought to do this even though knowledge – even at the elite level – about far-left politics in Western Europe was not particularly deep. Independent left-wing thought processes had largely been stifled in the GDR, and PDS leaders found themselves having to come to terms with the problems of implementing socialism after having seen the 'real-existing' socialist experiment fail.[24] PDS members had little experience of 'thinking outside the box', as they had been given so little opportunity to do so in the GDR. The SED permitted little internal dissent and those who did put their heads above the parapet knew that they were taking considerable personal risks in doing so. It was only in the last few weeks of the GDR that socialist critics of the SED made their voices heard on programmatic issues. The PDS rank and file and party elite were therefore unsure how a democratic socialist or communist party should behave in an open electoral market, given that they had little experience of genuine debate on what socialism was and how it might be achieved.

The PDS and Other Hard-Left Parties

Nevertheless it was also obvious that left-wing parties did still remain relevant actors in most other European states, and this rather vague ideological path offered the PDS a practical route to survival. In this sense, the PDS did see some mileage in what Richard Rose has termed 'lesson-drawing'.[25] The PDS looked westwards to see not just what policies other far-left parties proposed: they also took stock of what had *not* worked. They tried to assess whether failed left-wing experiments such as François Mitterrand's expansionist economic policies in France in the early 1980s were due to failures of policy or to unfortunate circumstances, and what the left should learn from this. PDS reformers around the Brie brothers (André and Michael, the head of the PDS-affiliated Rosa Luxemburg Foundation) then tried to assess whether modified versions of particular policies – or 'templating', in Jacoby's language – might be successful either in Germany or perhaps at the EU level.[26] This left the PDS open to a number of different sorts of policy transfer: voluntary transfer that the party adopted either because it had 'worked' for other actors elsewhere and PDS politicians thought it might work in Germany; semi-voluntary transfer where PDS politicians thought it politically expedient to adopt specific policy positions; and finally obligated transfer where the PDS absorbed ideas because it wished to join a broader network of left-leaning actors (such as the far-left parliamentary party in the European parliament).[27] The PDS developed its environmental policy, for example, after observing the discourse of left-wing parties at the Rio Summit in 1992. Aware that it possessed little credibility on this issue (on account of the SED's environmentally destructive policies prior to 1989), the PDS sought to import more or less wholesale the environmental agendas that had been developed by other left-wing forces, shaping them to the particularly complex problems of de-industrialization and environmental degradation evident in eastern Germany.[28] This saved the party valuable time and resources, even if many eastern Germans saw such policy importing as decidedly opportunistic and the PDS did not gain any genuine electoral ground as a result. Even more blatant copying of policies in a faithful (and voluntary) fashion, such as the call for a 35-hour working week (imported directly from the French PCF), also took place.[29] These forms of transfer generally occurred in areas where a form of international consensus already existed and the PDS could latch on to the ideas of others. More frequently, the PDS used the programmatic stances of other parties as broader templates, emulating programmatic positions by translating them into the uniquely German context. This is evident in much of the PDS's economic policy, which follows the anti-capitalist rhetoric of the West European hard left but is translated into the language of Germany's unique brand of social market capitalism. Other forms of less voluntary transfer were not as significant for the PDS as they were for other parties (no matter what their ideological persuasion) of Eastern and Central Europe. Once the PDS agreed to accept democratic norms and ideals, as it did in the first weeks of 1990, it was catapulted into an EU state that was already a member of NATO. No questions of possible accession to these organizations (or rejection by them) ever seriously influenced the PDS's programmatic debates. Germany remains anchored in both the European Union and NATO, and although the PDS claims to want to disband NATO this remains a relatively small and surprisingly uncontroversial part of its ideological self-understanding. Subsequently there was no need for discussions of how, or indeed whether, it should look to meet the requirements needed to enter such organizations since, of course, these debates were not taking place.

In more general terms, the PDS saw the programmes of parties such as the PCF, the Italian PCI and also the Scandinavian socialist parties as being strategically anti-capitalist enough for them to remain true to socialist ideals, yet pragmatic enough to be electorally viable. André Brie has stressed that the Swedish Party of the Left (*Vänsterpartiet*, VP) and the Finnish Left Wing Alliance (*Vasemmistoliitto*, VAS) were particularly interesting partners for the PDS elite as they have traditionally stressed a more libertarian form of socialism than that of the French and Italian communist parties. Given the PDS's wish to learn from the mistakes of the dogmatic socialism of the GDR, this has proved particularly attractive for PDS reformers.[30] There is also evidence of cherry-picking by the PDS as both André Brie and Judith Dellheim, another pivotal figure in the PDS's programme commission, have emphasized that, despite the good relationship between theses parties, the PDS is not interested in importing the Eurosceptic undertones that underpin much of the Scandinavian left's programmatic material, and it continues to be supportive of the European Union in principle, if not all its policies in practice.[31] Brie and reformers such as Gysi, Lothar Bisky and Dieter Klein have attempted to learn particular lessons from parties that they have thought applicable in their own context before developing their own ideas. Personal links have also been of significance in prompting individual PDS politicians to interact with particular parties: the Austrian-born PDS leader in Saxony, Peter Porsch, has attempted to maintain close ties with the KPÖ, while Hans Modrow, the PDS's honorary president and a former MEP, has traditionally maintained close links with the Czech communists.[32]

The PDS has adopted a similar approach with the communist parties of France and Italy (particularly the Communist Refoundation – PRC – in recent years). The PCF, PRC and the PDS certainly find themselves in very similar structural environments in terms of their general political situation (competing with a larger social-democratic party from the left and occasional support of that same social-democratic party at the regional and national levels), their ideological orientation (a rejection of traditional Marxism-Leninism, calls for a 'democratization' of capitalist democracy and a vague acceptance of the social market economy), and organizational developments (development of the party as a heterogeneous movement permitting internal debate and conflict, an ageing of the party membership, relatively outspoken leaders, and a reduction in the number of party workers), as well as similar political strategies (being on the one hand an electoral party, while on the other an extra-parliamentary movement; the creation of a network of like-minded organizations that are not controlled by the party but none the less remain close to it). Despite the differences in national cultures and in their own pasts, the PCF, PRC and PDS have found themselves in 'virtually identical political situations that have necessitated the development of compatible and interchangeable strategies'.[33] This is not really policy transfer as such; it is much more policy networking – and in its most explicit form.

The PDS has attempted to build up particularly deep links with the PCF as it perceives its own position within the German party system as very similar to that of the PCF in France. Patrick Moreau describes the PDS–PCF relationship as having grown to become 'the key one' in the international network of far-left parties, with the PCF and PDS joining forces to campaign against the Maastricht treaty and other international agreements, and the PCF actively supporting the PDS's attempt to gain European parliament observer status for the 1994–99 period (when the PDS narrowly failed to achieve full member status).[34] Indeed, Lothar Bisky and the PCF leader Robert Hue have stressed that the PCF and PDS will 'intensify' and 'deepen' their links in the future. The parties are particularly keen to coordinate their policy preferences *vis-à-vis* the European integration process and in tackling the 'social, democratic, ecological and peace-orientated dimensions' of the European debate.[35] Shortly before the French EU presidency in May 2000, Bisky and Hue went on record saying that the PDS and PCF had a special responsibility to work constructively to help create a new (socialist) Europe, indicating a clear wish to intensify dialogue and co-operation 'at all levels of our parties'.[36] Subsequently the parties have created joint working groups, looking to formulate common strategies for common problems.[37]

The PDS and the Institutionalized European Hard Left

How, then, do these bilateral links fit in with the broader European hard-left movement? Are there grounds for substantial policy transfer and policy networking? At the EU level, the PDS's policy package fits in well with that of the confederal Group of the European United Left/Nordic Green Left (GUE/NGL) parliamentary grouping in the European parliament – a grouping that the PDS joined in 1999. The group came into existence in July 1994, largely at the behest of the Spanish PCE–IU and Greek Coalition of the Left and Progress. The founding declaration states that the GUE/NGL is 'firmly committed to European integration, although in a different form to the existing model' and 'notwithstanding the different approaches that its various components may choose to follow'.[38] This clarification hints at some of the problems that the GUE/NGL has experienced: the ideological identities of the organization's member parties are diffuse, and finding common programmatic ground has frequently proved difficult. This has severely hindered the GUE/NGL in coordinating its work and it has prevented it from being a cohesive, constructive force for change. The group now contains outright communist parties, left-leaning social democratic forces and a variety of parties and individual MEPs – frequently exotic – somewhere in between. This has undoubtedly increased its numerical strength but diluted the opportunities for programmatic consensus, and the GUE/NGL remains the least capable of all EP parliamentary groupings in agreeing a coherent political programme and strategy.

The GUE/NGL has none the less developed a number of basic programmatic positions to which all member parties at least theoretically adhere – examples include the call for a fundamental democratization of the EU's institutions and a rejection of monetarist (and 'neo-liberal') economic policies – while still allowing individual delegations to develop their own national responses to problems.[39] The increasing intensity of these contacts illustrates that the far-left parties interact with the conscious aim of producing policy proposals that build on each other's individual experiences. The project of the West European far-left parties is relatively clear: to be anti-capitalist parties; to embrace environmental politics, the politics of gender and sexuality, anti-racism, 'social solidarity' and global peace; and to use national opportunity structures to produce policy proposals within the context of a coordinated European (and global) movement. Networking of this type most certainly assists the PDS in gathering information and assessing the possible programmatic models in existence.

In more concrete terms, the European hard left is unambiguously anti-capitalist and the PDS clearly has little difficulty fitting in with international partners in terms of its criticisms of Europe's free-market agenda. Arguments about whether parties are 'reformers' (such as the Danish Socialist People's Party) or 'revolutionary' (such as the Portuguese Communist Party) are not particularly relevant in this context. The entire hard left rejects the Maastricht consensus, embodied in the stability and growth pact and the introduction of the euro, but also encompassing a weakening of trade union rights, job cuts, privatization programmes and cuts in welfare expenditure.[40] The PDS has little trouble offering unequivocal support to these policies, making opposition to the entire Maastricht treaty a pivotal element of its 1998 Bundestag election campaign.[41] It clearly and consistently opposes capitalism and places anti-capitalist discourse at the forefront of its everyday work, espousing policies that are common to a number of other far-left programmes across Europe (see below). Yet while the basic orientation is clear – a rejection of 'neo-liberal' economics – there are tensions, both across the European hard left and within the PDS, on what this should mean in terms of policies and programmes to redress perceived imbalances and distortions. It is not clear whether the project of European monetary union (EMU), for example, should be opposed outright or whether it can be 'saved' and 'socialized' if more progressive forces gain the reins of power. Whereas the Portuguese and Swedish communists, as well as a number of smaller groupings, tend towards the former position, the less orthodox Spanish and Finnish communists, together with the Coalition of Left and Progress in Greece, tend towards the latter. Others – including the PCF and PRC – tend to hover somewhere between these positions. These ideological differences do not prevent parties from opposing the onward march of free-market liberalism, but they do hinder the process of creating clear and decisive programmes for change, prompting parties to slip back into making policy with national circumstances and national electorates very much in mind.[42] The PDS is no different in this, as internal debates on how best to oppose EMU – principled versus pragmatic – have illustrated.[43] Interestingly, the PDS sees itself as having 'grown into playing a mediatory role', balancing out the often diverse interests of the other far-left parties in Europe. The PDS claims to have 'contributed a great deal to helping differences of opinion to be solved in a constructive and friendly fashion', and the PDS claims that it is a positive influence in 'prompting broadly accepted Europe-wide left-wing policies'.[44]

The PDS – like other far-left parties – accepts Keynesian doctrines of economic demand management, with the state having a fundamental responsibility in both stimulating demand and providing its citizens with employment. There are strange echoes of the *Parti Socialiste* (PS) as well as the PCF in France, in that the PDS aims to counter high levels of unemployment by advocating policies such as legally enforceable reductions in the number of hours that employees are allowed to work (in weekly and yearly terms) and drastic reductions in the amount of overtime that is worked at present in both Germany and the European Union.[45] In concrete terms, this has been conceptualized as a maximum working week of 35 hours and, in the long term, a five-day week of just 30 hours.[46] The PDS also claims that drastic reductions in the 1.8bn hours of overtime that are worked annually in Germany could create a further 600,000 jobs.[47]

Despite the difficulties of co-ordinating policies across borders, the PDS continues to work with other far-left actors to find ways of defending the regional subsidies that come from the EU's structural funds. The PDS is very well aware that its core east German electorate benefits from considerable transfer payments originating in Brussels – and it has fought for their retention in the face of increasing calls for reform of EU regional policy to accommodate the expansion of the EU eastwards to include a number of poorer Central European states.[48] 'The PDS has continued to stress', claimed Gabi Zimmer, a newly elected PDS MEP and former party leader, in May 2004, 'that the border regions in eastern Germany need further direct funding from the EU's structural funds', echoing the sentiments of far-left politicians representing poorer regions of the EU in other countries.[49] The PDS group in the GUE/NGL sees itself as a key actor in defending such subsidies and it organized a conference for all member parties in Schwerin in September 2001 specifically to address questions of regional employment policies. PDS MEPs actively contribute to shaping future regional policy within the European parliament's committee system. MEP Helmut Markov was spokesman for the GUE/NGL group on questions of structural funds in 'ultra-peripheral' regions, and he published two reports outlining, first, the innovative measures that should be implemented through the EU's regional funds in the period 2000–06, and second, notes on altering the complex co-financing arrangements of the structural funds when the EU grew to 25 member states.[50] Sylvia-Yvonne Kaufmann, another very vocal PDS MEP, actively defended the importance of maintaining the subsidies distributed to poorer regions in the existing EU.[51] These interests clearly cross with those of both the soft left and the hard left in Finland, Spain and Italy, and policy co-ordination has been evident in the defence of regionally significant subsidies, with the PDS actively taking a lead in shaping policy preferences.

Similar sentiments apply in terms of policies for an envisaged democratization both of nation states and, in particular, of the EU. All parties of the far left are clear in their rejection of the undemocratic nature of the EU's institutions. They regard the EU as elitist, bureaucratic and intrinsically linked to corporate capitalism.[52] There is a list of institutions and practices that all the parties of the far left reject, ranging from the 'independent' nature of the European Central Bank to the alleged influence of multinational companies on policy implementation. As in other areas, however, formulating policies on how processes of democratization can be introduced in both nation-states and the EU – that all the parties can agree on – is much more difficult. Some parties wish to strengthen the institutions of the EU – others to do the exact opposite, strengthening national parliaments by clawing sovereignty back. There are – as is the case with attitudes to capitalism in general – a number of shades of grey in between. The PDS, again, has traditionally tried to find common ground by stressing the importance of bringing the citizen into the political process through the mechanism of direct democracy.[53] The PDS has been adept at defusing ideological battles between its erstwhile partners by developing practical policies to deal with practical questions. The PDS has, for example, actively been 'transferring out' (exporting) ideas on referendums that have now become central to the programmes of far-left parties across much of the continent.

The final area where considerable policy co-ordination and networking takes place is militarism and, in far-left language, the imperialism of the capitalist world. Anti-militarism does not always equate with the strong pacifism inherent in the PDS, but the unambiguous rejection of the military 'adventures' of NATO and the United States can act as a beacon bringing the far-left movement together. There is unanimity that the EU should not seek to militarize itself or, indeed, to produce weapons that would assist others in going down this route. Positions on the EU's common foreign and security policy (CFSP) and European security and defence policy (ESDP) may differ a little – some see it as a tool with which to rein the US back in, others reject it on principle – but the underlying trend is more consensual than in other policy areas.[54]

The GUE/NGL group of parties may well have only limited programmatic aims, but the newly created European Party of the Left (EPL), of which the PDS is an important member, has much more expansive goals.[55] Yet problems of coordination still exist. The EPL's founding congress in Rome highlighted some of the ideological differences still evident across the anti-capitalist left, and it is not likely that pan-European programmes of genuine substance will be practicable for the foreseeable future. At the founding congress in Rome (May 2004), for example, there was an undignified spat between the Czech KSČM and a number of other parties over the EPL's statute – with the Czech delegates refusing to sign up on account of disagreements over the place of Stalinism in the history of left-wing politics. If the anti-capitalist left cannot agree on even the most elementary of points then it is unlikely that it will be able to come together and produce programmes and manifestos that rise above tokenism and it will remain likely that parties will continue to work with those actors with whom they can find the most common ground. The PDS none the less sees the creation of an umbrella hard-left organization – with a leader (Faustino Bertinotti from the Italian Communist Refoundation), an executive made up of two members per party and a headquarters in Brussels – as a very positive initial step towards, first, increasingly interlocking election campaigns and second, more importantly, a genuine institutionalization of over 15 parties with broadly similar, anti-capitalist aims and ideals[56] – in other words, a qualitative step forward for hard-left politics. This institutionalization is seen as facilitating hard-left programmatic co-operation in three key areas: developing European anti-war initiatives, supporting the anti-globalization movement, and assisting broader social movements that oppose capitalism.[57] It will also act as a prompt for more concerted action among member parties of the GUE/NGL.

The non-involvement of the Czech KSČM will not stop the PDS from attempting to work closely with the party in the GUE/NGL and also in more informal, face-to-face, terms. The PDS has long enjoyed cordial relations with the Czech KSČM. The two parties possess a well-developed institutionalized basis for co-operation, and many personal links exist between party members (based largely on pre-1989 networks). The close geographical proximity of the Czech Republic and Germany also assists the parties in maintaining close contacts. The Czech neo-communist representatives have been very impressed by the PDS's attempts to engage in grassroots politics: the PDS is seen as being willing 'to get closer to the structures of civic initiatives in issues of peace, the environment and social affairs' and this is frequently seen as an 'inspiration for us [the KSČM] in the sense that it opens the party up on programmatic issues'.[58] An exchange of views on programmes has therefore developed, mainly during and around conferences and seminars. The two parties co-operated in the course of election campaigns in 2002 and there is a degree of similarity in their political language and political symbols: they revolve around an ideational and emotional bridge of positive continuity between the present capitalist reality, the flawed socialist past and the idealized socialist future. The 'survival strategies' of both parties have also been similar, focusing on the preservation of traditional memberships and radically democratizing internal party processes. Both share values and historical experiences and both were fortresses under siege through the 1990s. Furthermore, the most important representatives of both parties have developed good working relationships with each other, in particular Miloslav Ransdorf and Hans Modrow, but also Jiří Dolejš, André and Michael Brie, Jaroslav Kohlíček and Heiko Kosel. They share historical experiences and ideological similarities, even if they articulate them in slightly different ways. However, more recently, with the declining influence of Hans Modrow on relations between the PDS and the KSČM, the original closeness has not been so evident. German post-communists, such as André Brie or Lothar Bisky, seem to have difficulty in working with the heterogeneous conservative or neo-communist KSČM. The PDS, for example, clearly treated the KSČM as an outsider when the PEL was established. This may indeed prompt a careful recalibration of co-operative relations between the PDS and the KSČM in the future.

Conclusion

There is little evidence to suggest that PDS's electoral successes in eastern Germany have been directly related to the programmes that it has produced. This, in itself, need not come as much of a surprise: political scientists have long argued that party programmes are one factor in shaping voter preferences, and frequently some combination of contemporary issues, personality, rational self-interest and voter loyalty to a particular party can be much more significant electorally. Yet the party's programmatic offerings do not remain wholly unpopular. Its claim that it defends broad and somewhat ill-defined east German interests, its anti-capitalist rhetoric and its pacifist leanings all strike chords with segments of a disaffected east German electorate (even if there is widespread ignorance about what the PDS would actually do if given the opportunity). In truth, the rhetoric of skilful politicians such as Gregor Gysi has frequently touched nerves across eastern Germany, even if there is scant evidence that suggests that its *detailed* policy positions are actively supported by any societal groups over and above loyal PDS activists. It is factors outside the PDS's control – principally dissatisfaction and disillusionment with the other parties – that has undoubtedly played the most significant role in drawing voters towards the PDS so far.

The unique experience of unification has not prevented the PDS – particularly in the second half of the 1990s – from remaining true to the internationalist ethos of its political heritage. This should, theoretically at least, assist the PDS in transferring in (and latterly transferring out) policies from other actors pursuing similar agendas. This is not something that the PDS did – at least, not directly – until it joined the European parliament itself in 1999, and its policy development in the period before then was characterised by piecemeal adaptations to uniquely German circumstances. International forums in the shape of the GUE/NGL and more recently the European Party of the Left now offer springboards for co-operation and coordination, and the PDS has been one of the most active exponents of far-left policy networking within these arenas. But this has not been a straightforward process: disagreements have plagued the development of a coherent far-left agenda and the PDS has only slowly been able to engage with other international actors. One such actor is the Czech KSČM. While relations between the two parties have traditionally been good, the departure of more senior PDS politicians from leadership positions and the conservative communism of many KSČM deputies may well weaken links between the two parties in the future. After the PDS successfully re-entered the European parliament in June 2004, it is now looking much more optimistically towards the federal election of 2006. It sees the EPL as a genuine opportunity for co-ordinating a left-wing agenda based on anti-militarism, the defence of socially just economic policies and the welfare state, alongside the expansion of democracy, and it is through this forum that policy co-ordination and transfer is most likely to take place. Should the EPL run into stormy waters – which is quite possible, given the history of ideological and programmatic disagreement in the far left – then it is likely that the PDS will continue to stress its links with its socialist cousins but in practice develop policies that are specific to its own environment.

NOTES

1. See in particular M. Gerner, *Partei ohne Zukunft* (Munich: Tilsner, 1994). For a detailed discussion of the PDS's development out of the SED in 1989–91, see P. Barker, 'From the SED to the PDS: Continuity or Renewal?', in P. Barker (ed.), *The Party of Democratic Socialism: Modern Post-Communism or Nostalgic Populism?*, German Monitor, Vol.42 (Amsterdam: Rodopi, 1998), pp.1–17.
2. D. Roth, 'Die Wahlen zur Volkskammer in der DDR: Der Versuch einer Erklärung', *Politische Vierteljahresschrift*, Vol.31 (1990), pp.369–93; H. Rattinger, 'Parteineigungen, Sachfragen und Kandidatenorientierungen in Ost- und Westdeutschland', in H. Rattinger, O.W. Gabriel and W. Jagodzinski (eds.), *Wahlen und politische Einstellungen im vereinigten Deutschland 1990–1992* (Frankfurt am Main: Peter Lang Verlag, 1994), pp.267–315.
3. H. Bortfeldt, *Von der SED zur PDS: Wandlung zur Demokratie?* (Bonn: Bouvier, 1992), p.295; G. Smith, 'The "New" Party System', in G. Smith, W.E. Paterson, P.H. Merkl and S. Padgett (eds.), *Developments in German Politics* (Basingstoke: Macmillan, 1992), p.100; P. Moreau, *PDS: Anatomie einer postkommunistischen Partei* (Bonn and Berlin: Bouvier, 1992), p.459; Gerner, *Partei ohne Zukunft*, p.59.
4. D. Hough, *The Fall and Rise of the PDS in Eastern Germany, 1989–2000* (Birmingham: Birmingham University Press, 2002); F. Oswald, *The Party That Came Out of the Cold War: The Party of Democratic Socialism in Germany 1989–1999* (London: Praeger, 2002).
5. Although the PDS failed to surpass the electorally significant five per cent barrier in the 2002 federal elections, and was therefore ineligible for preference votes that were being redistributed, it is none the less represented in the Bundestag by Petra Pau, who was directly elected in Berlin Marzahn-Hellersdorf, and Gesine Lötzsch, who was directly elected in Berlin Lichtenberg-Höhenschönhausen.
6. F. Berg, *Die Mitte-Links-Koalition in Mecklenburg-Vorpommern* (Berlin: Rosa Luxemburg Stiftung, 2001); M. Gerner, 'Die SPD–PDS Regierungskoalition in Mecklenburg-Vorpommern: Nagelprobe für die Regierungsfähigkeit der SED-Nachfolgeorganisation', in G. Hirscher and P. Christian Segall (eds.), *Die PDS: Zustand und Entwicklungsperspektiven* (Munich: Hanns Seidel Stiftung, 2000), pp.97–108; L. Probst, *Die PDS – von der Staats- zur Regierungspartei: Eine Studie aus Mecklenburg-Vorpommern* (Hamburg: Verlag Dr Kovac, 2000).

7. D. Hough and J. Grix, 'The PDS and the SPD's Dilemma of Strategy in the Eastern German Länder', *Politics*, Vol.21, No.3 (2001), pp.158–67; M. Rueschemeyer, 'A Divided Left: The SPD and Reformed Communists in Eastern Germany', in P.H. Merkl (ed.), *The Federal Republic of Germany at Fifty: The End of a Century of Turmoil* (London: Macmillan, 1999), pp.123–34.
8. See, for example, V. Neu, *Das Janusgesicht der PDS* (Baden-Baden: Nomos, 2004); J. Lang, *Ist die PDS eine demokratische Partei? Eine extremismustheoretische Untersuchung* (Baden-Baden: Nomos, 2003); Hough, *The Fall and Rise of the PDS*, pp.23–31; P. Moreau, *Die PDS: Profil einer antidemokratischen Partei* (München: Hanns Seidel Stiftung, 1998); V. Neu, *Die Potentiale der PDS und der Republikaner im Winter 1997-98* (Sankt Augustin: Konrad Adenauer Stiftung, 1998); P. Moreau and J. Lang, *Linksextremismus: Eine unterschätzte Gefahr* (Bonn: Bouvier, 1996); P. Moreau and J. Lang, *Was will die PDS?* (Frankfurt am Main: Ullstein, 1994).
9. G.R. Kleinfeld, 'The PDS: Between Socialism and Regionalism', in M.N. Hampton and C. Søe (eds.), *Between Bonn and Berlin: German Politics Adrift?* (Oxford: Rowman & Littlefield, 1999), pp.137–54.
10. D.F. Ziblatt, 'Putting Humpty-Dumpty Back Together Again', *German Politics and Society*, Vol.16, No.1 (1998), p.36.
11. Sahra Wagenknecht – the talismanic figurehead of the KPF – was elected to the European parliament in the 2004 EP elections.
12. See D. Hough and V. Handl, 'The (Post-)Communist Left and the European Union: The Czech KSČM and the German PDS', *Communist and Post-Communist Studies*, Vol.37, No.3 (2004), pp.319–39.
13. See A. Grzymala-Busse, 'The Programmatic Turnaround of Communist Successor Parties in East Central Europe, 1989–1998', *Communist and Post-Communist Studies*, Vol.35, No.1 (2002), p.51; A. Grzymala-Busse, *Redeeming the Communist Past: The Regeneration of Communist Parties in East Central Europe* (Cambridge: Cambridge University Press, 2002), pp.9–10.
14. D. Hough, '"Made in Eastern Germany": The PDS and the Articulation of Eastern German Interests', *German Politics*, Vol.9, No.2 (2000), pp.125–48.
15. H. Neubert, *Internationalismus: Tradition und aktuelle Erfordernisse* (Berlin: Grundsatz Kommission der PDS, May 1998), p.5.
16. For further discussion, see C. Major, 'Ist die PDS ein Stück europäischer Normalität? Eine Fallstudie zur Europapolitik der PDS', unpublished manuscript, Otto-Suhr-Institut für Politikwissenschaft an der Freien Universität, Berlin, 2001, p.5.
17. See D. Mühlberg, 'Beobachtete Tendenzen zur Ausbildung einer ostdeutschen Teilkultur', *Aus Politik und Zeitgeschichte*, No.11 (2001), pp.30–38.
18. For a particularly provocative analysis of these differences, see M. Howard, 'An Eastern German Ethnicity? Understanding the New Division of Unified Germany', *German Politics and Society*, Vol.13 (Winter 1995), pp.49–70.
19. Hough, *The Fall and Rise of the PDS*, pp.92–6.
20. The old programme is still available at <http://www.pdsnetz.de/service/progd.htm>, while the new programme can be found at <http://www.pds-online.de/partei/grundsatzdokumente/programm/index.htm>.
21. Author's interview with Bernd Ihme, secretary of the PDS's programme commission, Berlin, 17 Dec. 2002.
22. D. Hough, *The Fall and Rise of the PDS*, p.28.
23. See V. Handl, 'Choosing Between China and Europe? Virtual Inspiration and Policy Transfer in the Programmatic Development of the Czech Communist Party'; in the present collection, pp.127–145.
24. Author's interview with André Brie, Schwerin, 20 Dec. 2002.
25. R. Rose, *Lesson Drawing in Public Policy* (Chatham, NJ: Chatham House, 1993).
26. W. Jacoby, 'Priest and Penitent: The EU as a Force in the Domestic Politics of Eastern Europe', *East European Constitutional Review*, Vol.8, Nos.1–2 (1999), pp.62–7; D. Dolowitz, 'A Policy-Maker's Guide to Policy Transfer', *Political Quarterly*, Vol.74, No.1 (2003), pp.100–108.

27. D. Dolowitz and D. Marsh, 'Who Learns What from Whom? A Review of the Policy Transfer Literature', *Political Studies*, Vol.44, No.2 (1996), pp.343–57.
28. See 'BAG Umwelt-Energie-Verkehr', available at <http://sozialisten.de/partei/strukturen/agigs/bag_umwelt_energie_verkehr/index.htm>, accessed 1 Nov. 2004.
29. Wade Jacoby writes of four modes of emulation, of which the faithful and voluntary copying of policies or institutions is just one; faithful but less voluntary emulation can occur (emulation in 'patches'), as can voluntary lesson drawing ('templating') and less voluntary coercive measures ('thresholds' that need to be met). For further analysis of this, see W. Jacoby, *The Enlargement of the European Union and NATO: Ordering from the Menu in Central Europe* (Cambridge: Cambridge University Press, 2004).
30. Author's interview with André Brie, Schwerin, 20 Dec. 2002.
31. Author's interview with Judith Dellheim, Berlin, 17 Dec. 2002.
32. Author's interview with Peter Porsch, Dresden, 16 Dec. 2002.
33. P. Moreau, 'Transnationale Vergleiche: Partei des demokratischen Sozialismus, Parti Communiste Français, Partito della Rifondazione Comunista. Politische, ideologische und strategische Konvergenzen', in Barker (ed.), *The Party of Democratic Socialism*, p.129.
34. P. Moreau, 'Die Partei des demokratischen Sozialismus', in P. Moreau, M. Lazar and G. Hirscher (eds.), *Der Kommunismus in Westeuropa* (Lansberg am Lech: Günther-Olzog-Verlag, 1998), p.318.
35. Hough and Handl, 'The (Post-)Communist Left and the European Union'.
36. 'PDS und FKP: Zusammenarbeit intensivieren: Meinungsaustausch zwischen Lothar Bisky und Robert Hue', *PDS Pressedienst*, 22, 2 June 2000; available at <http://sozialisten.de/politik/publikationen/pressedienst/view_html?zid = 8294&bs = 1&n = 1>, accessed 1 June 2004.
37. Ibid.
38. Confederal Group of the United European Left/Nordic Green Left (GUE/NGL), *The GUE/NGL Constituent Declaration*, 1994, quoted in R. Dunphy, *Contesting Capitalism: Left Parties and European Integration* (Manchester: Manchester University Press, 2004), p.172.
39. Major, *Ist die PDS ein Stück europäischer Normalität?*, p.7.
40. Dunphy, *Contesting Capitalism*, p.169.
41. B. Kühn, 'Garantieren Konvergenzkriterien die Stabilität des Euro?', in *PDS Disput*, Feb. 1998; available at <http://sozialisten.de/politik/publikationen/disput/view_html?zid = 1723&bs = 1&n = 19>, accessed 3 July 2004.
42. Dunphy, *Contesting Capitalism*, p.169.
43. See, for example, U. Kalinowski, 'Einmütig ohne Einheitsbrei', in *PDS Disput*, June 1998; available at <http://sozialisten.de/politik/publikationen/disput/view_html?zid = 1776&bs = 1&n = 15>, accessed 3 July 2004.
44. See PDS Delegation in the European Parliament, 'Halbzeit im Europäischen Parlament', in *PDS Pressedienst*, 14, 4 April 2002; available at <http://sozialisten.de/politik/publikationen/pressedienst/view_html?zid = 10136&bs = 1&n = 18>, accessed 3 July 2004.
45. PDS Mecklenburg-Vorpommern, 'Für eine andere Beschäftigungs- und Wirtschaftspolitik in Mecklenburg-Vorpommern. Beschluß der 4. Tagung des 4. Landesparteitages der PDS Mecklenburg-Vorpommern, Parchim, 15 and 16 February 1997', in *PDS Pressedienst*, 8, 21 Feb. 1997, p.8.
46. PDS, *Programme of the Party of Democratic Socialism* (Berlin: PDS, 2003); available at <http://sozialisten.de/partei/grundsatzdokumente/programm/3-5.htm>, accessed 3 July 2004.
47. *Deutscher Bundestag*: Drucksache 13/10015.
48. Five west German *Länder* can be found in the list of Europe's ten richest regions, while every east German *Land* fits into the category of Europe's poorest regions: see PDS, *Europawahlprogramm 2004*; available at <http://sozialisten.de/wahlen2004/wahlprogramm/langfassung/1-6.htm>, accessed 3 July 2004.
49. G. Zimmer, Vorschläge für den Osten – mit Blick auf die gewachsene EU', in *PDS Disput*, May 2004; available at <http://sozialisten.de/politik/publikationen/disput/view_html?zid = 20020&bs = 1&n = 1>, accessed 3 July 2004.

50. See S.-Y. Kaufmann, 'Fünf Jahre Brüssel – Bilanz der PDS-Europaabgeordneten'; available at <http://www.pds-europa.de/europarot/view_euro_html?zid = 1212&pp = 1>, accessed 3 July 2004.
51. PDS Delegation in the European Parliament, 'Halbzeit'.
52. Dunphy, *Contesting Capitalism*, p.170.
53. Hough, *The Fall and Rise of the PDS*, pp.160–62.
54. See S.-Y. Kaufmann, 'Die USA wollen den Krieg – Europa kann den Frieden gewinnen', in *PDS Betrieb und Gewerkschaft*, May 2003; available at <http://sozialisten.de/politik/publikationen/bg/view_html?zid = 1555&bs = 1&n = 6>, accessed 3 July 2004.
55. For further details, see 'Programm der partei der Europäischen Linken (EL)'; available at <http://sozialisten.de/politik/publikationen/disput/view_html?zid = 20028&bs = 1& n = 12>, accessed 3 July 2004.
56. J. Reinert, 'Startschuss für europäische Linkspartei'; available at <http://www.pds-online.de/partei/international/dokumente/view_html?zid = 61&bs = 1&n = 0>, accessed 8 Jan. 2004; EPL, *Statut der Partei der Europäischen linken (EL)*; available at <http://sozialisten.de/sozialisten/el/statut.htm>, accessed 20 May 2004.
57. PDS Parteivorstand, 'PDS engagiert sich für die Gründung einer europäischen Linkspartei', in *PDS Pressedienst*, 48/2003.
58. Interview with KSČM MP Jiří Dolejš, quoted in Hough and Handl, 'The (Post-)Communist Left', p.335.

Conclusion

WILLIAM E. PATERSON AND JAMES SLOAM

Introduction

The fall of the Iron Curtain brought with it regime change across all of Eastern and Central Europe (ECE).[1] With the birth of new democracies came new political parties that had to adapt to the new political environment. Contrary to the predictions of many observers, communist successor parties (CSPs) re-emerged from heavy defeats in the first wave of free elections, to find a place for themselves in their new democratic surroundings. These parties nevertheless remained attached to the past to varying extents – whether in terms of the personal biographies of their leading politicians or the nature of their electoral support and party membership. The main objective of the parties that led the states of Eastern and Central Europe after 1990 became accession to the European Union, which appeared to offer the prospect of both material prosperity and political stability. As the political systems of the region adapted themselves to the EU's accession demands, political parties in these countries naturally sought to learn from similar parties in Western Europe and international socialist and social-democratic organizations in the development of their policy programmes. For CSPs, this had a strong 'instrumental' dimension: to restore legitimacy, secure resources and improve their electoral appeal. Many successor parties nevertheless made serious efforts to modernize their party programmes. The gradual Europeanization (or 'EU-ization') of Eastern and Central Europe was finally crowned by the eastern enlargement of the European Union in May 2004.

Deeper European integration in the 1990s created greater interest among both policy makers and academics in learning across space and how 'best practice' could be promoted in the EU. The apparent diffusion of ideas and policy concepts led to an explosion of literature on the concepts of 'lesson

---

William E. Paterson is Professor and Director of the Institute of German Studies, University of Birmingham.
James Sloam is Lecturer in European Studies at King's College London, and an honorary Research Fellow in the Institute of German Studies, University of Birmingham.

drawing' and 'policy transfer' within the broader idea of 'policy learning'.[2] While formal rules and procedures for policy co-ordination were laid down in, for example, the European growth and stability pact (agreed in 1996), more informal processes for 'benchmarking' were also established, most notably with the Lisbon agenda (2000).

One of the key aims of this collection of studies has been to examine the validity of policy transfer as an analytical tool for understanding the external influences on CSP programmatic change. More specifically, it focused on how these parties had learnt from the West, from their sister parties in the 'old' EU, concentrating on West European social democracy as a model for programme change. Although the various contributions have found that diversity continues to exist among CSPs – based on their institutional and national contexts – environmental change in the European context has had a deep impact, facilitating analysts in their attempts to explore common trends in EU policy, welfare policy and security policy. It is with this background in mind that the contributions to this collection have confirmed the suspicion that party-to-party policy transfer has had a good deal of relevance for CSP programmes within the broader Europeanization process. Successor parties have learnt from their sister parties in Western Europe (and even adopted or adapted policies into their own programmes) – even if these policies have been instrumentalized, and frequently lacked feasibility, in particular national political and socio-economic contexts, or have been imported as a result of more general Europeanization pressures. Despite the many obstacles to policy transfer and the complex matrix of actors and structures that influence policy, transfer has a continuing relevance for policy makers and academics alike in an ever-closer Union.

Environmental Change

Structural change, and more specifically European integration, has promoted three dimensions of Europeanization with respect to CSPs: 'downloading' from the EU level, 'uploading' to the EU level (European policy), and horizontal 'cross-loading' between political parties.[3] In this volume Marcin Zaborowski discussed the influence of these EU-level actors on the states where successor parties are active as well as the successor parties themselves. He writes that, although external influences have been neglected in much of the literature on post-communist politics, they have nevertheless played a major part in the development of CSPs – from long before the collapse of communism to this day. Zaborowski argues that the collapse of communism provided fertile ground for the implantation of policies from a wide range of external influences, from the European Union and NATO to the ideas of the Chicago Business School.

Michael Dauderstädt argues strongly that, setting the special case of the German Party of Democratic Socialism to one side, 'the defining issue for the three other parties has been the question of accession and membership', even if their programmes have tended to reflect national rather than European preferences. Nevertheless, he finds a common thread in the policies of all four successor parties examined in this volume in their desire to preserve and protect a European welfare state model from the forces of globalization. Even the more orthodox parties in Germany and the Czech Republic advocate a form of European integration, although they give priority to a more clearly social (or socialist) EU. Dauderstädt also underlines the importance of the process of intensive dialogue and networking for the successor parties in their adaptation to the policy framework of the European Union, and further points to the impact of accession on these parties' European policies, after which they have come to focus more on the 'core business' of the EU. It is on these issues that party policies are more likely to reflect national issues.

Policy Transfer and Programme Change

We have already explained how policy transfer and policy learning have become increasingly relevant for a deepened and widened European Union, and this is emphasized by William Paterson and James Sloam's contribution. By policy transfer we mean the transfer of knowledge about policies across time and space,[4] and the utilization (but not necessarily the actual adoption) of this knowledge.[5] This broader definition of policy transfer fits with the more subtle diffusion of policy that takes place in practice – and that is frequently identified in these studies. Policy transfer, as an analytical tool, has allowed us to focus on the influence of one political party upon another – to understand, in Dolowitz and Marsh's terms, 'who learns what from whom'.[6] Through these means researchers can interpret political and policy change. Furthermore, by looking more generally at the contexts within which this programmatic change has taken place, we can understand – given parties' individual opportunity structures – why and how policy learning has taken place. Contexts also explain the meaning of these transfers given the different nature or 'value' of programmes for individual political parties.

Voluntary transfer between political parties (cross-loading) has been found to take place through two main channels: 'emulation' through ideational transfer, and the active engagement of parties with each other through 'transfer networks'. The case studies in this volume concur that these types of transfer have usually taken place on the basis of proximity (geographical, ideological and cultural) of an importer party to an exporter party. For this reason, the West European social-democratic tradition, in a general sense, has provided a good model for centre-left CSPs and – to varying degrees – a source for policy transfer, and the German Social Democrats (together with the Austrian Social Democrats) have proved particularly important in this respect. Policy transfer is nevertheless dependent upon the desire of the individual CSP to learn lessons, and upon the applicability of these new policies in very different institutional and national contexts.

Learning from the West

The collection, while examining the external influences on successor party programmes, concentrated on West European social-democratic parties (SDPs) as the source of policy transfer. James Sloam studies this transfer from the perspective of the exporter party, which has been a much neglected part of the transfer equation, exploring the 'push' and 'pull' factors of policy transfer: the attractiveness of social democracy as a model, and transfer through interaction in transfer networks. His contribution investigates SDP policies: what is available to be transferred and why, in some cases, these policies have proved appealing to CSPs. He argues that, although the 'desirability' of a policy or policy programme may be largely dependent on the political success of a potential exporter party, proximity can frequently determine the 'feasibility' of a particular policy. The levels of interaction of SDPs with their sister parties to the East – through networks – is largely dependent upon proximity. He also highlights the Socialist International and the Party of European Socialists as important factors in the diffuse spread of social democracy to the East. Sloam, like other contributors to this collection, makes the point that German Social Democrats, when compared with the SDPs of other large, 'old' EU states, has exerted the most influence over centre-left successor parties in Eastern and Central Europe,[7] but that CSPs have not adopted policies from the social democratic menu on an *à la carte* basis.[8]

The four case studies of the successor parties in Poland, the Czech Republic, Slovakia and Germany examine policy transfer and programme change from the perspective of potential importer parties. The in-depth studies look first at the motivations or 'opportunity structures' for policy transfer. First Buras, and then Handl and Leška, describe how the leaderships of the (at least in part) reformist, centre-left-oriented parties in Poland (Alliance of the Democratic Left – SLD) and Slovakia (Party of the Democratic Left – SDL) paid considerable attention to international contacts in the early 1990s for three main reasons: because they wished to help legitimize the successor parties of the previous (discredited) regimes; because they desired to be regarded as modern European parties by their domestic electorates; and because they were inspired, to various degrees, by programmes of their sister parties in Western Europe. The impact of Western policies was quite different in these two cases, however. In Poland, while many of the policies of the Western parties were brought into the party's first programmatic documents, their adoption was a largely 'instrumental step' to adapt to the new political environment. The Polish SLD was influenced by a number of social-democratic policies, which were selected – according to their potential appeal and applicability – into the Polish context on an area-by-area basis. The programmatic path of the Slovakian SDL was deeply influenced by West European social democracy in the 1990s. At the same time, the nature of this influence has reflected the societal and socio-economic context in which the party was active – placing an altogether different emphasis on 'who and what they looked to for programmatic inspiration'. A group of SDL modernizers had already looked to the centre-left in Western Europe for programmatic inspiration before 1989, proceeding to work with the 'templates' set out by the Socialist International in the mid-1990s. Although this leading group of SDL politicians was genuinely supportive of West European social democracy, and ensured that much of this discourse founds its way into party policy, the conservative majority only superficially accepted these programmatic changes and began to develop a separate, critical discourse. Policy transfer for these parties was clearly important in their programme development within the context of a more general process of Europeanization. In both cases the policies of the Socialist International and the Party of the European Socialists, and legitimization by these bodies, played a pivotal role in the parties' 'modernization'. Individual parties were important in this process, and here proximity – as set out above – does appear to be the determining factor. Although bilateral contacts have not led to clear programmatic change, interaction through transfer networks has played a prominent part in these successor parties' policy learning. Here, a subtle diffusion of ideas took place as the Western SDPs assisted the CSPs in adjusting to the norms of the EU. In this process, the importer successor parties 'cherry-picked' the policies most suitable to their own political environments.

Although the German Party of Democratic Socialism (PDS) and the Czech Communist Party of Bohemia and Moravia (KSČM) have usually been characterized as 'retreatist' successor parties, they have nevertheless, at times, also been open to influence from their sister parties in the European far left. Dan Hough argues that after 1990, as the PDS was attempting to establish itself in the political system of the Federal Republic, it found itself in a programmatic vacuum largely devoid of contact with other parties in other countries. The immediate aim of its programmatic positions was self-preservation. From this initial position of isolation, the PDS has, however, come to place a high priority on co-operation with its sister parties on the European level and stressed bilateral ties with similar parties in Europe. In this vein, the party has sought to realize its internationalist aspirations, and in recent years has proved 'one of the most active exponents of far-left policy networking' in Europe.[9] In bilateral terms, the PDS's relations with the Czech KSČM have been strong for reasons of geographical and ideological proximity. Its commitment to EU-level cooperation and strong ties with selected sister parties – in particular the Czech KSČM – provides fertile ground for policy transfer. Vladimír Handl argues that the role of policy transfer for the KSČM has been greater than has been traditionally acknowledged in the Czech and English-language literature on the Czech communists as well as within the party itself. The two main streams in the party, however, have looked to different models for inspiration: the conservatives ('retreat coalition') towards China (although still engaging in largely unacknowledged transfer from the non-communist left in the EU); and the 'neo-communists' towards the European left. Although no 'single pattern of programmatic borrowing' can be identified, these two streams 'engaged actively in the search for, and export of, ideological and policy inspiration'. Handl argues that, while the impulses for programmatic change in the KSČM emanated mostly from the Europeanization process, the Czech party has sought to legitimize these changes through reference to other 'hard left' parties – 'most often the German post-communist PDS'.

In general, the case studies have shown that there has been a significant amount of learning from the West, increased in its extent as a consequence of democratic and economic transition and the EU accession process (leading to more similar external environments), and based on proximity to the source of new policies. They nevertheless underline the 'pragmatic' or 'instrumental' nature of much of this learning, which has been geared towards achieving legitimacy for the parties of the former communist regimes (for example, by entering one or both of the Party of European Socialists and the Socialist International) and, in simple terms, presenting attractive rather than feasible policy programmes to voters. For the parties in Poland and Slovakia that moved towards social-democratic ideas, the 'cherry-picking' of policies was common, and many of the policies that were imported remained rather dislocated from the parties' core electorates and core identities. For the SLD in Poland, this was possible because programmes meant little for the party; for the SDL in Slovakia, it resulted in the establishment of two separate discourses within one party.

For all these parties, the Europeanization process was the key to their programmatic development – whether this meant adapting policies to EU norms (the SLD and SDL in the 1990s) or refocusing policies to give priority to reform of the European Union (the KSČM and the PDS). This Europeanization was central to promoting congruence between parties of similar ideological leanings, and encouraging policy transfer and policy learning. Despite the diverse programmatic paths taken by CSPs in the transition states, European integration continues to make policy transfer attractive.

There can be no doubt about the relevance of policy transfer within the process of Europeanization. The cross-loading described in this collection is

CONCLUSION

progressively more relevant given the increasing penetration of the European Union and its rules and regulations. David Dolowitz illustrates clearly how policy transfer can assist policy makers in their efforts to learn across space by benchmarking 'best practice'.[10] For academics, the concept of policy transfer can help us focus on the central actors at work within the more general diffusion of policy analysed in the European integration literature. This offers a more agent-centred approach to explaining change, convergence and divergence within an increasingly integrated EU. From this agent-centred perspective, we also gain a better understanding of national and institutional opportunity structures that come into play when policy makers decide to adopt or adapt policies. The contextualization of the policy-making environment and the diffusion, in its various forms, of ideas and policy concepts lie at the heart of a diverse Europeanization process.

NOTES

1. The work used in this article is based on the research carried out for a Leverhulme-funded project (F/00094/O) on 'Policy Transfer and Programmatic Change in the Communist Successor Parties of East Central Europe'
2. See, for example, R. Rose, *Lesson-Drawing in Public Policy: A Guide to Learning across Time and Space* (Chatham, NJ: Chatham House, 1993); D. Dolowitz and D. Marsh, 'Who Learns What from Whom: A Review of the Policy Transfer Literature', *Political Studies*, Vol.44 (1996), pp.343–57; C. Bennett, 'Understanding Ripple Effects: The Cross-National Adoption of Policy Instruments for Bureaucratic Accountability', *Governance*, Vol.10, No.3 (1997), pp.213–33l; D. Stone, 'Learning Lessons and Transferring Policy across Time, Space and Disciplines', *Politics*, Vol.19, No.1 (1999), pp.51–9; M. Evans and J. Davies, 'Understanding Policy Transfer: A Multi-Level, Multi-Disciplinary Perspective', *Public Administration*, Vol.77, No.2 (1999), pp.361–85; E. Page, 'Future Governance and the Literature on Policy Transfer and Lesson Drawing', prepared for the ESRC Future Governance Workshop on Policy Transfer, 2000, available at <http://www.hull.ac.uk/futgov/Papers/EdPagePaper1.pdf>, accessed 18 Nov. 2004; K. Mossberger and H. Wolman, 'Policy Transfer as a Form of Prospective Policy Evaluation', Future Governance Paper 2 (2001), available at <http://www.hull.ac.uk/futgov/Papers/PubPapers/KMPaper2.pdf>, accessed 18 Nov. 2004; W. Jacoby, 'Tutors and Pupils: International Organizations, Central European Elites, and Western Models', *Governance*, Vol.14, No.2 (2001), pp.169–200; H. Wolman and E. Page, 'Policy Diffusion Among Local Governments: An Information-Theory Approach', *Governance*, Vol.15, No.4 (2002), pp.477–501; S. Padgett, 'Between Synthesis and Emulation: EU Policy Transfer in the Power Sector', *Journal of European Public Policy*, Vol.10, No.2 (2003), pp.227–45.
3. For a similar typology of Europeanization, see I. Bache, 'Europeanization: A Governance Approach', *ESRC/UACES Series of Seminars on EBPP*, available at <http://www.shef.ac.uk/ebpp/bache.pdf>, accessed 18 Nov. 2004.
4. Stone, 'Learning Lessons'.
5. Wolman and Page, 'Policy Diffusion'.
6. Dolowitz and Marsh, 'Who Learns What from Whom'.
7. The finding that the Austrian Social Democrats were the German Social Democrats' main rival for influence in the centre-left parties of Eastern and Central Europe further supports the geographical proximity hypothesis.

8. This analogy is used by Wade Jacoby with respect to the external influences on the states of Eastern and Central Europe: W. Jacoby, *The Enlargement of the European Union and NATO: Ordering from the Menu in Central Europe* (Cambridge: Cambridge University Press, 2004).
9. The PDS was a keen advocate of the creation of the Party of the European Left in 2004, and this is likely to provide an opportunity for intensified interaction through policy networks and the diffusion of policy through policy transfer and policy learning.
10. D. Dolowitz, 'A Policy-maker's Guide to Policy Transfer', *Political Quarterly*, Vol.74, No.1 (2003), pp.101–8.

INDEX

Page references for notes are followed by n

Adamec, Ladislav 131
agency 41–2
Alfred Mozer Foundation 62
Alliance of the Democratic Left (Poland) *see* SLD
Austria 117

background variables 18, 19–22
Balcerowicz, Leszek 18, 114
Balín, Vlastimil 127
Bara, J. 37
Bennett, Colin 35, 136
Bertinotti, Faustino 155
Bisky, Lothar 145, 149, 150–1, 156
Blair, Tony 76, 96
Bokros, Lajos 114
Börzel, Tanja 27
Bozóki, A. 125
Brandt, Willy 90
Brie, André 147, 148, 149, 155, 156
Brie, Michael 148, 155
Britain, *see also* Labour Party
BSP (Bulgaria) 5
Budge, Ian 36, 37, 40, 41
Buras, Piotr 77

CDU (Germany) 25
Celiński, Andrzej 88, 98, 99, 101
Centre Party (Estonia) 52, 53
China 124, 126, 131–2, 136, 137, 166
Chmelár, Eduard 112–13
Cimoszewicz, Włodzimierz 55–6, 96, 99

Civic Democratic Party (Czech Republic) 52, 53
Clinton, Bill 126
Communist Party of Bohemia and Moravia (Czech Republic) *see* KSČM
Communist Party (Portugal) 131
Communist Party of the Russian Federation 128
Communist Party of Slovakia 49, 106, 107, 108, 112, 117, 130
Communist Party of the Soviet Union (CPSU) 1–2, 13n
Communist Refoundation (Italy) 128, 131, 150
communist successor parties (CSPs) 1–4, 49, 80–1, 161–3; and European integration 49–54; European policies 54–63; policy transfer 9–10, 163–7; political appeal 69–71; and programmatic change 4–7, 10–12; programmes 38–9; and social-democratic parties 33–4, 41–4, 67–9; transfer networks 72–80, *see also individual parties*
conditionality 23–5, 27, 30
contextual analysis 40, 44
convergence 23, 24–7, 28
Copenhagen Criteria 23, 24
Council of Europe 22, 23, 30, 130
Crook, Nick 51
CSCE 97, 98
ČSSD (Czech Republic) 63, 113, 116
Cuba 126, 136

169

Czech Communist Party *see* KSČM
Czech Republic 2, 5; background variables 19, 21; and EU 50, 52, 124; external influence 27; political orientation 51; post-communist transformation 106, *see also* KSČM
Czechoslovakia 2, 19, 20, 29, 48, 49

Dauderstädt, Michael 37, 51
Davies, Jonathan 43, 68
Dellheim, Judith 149
desirability 35, 42
diffusion theory 35
Dimaggio, P. 42
discourse analysis 40, 41, 44
Dolejš, Jiří 131, 134, 155
Dolowitz, David 7, 8, 67, 163, 167
Dubček, Alexander 111

East Germany 2, 20, 49, 60
Eastern and Central Europe (ECE): background variables of post-communist transitions 19–22; domestic norms, institutions and external influences 27–9; and EU 48–9; forms of external influence 23–7; inhibitions 18; post-communist transitions 16–17, 29–30
EK (Estonia) 52, 53
election manifestos 37
electoral success 69–71, 80
electoral success *see* political appeal
electoral system 27
elite interviews 40, 41
engagement 73, 74–6
environmental policy 148–9
Esping-Andersen, G. 89
Estonia 50, 51, 52
EU-ization 24, 27, 30

European Convention on Human Rights 23
European Forum for Democracy and Solidarity 62, 77, 112
European Parliament: Socialist Group 78, *see also* Group of the European Left/Nordic Green Left
European Party of the Left (ELP) 130, 137, 144, 154–5, 156, 157, 168n
European Union (EU) 10–11, 17, 22, 35–6, 48–9, 161, 163; co-operation and conflict 61–3; and communist successor parties 49–61; conditionality 23–4, 30; conditionality and convergence 27–8; enlargement 73–4, 76, 81; and KSČM 124, 129, 132–5, 137; and PDS 149, 153–4; penetration 39; policy transfer 8; and SDL 110, 115–16, 118; and SLD 92, 95–6; and social-democratic parties 42
Europeanization 23–4, 27, 36, 103n, 161, 162, 166–7; SDL 109; SLD 96
Evans, Mark 43, 68
Exner, Václav 58, 128
external influences 17, 18, 21–2, 29–30; conditionality 23–5; convergence 24–7; domestic norms and institutions 27
external security *see* security policy

Fassino, Piero 110
FDP (Germany) 25
feasibility 35, 42
Fico, Robert 108
Fidesz (Hungary) 52, 53
Finland 134, 149
Fischer, Heinz 110, 117
Fogaš, L'ubomír 110

INDEX

Fondation Jean Jaurès 62, 80, 83n
Ford Foundation 22
foundations 22, 25–6, 30, 32n, 62,
  79–80, *see also* Friedrich Ebert
  Foundation
France 18, 30, 72, 148, *see also Parti
  Socialiste*; PCF
Friedman, Milton 114
Friedrich Ebert Foundation (FES) 22,
  25, 26, 32n, 62, 74, 80, 83n;
  Poland 91, 102n; Slovakia
  109–10, 116, 117
Friedrich Naumann Foundation
  (FNS) 25, 26, 32n
Ftáčnik, Milan 108, 110

Gál, Fedor 111
GDR 2, 20, 49, 60
German-Czech Forum 22
Germany: convergence 27;
  foundations 25–6, 32n; influence
  17, 22, 30; inhibitions 18; in PES
  77–8; Polish-German border 21;
  proximity 11, 71–2; and Slovakia
  115, 117; social market economy
  88–9; trade 42; unification 12, 20,
  see also PDS; SPD
Gerrits, André 51
Giddens, Anthony 99
Grebeníček, Miroslav 131
Group of the European United
  Left/Nordic Green Left
  (GUE/NGL): and KSČM 129–30,
  134; and PDS 62, 151–2, 153,
  154, 155, 156
Gysi, Gregor 144, 145, 149

Haló noviny 126, 127, 131–2, 134
Handl, Vladimír 77
Hanley, S. 125
Hartl, Jan 126–7
Haughton, Tim 108

Hollande, François 38
Hue, Robert 150–1
Hungary 2, 3, 49; background
  variables 19; and EU 48, 50;
  external influence 26, 27; political
  orientation 51
HZDS (Slovakia) 52, 53, 58, 107,
  108, 118

ideational transfer 34, 35, 42, 67,
  68–9, 80, 163; political appeal
  69–71; proximity 71–2; SDL
  111–17; SI and PES 76, 77
informal institutions 27–8
information networks 43, 47n
Institute for Marxism-Leninism 111
international institutions 22, *see also*
  European Union; International
  Monetary Fund
International Monetary Fund (IMF)
  8, 22, 114
internationalism 146
Iraq 126
Ireland 134
Ishiyama, J.T. 125
Italy 109, 112

Jacoby, Wade 8–9, 35–6, 136,
  148, 159n
Jean Jaurès Foundation 62, 80, 83n
Jospin, Lionel 38, 99

Kanis, Pavol 110, 111, 116
Karl Renner Institute 62, 109, 117
Kaufmann, Sylvia-Yvonne 153
Kelles Krauz Foundation 91
Keohane, Robert 71
Kik, Kazimierz 90
Kitschelt, Herbert 3, 16
Klaus, Václav 52, 64n, 127, 133
Klein, Lothar 149
Koch, Roland 9

Kohlíček, Jaroslav 155
Kołodko, Grzegorz 94
Komunistická strana Čech a Moravy see KSČM
Koncoš, Pavel 110, 112, 113, 116
Konrad Adenauer Foundation (KAS) 25, 26, 32n
Kosel, Heiko 155
KPÖ (Austria) 150
KSČM (Czech Republic) 5, 10, 11–12, 49, 53, 72, 75, 123–5, 135–7, 147, 165, 166; and European Party of the Left 154; European policies 54, 56–8, 62, 63, 133–5; external inspiration in practice 130–3; international relations and programmatic development 128–30; and PDS 150, 155–6, 157; post-1989 transformation 125–7; and SDL 111
KSS (Slovakia) 49, 106, 107, 108, 112, 117, 130
Kwaśniewski, Aleksander 97

labour market policy: Poland 93–5, 100; Slovakia 114–15
Labour Party (Belgium) 128
Labour Party (Britain) 11, 34, 67, 117; engagement 76; European policy 73, 74, 82n, 96; labour market policy 94, 95; leadership 36, 37; policy goals 78; political appeal 69, 70; programmes 36, 37–8, 39, 46n; resources 79, 80; and SDL 110, 113; and SLD 91, 101
Ladislav Novomeský Foundation 109
Ladrech, Robert 103n
Lafontaine, Oskar 114
Latvia 50, 51
leadership 3, 36–7

left-wing parties: European institutions 151–6; and KSČM 128–9; and PDS 148–51
Leška, Vladimír 77
lesson drawing 7–8, 30, 11, 148, 161–2
Lithuania 50, 51, 54
LSDP 63

Magvaši, Peter 115
Manka, Vladimír 59
Markov, Helmut 153
Marsh, D. 7, 8, 163
Mason, David 16
Mauroy, Pierre 98
Mečiar, Vladimír 58, 107, 108
Meckel, Markus 110
Migaš, Josef 59, 107, 108, 110, 113, 116
Miller, Leszek 56, 69, 76, 91, 96, 98
Mitterand, François 81n, 148
Modrow, Hans 129, 150, 155, 156
Mohorita, Vasil 125
monetary systems 27
Moreau, Patrick 150
Moscovici, Pierre 74, 76
Mossberger, K. 35
Movement for a Democratic Slovakia 52, 53, 58, 107, 108, 118
MSzP (Hungary) 5, 52, 53, 63

nationalism 6, 29
NATO 22; conditionality 23; KSČM 57, 135; PDS 149; and Poland 55, 97–8; SDL 60, 116, 118
Netherlands 110, 117
networks *see* transfer networks
Nikolski, Lech 88
norm entrepreneurs 27, 29
North Korea 126, 136
Nye, Joseph 71

INDEX

ODS (Czech Republic) 52, 53
Offe, Claus 16
Oleksy, Józef 54, 55, 56
Olof Palme Institute 62, 111
Ondryáš, Pavol 113
OSCE 23, 97, 98

Parti Socialiste (France) 11, 34, 67, 81n, 153; engagement 74; EU enlargement 73, 74; leadership 37; policy goals 78; political appeal 69, 70; programmes 36, 38; resources 79, 80; and Third Way 98
Party of the Democratic Left (Slovakia) *see* SDL
Party of the European Left *see* European Party of the Left
Party of European Socialists (PES) 33, 43, 62, 69, 75, 76–8, 164, 165; and EU 96; policy goals 79; resources 79; and SDL 110, 111, 112, 113, 115, 117, 118; and SdRP/SLD 11, 92, 100, 101
party programmes 36–40, 44; channelling transfer 41–3; KSČM 124; qualitative programmatic analysis 40–1; SDL 107–8, 111–17, *see also* programmatic change
PCF (France) 128, 149, 150–1
PCI (Italy) 109, 110, 112, 117, 149
PDS (Party of Democratic Socialism) (Germany) 10, 12, 53, 54, 75, 142–4, 156–7, 165–6; European policies 60–1, 62; formation 144–5; and institutionalized European hard left 151–6; international and challenges 146–8; and KSČM 128, 129, 131, 132, 137; and other hard-left parties 148–51; and Party of the European Left 168n

PDSR (Romania) 5
Petráš, Michael 110
Poland 2, 3, 49, 84–6; background variables 19–20, 21; constitution 30; and EU 48, 50, 51; European policy 95–6; external influence 26, 27; informal institutions 28; labour market policy 93–5; NATO membership 23; policy contexts 86–92; policy transfer 99–101; political orientation 51; *powiat* 18; security policy 97–8; shock therapy 18, 30; and Slovakia 112; Third Way 98–9; welfare policy 92–3, *see also* SdRP; SLD
policy contexts 34, 38–9, 40, 44, 85, 86–92, 163; Poland 86–92
policy learning 7, 33, 34, 44, 162
policy transfer 30, 33, 34–6, 44, 67–8, 162, 163; analytical framework 7–10, 159n; convergence 24–7; PDS 148–51; and political appeal 69–71; proximity 71–2; SDL 106, 108–19; SdRP/SLD 84–6, 92–101; social-democratic parties 41–3, 164–7, *see also* voluntary policy transfer
political appeal 69–71, 80
Porsch, Peter 150
Portugal 134
post-communist transitions 16–17, 29–30; background variables 19–22; domestic norms, institutions and external influences 27–9; forms of external influence 23–7; research difficulties 17–18
Powell, W. 42
powszechność pracy 93
PRC (Italy) 128, 131, 150
Pridham, Geoffrey 18, 19

Prodi, Romano 56
programmatic change 4–7, 10–12, 40, 41, 44, 163; PDS 143–4; SDL 117, 118–19
proximity 34, 42, 71–2, 117
PS (France) see Parti Socialiste (France)
PSSH (Albania) 5
public spending 39, 46n, 70–1
PZPR (Polish United Workers' Party) 84, 87, 90, 100

qualitative discourse analysis 40, 41, 44
qualitative programmatic analysis 34, 40–1, 44

Rakowski, Mieczysław F. 90
Ransdorf, Miloslav 113, 127, 128, 129, 130, 155
rational institutionalism 27, 28
Return to Europe 24, 26, 49
Richter, Ján 110, 111
Risse, Thomas 27
Romania 2, 30
Rosa Luxemburg Foundation 62, 129, 148
Rose, Richard 7–8, 42, 68, 148
Roth, Wolfgang 110

Sachs, Jeffrey 18
Samoobrona (Poland) 52, 53, 55
Schmögnerová, Brigita 58, 59, 108, 110, 114
SDA (Slovakia) 108, 119
SDL (Slovakia) 5–6, 10, 12, 49, 53, 75, 105–6, 107–8, 164, 165, 166; European policies 54, 58–60, 62; international co-operation 108–11; programmatic inspiration 111–17; transformation and policy transfer 117–19

SdPl (Poland) 85
SDPs see social-democratic parties
SdRP (Poland) 5, 11, 84–6, 99–101; European policy 95; institutional context 86–8; international context 89–91, 102n; labour market policy 9; security policy 97–8; welfare policy 92–3
SDSS (Slovak Social Democratic Party) 109, 118, 119
security policy: KSČM 135; SDL 116; SdRP 97–8
SED (East Germany) 2, 13n, 142, 143, 144, 148
shock therapy 18, 29, 30
SI see Socialist International
SLD (Poland) 10, 11, 53, 63, 72, 84–6, 99–101, 164–5, 166; European policies 54–6, 62, 63, 95–6; institutional context 86–8; international context 91–2; labour market policy 93–5; and SPD 76; Third Way 98–9; transfer networks 83n; welfare policy 92–3, 103n
Slovakia 2; and EU 50; external influence 27; political orientation 51; post-communist transformation 106–8; public spending 70–1, see also SDL
Slovenia 50, 51, 54
Smer (Slovakia) 106, 108, 119
Social Democracy of Poland 85
Social Democracy of the Republic of Poland see SdRP (Poland)
Social-Democratic Alternative (Slovakia) 108, 119
social-democratic parties 34, 44, 62, 68–9, 80–1, 163–4; policy transfer 11, 42–3, 164–7; political appeal 69–71; programmes 36–40; and SDL

109–13, 117; and SdRP/SLD 85, 90, 99–101; transfer networks 72–80, *see also* Labour Party; *Parti Socialiste*; SPD; SPÖ
Social Democratic Party (Czech Republic) 75
social market economy 88–9, 149
Socialist International 9, 11, 39, 43, 62, 69, 76–7, 164; and KSČM 128, 131, 132; and SDL 108, 111, 112, 113, 115, 117, 118, 165; and SdRP/SLD 90–1, 100, 101, 102n
Socialist Unity Party (East Germany) 2, 13n, 142, 143, 144, 148
socio-economic issues: KSČM 133–5; Slovakia 113–15
sociological institutionalism 27–8
Sojusz Lewicy Demokratycznej (Poland) *see* SLD
Solidarity (Poland) 19, 49, 87
Sorino, Fausto 125
Soviet Union 2, 19, 48, 49, *see also* Communist Party of the Soviet Union
Spain 129
SPD (Social Democratic Party) (Germany) 11, 22, 25, 34, 42, 67, 68, 81, 129, 164; engagement 74, 75–6; EU enlargement 73–4; labour market policy 94; leadership 37; and PDS 143; policy goals 78; political appeal 70; programmes 36, 37, 38, 46n; proximity 71–2; and PZPR 90; resources 79, 80; and SDL 109, 110, 113, 114, 117; security policy 98; and SLD 91, 100–1; social state 92
SPÖ (Social Democratic Party) (Austria) 74–5, 81, 109, 110, 112, 117, 164

Štěpán, Miroslav 126
Stone, Diane 7, 111
Strany Demokratickej L'avice (Slovakia) *see* SDL
Svoboda, Jiří 125, 131
Sweden 110, 117, 134, 149

Third Way: KSČM 134; SDL 112, 113, 114; SpRP/SLD 94, 98–9
transfer networks 34, 35, 43, 44, 47n, 67, 72–3, 83n, 163; engagement 74–6; EU enlargement 73–4; international plane 76–8; policy goals 78–9; resources 79–80
Turkey 21

Union of Communists (Slovakia) 107
Union of the Democratic Left (Poland) *see* SLD
United States 17, 20, 21, 22; and communist successor parties 63; foundations 25; and KSČM 57–8, 126; shock therapy 29; and SLD 55–6
USAID 22, 25

Valenčík, Radim 131
van den Broek, Hans 64n
VAS (*Vasemmistoliito*) (Finland) 149
Verheugen, Günter 110, 115
voluntary policy transfer 18, 86, 148–9, 163
VP (*Vänsterpartiet*) (Sweden) 149

Waniek, Danuta 90
Wehner, Herbert 90
Weiss, Peter 59, 74, 106–7, 108, 110, 111–12, 114, 115
welfare state 70; Poland 89, 92–3
Westminster Foundation 22, 80, 83n

WEU 97
Wiersma, Jan 110, 115
Wolman, H. 35
World Bank 22

Yugoslavia 29, 49, 126

Železný, Vladimír 127
Zeman, Miloš 75, 96, 109
Zimbabwe 126
Zimmer, Gabi 153
ZSLD (Slovakia) 5
Zväz kommunistov (Slovakia) 107